Marcus Ne̶l̶

118 Falconer St

Frewsburg ny 14738

Other books by Iyanla Vanzant

IYANLA VANZANT

Yesterday, I Cried

Celebrating the Lessons
of Living and Loving

SIMON & SCHUSTER

SIMON & SCHUSTER
Rockefeller Center
1230 Avenue of the Americas
New York, NY 10020

Designed by Bonni Leon-Berman

Manufactured in the United States of America

ISBN 0-684-86424-X

Acknowledgments

THANK YOU, GOD, "DIVINE MOTHER," by all the names you are known and called, for all the second chances you have given me, and for never asking me to do anything I was not equipped to do. It is only by your grace, and through your divine mercy, that I have made it this far. Thank you! Thank you! Thank you!

Thank you, God, for spirit in the body that I know and recognize as Blanche Richardson of Marcus Books in Oakland, California. Had you not shown up as Blanche to breathe with me through the process of this birth, I know this project would not have been born with such great joy and love and ease.

Thank you, God, for Terry McMillan, who said yes to what Blanche and I needed.

Thank you, God, for all the Mothering Angels you sent to love me in the most intense hours of my insanity. I thank you for showing up as Elvia Myrie, Wilhelmina Myrie, Tulani Kinard, Roseanne Logan, Stephanie Weaver, Denise DeJean, Linda Beatty-Stevenson, Melba Ramsay-Fernandez, Majorie Battle, the entire Inner Visions team, and of course, Carmen.

Thank you, God, for being a strong shoulder I could rest upon in the bodies of the Reverend Dr. Barbara Lewis King and David Phillips, Ph.D.

Thank you, God, for showing up at Simon & Schuster in the bodies of Christine Saunders, Trish Todd, Sue Fleming, Victoria Meyer, Annik LaFarge, Carolyn Reidy, Marcela Landres, David Rosenthal, Chris Lloreda, and Mark Gompertz.

Thank you, God, for the staff of the Oakland Marriott Hotel for their support throughout the writing of this book.

Thank you, God, for my friend, my lover, my pumpkin, my husband.

Thank you, God, for making a way out of no way, and for making me a brand-new instrument.

Thank you, God, for Mahogany, a Division of Hallmark Cards, Inc., who donated the beautiful cover art and supports my work and my vision and helps me spread the message.

This book is dedicated to
Ms. Oprah Winfrey,
for your "holy boldness" and willingness to demonstrate to the world
how to heal in public without losing God's grace or your own dignity;
and to
my children,
Damon Keith, Gemmia Lynnette, and Nisa Camille
for all the yesterdays you cried when I didn't have enough compassion
for myself, or the strength required to wipe your tears;
and in loving memory of
Sarah Jefferson, my mother,
Lynnette May Brown-Harris, my "Mommy" and best friend,
Nancy McCullum, my aunt,
Ruth Carlos, my first real sister.

Contents

Preface

Dear Iya:

Yesterday, I Cried will be a blessing to the world as you have been a blessing to me. I remember when I first heard your voice on tape (the National Black Wholistic Health Retreat tape). I could not sit down. I started pacing. Was this because of the truth you were sharing? I thought so then, and as the years have passed, I know that it really was because I was hearing a member of my "soul's" family.

When I met you in the flesh, I could see your apprehension, and your love. I remember how much you gave of yourself. Iya, you were so available to the women who were present. I felt very protective of you, then and now. I did not want people to use you up, or burn you out. I also remember how unconcerned you were about the money. It wasn't because you were financially set, either. You set the basket of money in the sun, telling me it would grow, and the very next day, one of the women we were working with gave you a large sum of money.

I remember all of the little notes to yourself (on the walls, in the bathroom, near your bed) in your house on Pine Street. I remember how thirsty you were for truth and the "clarity" of truth. I remember all of our conversations, processing, laughing, cussing, crying, and laughing some more. I find it absolutely incredible how you have moved through some very serious and heavy stuff with a sense of humor. Your humor is a gift!

I want to say some things to you that you perhaps do not realize about yourself. You have really, really paid your dues. People don't know the risks you took to be where you are, the "stable" jobs you said no to so that you could remain free enough to walk on nothing, absolutely nothing, but faith. You put your trust in the process. I have been a witness to your "acts of faith." You are more focused than you realize. People don't know how you opened your home to everyone and anyone, and how you gave of yourself so unselfishly. People don't know about the health challenges that presented themselves, or how you said no to them, aligned yourself for healing, and found it. People don't know the toll and the price you have paid, traveling with the "word" in your belly.

What I have loved about you is your honesty, even about your dishonesty. I love that you have the tenacity to operate effectively in the world. I have enjoyed the process of watching you grow and heal yourself and others. I am so very proud of you. I feel that I am a part of the process and of you. When they speak of you, I feel they're talking about me too! You have been a sister to me, a friend, a teacher, a student, and my baby. I really believe I came into your life to love you unconditionally.

When you became famous, I really missed our time—you eating coffee ice cream and me subs. But you stayed connected, and I adjusted. I was happy with you, and for you, for the way Spirit was using you. Yet I felt the loss. This was all a part of the process. Your process. My process. Our process. I have watched you reframe your history. I have watched you take leaps. I have watched you, and it has been a joy. I'm loving you, Iya.

Shaheerah (Reverend Linda Stephens)
Detroit, MI

Introduction

I AM NOT THE TYPE OF FATHER FIGURE that showed up when things started going well—when the child did or became something, someone a parent could be proud of. It has been my duty and honor to be a constant in Iyanla's life. Ours is a relationship born in our souls, many centuries ago. It is a relationship that I have not always understood but always respected. Today, I realize that trying to define and describe my relationship with Iyanla would be something akin to a television miniseries. She is, as I am sure you, her readers, know, a mouthful.

When I met her, at the age of twelve, she was a handful. Some called her rambunctious and loose. I called her talented, creative, but unguided and powerful. She was my younger sister's best friend and became a part of my family. At the time, I was her "older brother." My task was to guide and protect her. I did so with such fervor that my own sister became jealous. She did not realize or understand, as I did, that Iyanla was my "child" born to others, but destined to be a part of my life forever.

As a young woman, Iyanla was politically and culturally active and aware. She was a dancer and an organizer. She and my sister started a dance group, which I managed between the hectic duties of my own life. In the early 1960s, African culture had not yet become fashionable. It was new, something that was questioned and scrutinized. Yet it was a part of Iyanla's soul. When she moved to the drumbeat, she was amazing, and I was amazed. How did this young woman, born and raised in the United States, have such a feeling for the culture of her ancestors? Iyanla did the research and the study required to embrace and understand what being a young African woman really meant. It was more than just an interest to her. It was an identity, something she needed. I supported her in her study, and in the process, I too learned.

When most high school girls were chasing boys, Iyanla was on the picket line. As a student leader, she ran the risk of being thrown out of high school, and she challenged the authorities. The curriculum did not meet the needs of the students. There were no African studies. The teachers, who had been engaged in a long strike, were demanding that the students attend school for additional hours to make up for the time they had lost. Adults who watched from the sidelines seemed not to know what to do. They talked but took no action. I was not surprised to discover that Iyanla was on the committee of students that was making certain demands of the school system. I knew she was a leader. I knew she had the gift of gab. I was, however, quite surprised when my sister called to say that Iyanla was in jail as a result of a student protest.

In the midst of it all, there were problems at home. Problems Iyanla rarely spoke about, but problems she wore in her eyes. My role in her life changed. She needed a father, and I was willing to fill the need. When she told me she was pregnant, I was, like any father, disappointed. I was concerned. This was a young girl who had rarely been cared for—in fact never, as far as I could see. Now, she was faced with having to provide care for another human being. I watched her dance her way through a pregnancy. I watched her plan and prepare for a baby. She never spoke to me about her fears or her pain, and I never raised the issue. When the baby was born, I realized it meant that I now had a son to raise.

I think it was her fire that sustained Iyanla. She has always been ablaze. There was so much she wanted to know and do, and she was willing to work for it. It was that fire that enabled her to complete high school. It was that fire that kept her alive through dismal relationships. It was that fire that kept her eyes bright and her heart open as she lived through one abusive situation after another. It was Iyanla's spiritual fire that brought us to a point where there was little I could do for her or say to her. I had to let her go. She had to walk a path that most fathers pray their daughters will avoid. I had to pray Iyanla would survive.

When I saw her again, she had three children, two exes, and a college degree. When she announced to me that she going to law school, I almost had a heart attack! "How," I wondered, "is she going to do that with three children and no help?" But Iyanla had help, the help of invisible beings who walk by her side. She had always had my prayers and my love. She was earning my respect. I realized that Iyanla was now a grown woman, and once again, my role in her life had changed. I was a mentor and a friend. I was the one person she *knew* believed in her, stood by her, supported and loved her. I had always "been there and done that." I was not about to stop. Before I could figure out what to tell her, she had a law degree and was off in another direction in her life.

I have never once told the woman you call Iyanla what to do or what not to do. I have always helped her question and explore why she was doing a particular thing, in a particular way. She has always taken my words in, understanding them at a level well beyond her years. To say she is an old soul would be an understatement. She is an eternal soul, filled with a light that many seek, some try to buy, and few ever realize. I have done my best to guide and protect her. It has not always been easy. Iyanla has been her own greatest challenge. She has a strong mind and an even stronger will. Iyanla has to try something before she will be willing to give it up, and even then, she will want to know how or why it didn't work. It is the questioning and her willingness to try that gives her the fire. It is the fire most people see, do not understand, and cannot contend with. It is the fire that has kept her alive.

I have never known this woman to do a mean or malicious thing. She has made mistakes. She has made poor choices. Yet, I know she has done everything to the best of her ability in order to stay alive. The aliveness she sought was not in the physical world. It was a spiritual aliveness. She has endured life circumstances others cannot imagine and things the impact of which others cannot understand. Through it all, she has been available to help others and share whatever she has had. It is this about Iyanla that has endeared her to so many. I am among them.

Many have not understood Iyanla. They have questioned her motives, her authority, and her wisdom. This is because for most of her life she did not understand herself. Others have been quite openly demonstrative of their disdain or dislike of her. Rather than crushing her, it sent her on a *soul search*. Quite frankly, I believe it has been the work of her greatest adversaries that has fostered her greatest growth. As her friend, I am excited by and supportive of what she is doing and all that I know she will do. As her mentor, I am proud of her accomplishments, knowing that something I had to offer has been useful in her life. As her father figure, I am humble and grateful that such a human being is a part of my life. The love we share goes beyond words or comprehension. It is, as she has told me, the love of God, alive on the planet.

And So It Is!

Awo Osun Kunle Erindele

Yesterday, I Cried

Yesterday, I cried.
I came home, went straight to my room, sat on the edge of my bed,
    kicked off my shoes, unhooked my bra,
    and I had myself a good cry.
I'm telling you,
    I cried until my nose was running all over the silk blouse I
        got on sale.
    I cried until my ears were hot.
    I cried until my head was hurting so bad
        that I could hardly see the pile of soiled tissues lying on
        the floor at my feet.
I want you to understand,
    I had myself a really good cry yesterday.
Yesterday, I cried,
    for all the days that I was too busy, or too tired, or too mad
        to cry.
I cried for all the days, and all the ways,
    and all the times I had dishonored, disrespected, and discon-
        nected my Self from myself,
    only to have it reflected back to me in the ways others
        did to me
    the same things I had already done to myself.
I cried for all the things I had given, only to have them stolen;
    for all the things I had asked for that had yet to show up;
    for all the things I had accomplished, only to give them
        away, to people in circumstances,
    which left me feeling empty, and battered and plain
        old used.

I cried because there really does come a time when the only thing left
*   for you to do is cry.*
Yesterday, I cried.
I cried because little boys get left by their daddies;
*   and little girls get forgotten by their mommies;*
*   and daddies don't know what to do, so they leave;*
*   and mommies get left, so they get mad.*
I cried because I had a little boy, and because I was a little girl, and
*   because I was a mommy who didn't know what to do, and*
*   because I wanted my daddy to be there for me so badly until*
*   I ached.*
Yesterday, I cried.
I cried because I hurt. I cried because I was hurt.
I cried because hurt has no place to go
*   except deeper into the pain that caused it in the first place,*
*   and when it gets there, the hurt wakes you up.*
I cried because it was too late. I cried because it was time.
I cried because my soul knew that I didn't know
*   that my soul knew everything I needed to know.*
I cried a soulful cry yesterday, and it felt so good.
It felt so very, very bad.
In the midst of my crying, I felt my freedom coming,
Because
Yesterday, I cried
*   with an agenda.*

The Beginning

IT WAS HAPPENING. I had seen myself on television before, but not like this. I had never been on a mainstream national television show until now. This was special. This was big! This was the culmination of sixteen years of hard work, of three years of waiting for a producer to get back to me, and an entire day of filming. The results: one twelve-minute segment about my life and my work on CBS *Sunday Morning*. It felt great! Definitely something to celebrate. Instead of throwing a party, I felt awful, dishonest, like a fraud. I guess that's why I began to cry as the music began, heralding the start of the program. These tears were quite different from the tears I cried the day the segment was filmed.

Throughout our many experiences of life, we cry different kinds of tears. What we are probably not aware of is that each type of tear emanates from a specific place in the body, and that each type has certain distinct characteristics. We may realize that shedding tears at certain times will have a particular effect upon us and those around us. What we are probably less conscious of is that each tear, regardless of its origin, or its effects, contains a seed of healing.

Angry tears spill forth from the outside corner of the eye, making them easier to wipe away as they come at unexpected moments and inappropriate times. They originate in the ego—the part of our being that presents to the world who we *think* we are. Angry tears create heat and stiffness in the body, because when we are angry, we usually don't know how to express what we feel. We definitely don't want anyone to know when we are angry, because anger is not acceptable or polite. Rather than display anger, we hold back, and the tears rage forth, shattering our self-image. More important, angry tears reveal to those around us our vulnerabilities. This, we believe, is not a wise thing to do.

I cried angry tears the day the CBS film crew came to my home. I had just moved into a new house. I had very little furniture to fill the empty spaces in my large home. The garage was full of boxes, one of which contained the outfit I had planned to wear. It was an unmarked box that I could not find. I was also angry because my new mother-in-law was on her way to our home, and I had no place for her to sleep. *What would she think of me?* I thought I was angry because I had waited so many years for the segment to be filmed, and now that it was happening, I didn't feel ready. I realized that I was angry because I didn't have the courage to tell the segment producer or my manager that I wasn't ready to film the show. I wasn't ready because I didn't feel worthy. I cried because one of my favorite news correspondents was coming to my empty home, two days before Thanksgiving, and I couldn't locate four plates that matched. *What would he think of me?* I was angry because I felt so vulnerable, so exposed, and so inadequate. I was angry because I felt so powerless, and that made me sad.

Sad tears spill forth from the inside corner of the eye, finding their way across our nose, cheeks, and lips. For some reason we always lick sad tears. We know that they are salty, and the things that bring them forth are usually the bitter experiences in life. Sad tears come from the heart. They usually bring a bending of the shoulders and a drooping of the head.

When you are about to be interviewed for a national television program, you must hold your head up. And you must wear mascara. It is hard to put your mascara on when you are drooping and crying. I had found something to wear. It wasn't what I wanted to wear, but it would do. So now I was crying because of the incredible experience of sadness that I felt in my heart. I had worked long and hard to get to this day, this twelve minutes on CBS. There had been many hard times and many hard lessons. Weathering it all, my work had moved forward. My life had certainly moved ahead. In my heart, I knew that moving ahead would mean leaving certain things, and certain people, behind. I knew that this level of exposure would mean advancing to another level. It was no one's fault. It was simply about time. Life has a way of doing that *to* you and *for* you. Life will propel you into situations where the things that once worked, no longer work. Time passing, carrying things or people out of our lives as it brings new things and people into our lives, makes us sad. And it always makes us cry. I also knew that once the segment of *Sunday Morning* aired, if I had not made certain decisions, they would be made for me. That was frightening.

Frightened tears take up the entire eye, clouding our vision, as fear will do. When we are frightened, we cannot see or think. Frightened tears are usually big tears that well up in the eye. They spill over the whole face. Frightened tears come from the soles of the feet. They shoot through the body and create trembling or shaking.

I was scared to death that I would be found out. People would find out that I was frightened, angry, and sad. When you arrive at a certain station in life, people do not expect that you experience certain emotions. People believe you are above "all that," and they tell you so. That is simply not true. All teachers must learn. All healers must be healed, and your teaching, healing work does not stop while your learning, healing process continues. In fact, healing in public is an awesome task that requires you to lovingly point out the defects of others while you are healing your own.

I had no idea what I would be asked during the interview. This was, after all, the award-winning CBS *Sunday Morning*. They could ask me anything about anything, and I would be obliged to respond. What if I was asked about something that I had not yet healed? Suppose I couldn't get my mouth open to respond? What would people think if I were asked a question on national television about the little challenge I was now facing in my own life? And what if I got angry or frightened with millions of people watching me? Would they know? How would I live with that? *What would people think about me?* I didn't have time to figure any of it out. I had to get dressed. I had to be interviewed.

Then there are shame-filled tears, which fall when we are alone with our thoughts and feelings. Shame-filled tears come when we're judging ourselves, criticizing ourselves, or beating up on ourselves for something purely human that we have done yet can't explain to ourselves or to others. Shame-filled tears come from the pit of the stomach and usually cause us to bend over—not in pain, but in anguish.

There I stood, about to experience something that many people in my position would sell their two front teeth to experience, and I didn't feel ready or worthy. There I stood, about to realize a dream come true, and I was so ashamed of myself I couldn't get dressed. I was afraid, ashamed, and furious with myself that I had not yet mustered up the strength to confront a personal challenge. It had nothing to do with money. It was not about a relationship. Thank goodness, those two areas of my life are finally in order. This was about me. Me, the big-time, bestselling author. I was ashamed that I had come so far only to get stuck on something so small, so trivial. But was it trivial? You cannot trivialize the need to do, for your own well-being, something that you know will upset someone you care about. It is not easy or trivial to say to someone, I love you, but I must leave you. It is no small feat to try to wipe running mascara from your cheeks after you have put on your foundation and powder. Talk about PMS! The Poor-Me-Syndrome was making it impossible for me to get my face together, and the film crew had just entered my half-empty house.

Combination tears are the worst tears of all. They are filled with anger and sadness, with fear and shame. They have a devastating effect on the body, bringing the stiffness of anger, the drooping of sadness, the trembling of fear, and the bending of shame. They make you cold when you are hot. They make you tremble when you are trying to keep still. Most of all, they make you nauseated.

Suppose I threw up in the middle of the interview? Oh great! My imagination had taken a turn for the worse. I was standing in front of the mirror, terrorizing myself. Feeling unworthy. Feeling afraid, and being mad at myself for all that I was feeling. I would have slapped myself, but that would have made my eyes run again. Instead, my angel showed up at the bathroom door. My husband, Adeyemi, had come to tell me that the film crew was waiting for me. As soon as he saw the redness in my eyes, he stretched his long arms out toward me so that I could fall into them. I did. And I cried all over his clean white shirt.

"Come on, now. Don't be nervous. This is no different from anything else you've done. You can do this with your eyes closed." Closed, yes. Smeared with mascara, no. I would have to start all over again. That is exactly how I felt about my life. It seemed to me that, on what should have been one of the happiest days I had ever known, I kept arriving at the place where I would have to start all over, and it pissed me off!

The interview went smoothly. I did not shed a single tear. Terrence Wood, the CBS correspondent and interviewer, along with the camera-person and the producer, commented on my home. It was, they said, beautiful and peaceful. No one believed we had just moved in. No one seemed to notice, or care, that we did not have what I thought was the appropriate amount of furniture, in the appropriate rooms. Why do we subject ourselves to the hysteria of expecting the worst? I guess it is part of our nature as human beings. I also believe it is the natural outgrowth of postponing the inevitable. You can put off what you need to do, but the longer you put it off, the more hysteria and conflict you will experience. The more tears you will shed. The more anger, sadness, and fear you will create in your own mind. I had something unpleasant to do that I had resisted doing. I had put it off long enough. Now it, and I, were about to show up on national television. I knew that the moment the show was over, I would have to go upstairs and cry in my favorite place. The Jacuzzi.

Of all things to master, why did I have to pick tears? I've learned about tears and through tears. I haven't figured out whether it's a blessing or a curse that I can assess the tearful experience of a person. With a breath, I can feel in my own body what the person is going through. I can process others through their tears, with words and thoughts and images. I had come to the place and point in my life where I now had to do the same for myself. I had to get beyond my own tears to the core of the issue. I knew it was my core issue, my subconscious pattern, that was making it so difficult for me to fire my manager.

After all I had experienced and learned, I had to revisit my own past, which was filled with bitter tears, in order to move into the future. I would have to live through the present, knowing that millions of people would be watching me on television, people who did not know that I could not find the strength to do for myself what I felt I needed to do. It was this feeling that made me feel like a fraud. A fraud about to be found out.

The show had begun with the segment featuring me. Charles Osgood, the host of *Sunday Morning,* was talking about me. He was telling the world about all the books I had written and how many had been sold. He was revealing to the world how I had propelled myself from poverty in the projects in Brooklyn, New York, onto the stage of the world-famous Apollo Theatre. My husband squeezed my hand. My children beamed with pride. The dog was chewing on the leg of the sofa. It could have been a time of joyous celebration. Instead, I was trying to discern which type of tears were about to spill forth from my eyes and across my face, realizing that, whatever the type, everyone in the room would misinterpret their meaning. Everyone, that is, except me.

How much pain and shame and fear and anger can one body stand? That's a good question, I thought. How much pain *can* one body stand? I, like many people, have stood years and years, countless years of pain. We have held on to our mother's pain, and the pain of our fathers, not knowing what it was or how to get rid of it. We have held on to our children's pain, our lovers' pain, and most of all—on to the pain of those who stand closest to us. Sometimes we're able to cry through the pain. Sometimes we stomp through the pain. Sometimes we move through the pain in fear and in anger, without the strength to cry. When we do find our strength again, we move on to the next thing without taking a moment to breathe or celebrate.

It is the tears that have got us through the darkest days and the hardest times. Many of us have been able to float on our tears to a new and better understanding of ourselves and the things we have experienced in life. Through our tears, we get in touch with those experiences that we have forgotten, hidden, or buried away in the pit of our souls. So one

Sunday morning, I sat crying because my soul and my life were being shown on television, and I, the "guru" of faith and hope, wasn't sure it was a true picture.

The unshed tears of our many experiences color and cloud our thoughts. As we try to move forward without allowing the tears to flow freely, we find ourselves repeatedly in similar experiences. I was sitting in that place, a familiar place. A frightening, sad, and angry place. I was trying to suppress the tears of the things I had said and had not said. Tears of things I had done and now needed to undo. Unshed tears get caught in our throats, making it hard for us to speak our truth and honestly express who we are as we move through life. My life was moving, and if I did not find the courage and strength to speak, I knew I would choke out any possibility of the new life about to be born through me.

I've cried many tears for myself and, in the work I do, for other people. What I've discovered is that most tears come from our inability to tell our story. One of my teachers once told me, "Tell your story. Your story will heal you, and it will heal someone else." My story is full of tears: sad tears, shame-filled tears, angry tears, and of late, tears of joy. Watching myself on television, I realized that my story and my tears were not uncommon. Being a bestselling author does not make me uncommon or different. I am still human. I still cry when I am faced with the uncomfortable or the unpleasant. I still cry when I think about the sad parts of my story. I cry when I am angry or ashamed.

Sitting in my own home, surrounded by a loving husband and family, was reason enough to celebrate, and still I needed to cry. I wasn't crying because I had been able to move through my experiences, telling my story in a way that supports and facilitates the healing of other people. I was crying because I had ignored the need to celebrate that fact. Yesterday, I cried because the story was so tragic, so devastating and painful, that all I could do was cry. On this Sunday morning, I was crying because I realized that I still had work to do. Even though I had "made it," I still had healing work to do.

I've discovered the need not only to tell our story, but also to cry at the appropriate episodes. There are the times when we were unable to cry, unable to speak, unable to express ourselves, unable to lift ourselves up. In those times, we need someone else to cry for us. Crying for others and myself has led me to the belief that certain aspects of my story must be told. If I am truly to heal myself and help others in the process, I must tell the parts I am uncomfortable about telling. Not because my story is different or unique, but because I have been blessed to be able to cry myself through to a day and a time when joyful tears spring forth from my heart and allow me to stand straight. Joyful tears move up the spine and across the brain and bring you to a new perspective and a new understanding that the sad tears were necessary, that each tear was a prayer, that tomorrow will be better than today. Joyful tears free you up to celebrate your Self, your healing, and your progressive process.

My story is not so much a story of the things that I have been through and done, but the things that I have grown through, the things that I have learned, the things that I now understand. My story is what some would call "a triumph of spirit." Others would call it "a victory of goodness over evil." I just call it a story, and I tell it because I have learned that the telling helps me continue healing. Telling my story gives me something to celebrate.

I don't know who or what I would be if I had not cried through the many experiences of my life. I know today that it is a life of peace, a life of joy, and a life of healing. What I find most amazing is the number of people who have not yet been able to tell their story. These are the same people who do not realize that they have victories that have gone uncelebrated. I have found, though, that as I tell my story, there are places and pieces that other people can tap into so that they may somehow find the courage to revisit their own experiences, bring forth the tears, and grow into their greatness. Life is about so much more than moving from incident to incident, issue to issue. When we take this path, we find ourselves crying without hope.

That is what I experienced one Sunday morning. I had forgotten to celebrate my strength and my victories. I thought that would be selfish. I had forgotten to embrace myself or pat myself on the back. I had been told that it would be egotistical. I had never thanked my Self for all that

I had gotten me through. And now others would be celebrating my victories, and I did not feel worthy or deserving of such praise. I know there are far too many people suffering alone from experiences that are common to us all. Experiences that we have come through with flying colors but are ashamed to talk about and afraid to celebrate. After all, *what would people think* should we be caught smiling in our own mirror?

And that is all I have been able to do. I've done it in workshops; I've done it in lectures and in my books. I have been able to share with others a process that allows them to cry, and then celebrate. Unfortunately, I became so busy sharing, I forgot to cry and celebrate for myself. I had given everyone credit but me. I had thanked everyone but me. I felt obliged and indebted to everyone but me. One Sunday morning, I decided that the time had come for me to figure out where I had learned how to do that, and why I continued doing it when I no longer wanted to.

I cried yesterday. I cried when I was a child. I cried when I was a teenager. I cried when I was a young woman. And it is the fear, the shame, and the pain of those tears that have allowed me to stand up today, to tell my story and to celebrate my healing. This book is not just *my* story, it is *our* story. It is the story of the common things that we experience that we have not learned to express. It is the story of the things that keep us crippled because we hold them down in fear, in anger, and in shame. My prayer is that my story will help people throw away their crutches of dysfunction and addiction so that we can all stand together in a new time, in a new place, with a new understanding that enables us to celebrate the fact that we are still alive.

When Grandma said that God never gives you more than you can bear, she was saying that all the tears you need to grow, all the tears you need to cleanse, all the tears you need to share are available. Do the crying. Do the healing. And do the growing so that you can be all and celebrate all that God created you to be. That's what this story is about, and that's why this book had to be written.

Even as I write, I cry. I cry when I think about what people will say about me, what people will think of me. But because my tears now flow freely, with understanding, I am willing to take the chance. I know that I cannot lose. If this book, this story, these tears can help somebody, then I know that all I have lived through has not been in vain. I pray that as you read this book you will find the courage to cry and the understanding of why you're crying. I pray that you find the lessons beneath the tears, and the ability to love yourself no matter what, and in spite of it all. I pray that tomorrow your tears will wash away the fear or shame or sadness that has prevented you from telling your story.

Yesterday, I cried for the woman that I wanted to be. Today, I cry in celebration of her birth. Yesterday, I cried for the little girl in me who was not loved or wanted. Today, I cry as she dances around my heart in celebration of herself. I pray that your yesterday tears will be wiped, that you will find the courage to celebrate yourself and the lessons you have lived through, grown through, and learned through. The lessons that have brought you to a deeper realization of yourself, of the child within you, and of the constant mercy and grace of God. Now, let's have a party and enjoy!

CHAPTER ONE

What's the Lesson When You Think You Figured Out the Lesson, and You Really Haven't?

Pain is a wrong perspective.
When it is experienced in any form,
   it is proof of self-deception.
It is not a fact at all.
There is no form it takes
   that will not disappear if seen aright.
A Course in Miracles

DOES IT EVER STOP? Does the crap ever stop? Does it ever get to the point where everything in your life is going great at the same time, for any length of time? Does there ever come a day when the warm, sunny days come more frequently and last longer than the blistering, cold nights? I once thought that if I had the man of my dreams and the love of my life, all would be well. WRONG! I also thought that if I had money, not a lot of money, just enough to pay the bills on time and have a little bit of change left over, things would be just great. NOPE! Then I figured if I could identify the career of my dreams, and be fully and happily engaged in that career, I would be flying high. WRONG AGAIN! Now, after overcoming seemingly insurmountable obstacles, weathering devastating disasters, moving through mind-boggling challenges, and after watching myself on a national television program, I had finally figured life out.

As I lay in my Jacuzzi, watching my thousand-dollar dog poop on my carpet, I finally got it! Life is about cleaning up the crap and, while you're doing it, being okay with the fact that you have to do it.

I haven't always had such deeply profound insights about life or the process of living. Like most of the world, I thought life was about doing better than you were doing at any given moment. Doing more, I believed, would result in your having more, which would result in your feeling better. I thought this was the total essence of living. Of course, I didn't come up with this life philosophy on my own. I was taught to think and feel this way by most of the adults who have influenced my life. I have been taught this by every television commercial I have ever seen; by schoolteachers and college professors who shaped and molded my attitudes; and by my own secret desires to do better and have more than any of those adults were capable of. Now, I have a different perspective. And while it makes me somewhat sad to think of all the time, energy, and money I expended doing and getting, it sure takes a great deal of pressure off my mind to know that I was wrong.

The thing that makes the Jacuzzi, the money, the love, or anything that you may desire to have or experience in your life worthwhile, is your willingness to clean up the crap. Most of the time, it's not even your stuff! It could be something that someone else dropped off in your life. It could be something that you picked up because at first you didn't realize what it was. Sometimes you pick up something, thinking it's something else, and by the time you realize what it really is, you've got a real mess to clean up. Life is about being willing to take your naked body, your most vulnerable self, out of the warm water where you are comfortable and clean up the crap without getting angry and without losing your Self in the process. When you can do that, life becomes a joy rather than a chore. Cleaning up crap becomes an everyday experience that you know you are equipped to handle and that you realize can be accomplished without taking anything valuable away from the real you.

A word of caution. You can't get caught up in the crap! If you do, you will surely lose sight of the real meaning of life and lose your Self. You cannot, under any circumstances, get caught up in whether the crap is yours or someone else's. You can't get caught up in what it looks like, smells like, or how much of it may be piled in front of you. You can't get caught up in where it came from, or why it keeps coming your way. "Caught up" is another way of saying "being stuck." You can't get stuck in the right or wrong, good or bad, injustice or fairness of cleaning up the crap in your life. You cannot compare how much of it you have to the amount someone else may have. Life is like a crap-cleaning test. It is a test that we all signed up for, one we must all take. *The best students get the hardest tests.* Our *only* job, whether we like it or not, is to keep a vigilant guard over our lives and to clean up the crap as soon as it comes to our attention. Our ability to do this without getting caught up is what some folks call "success" and others call "personal growth" or "evolution." My experience has been that, no matter what you call it, the result of cleaning up crap is spiritual growth and development. That was the task that presented itself before me: cleaning up crap. First my doggie's, then my own.

I cleaned up after the dog, returned to the Jacuzzi, and stuck my toes back in the bathtub—my favorite personal crap-cleaning spot. The water in the tub had gotten cold. I shook my head and smiled to myself. "Does it ever stop?" As I reached over, turning the knob to replenish the water, Rhonda's thoughts began to fill my head. *Why bother? Is it really worth it? How many times are you going to drag yourself through this kind of hydro self-analysis, this waterlogged self-evaluation? Forget about it! Things aren't that bad. Leave well enough alone.*

Suddenly, there were two voices in my mind. Iyanla said, "No! Do it now. DO IT RIGHT NOW!" The bathroom began to steam up from the hot water as I refilled the tub. It was a definite sign. "Trying to make it through the fog again?" As I asked myself the question, I realized just how much I had grown. There were days when I would leave little things in my life undone, or half done, in fear of making someone mad at me, in fear of losing their love. There were times when I would sulk and cry about what I thought someone was doing or had done to me, believing that I was totally powerless to do anything about it. In many clever ways, I had allowed myself to duck and dodge unpleasant situations in my life to avoid confrontation.

This, however, was not one of those days, times, or ways. I was choosing not to live like that any longer. I had spent enough days reflecting on this in other bathtubs to know that if you leave even a little bit of crap lying around in your life, eventually it will start to smell really, really bad.

"How," I thought to myself, "do you get from begging for a job to keep a roof over your head, to being in a position to fire somebody, all in less than ten years?" I had done it, and done it in a big way. I had gone from not having a roof, to owning a half-million-dollar roof. From begging and pleading for what I needed, to having people beg and plead with me to share what I had to offer. I had grown through the dark, dank, funky pits of hell to a corner of heaven in such a short time that I was having trouble catching up with my own life. Still, in my own little corner of heaven, there were piles of crap that needed to be cleaned up. There were things in my life and about my life that had absolutely nothing to do with who I now was, what I did, and what I now knew to be the truth about me. I had to figure out what that truth was. I had to figure out how to rid my life of the nagging little struggles, bits and bouts of confusion, and unexpected chaos that continued to crop up. It was time to tell the truth—again.

Although I would be the first to gratefully and humbly admit that things in my life had gotten infinitely better, there were still some things that simply did not belong. Obviously, I had missed some part of some lesson that I, "The Lesson Queen," thought I had mastered. Admitting that to myself was half the battle. I had built my career on helping people to find and accept their lessons. Now it was my turn—again.

Over the years, I have discovered that hot water has a way of bringing things to the surface. I closed the bathroom door to keep the dog out. I had run a nice hot bath. I had scented it with lavender and chamomile bath salts. I was prepared to stay in the water until I got an answer to my least favorite question relative to my personal and spiritual growth: *What is it that I am doing to create the present situation in which I find myself?*

Lowering myself into the tub, I did a quick review and a mental celebration of the place in which I now sat. Spiritually centered. Decent person. Minister. Wife. Grandmother. Priestess. Bestselling author. Internationally heralded speaker. Home owner. Business owner. And I was clean! I closed my eyes and sank lower into the water, and Rhonda's thoughts filled my mind. *Confused wretch! Overweight and ugly! Whore! Tramp! Misfit!* Frantically, I felt around in the water for my washcloth and remembered Rhonda, the person I used to be. I decided not to respond, not to fight myself. *Pig! Dog! You really think you're hot s———t!* I pulled the washcloth out of the water and squeezed the warm water over my head.

"*Talk to me*," I whispered. "*Tell me what you want.*"

"*I want you to die! You don't deserve to live.*"

"*Shut up! You're just being dramatic. What do you want?*"

I closed my eyes and listened to myself. Rhonda was raging again.

She was angry and she wanted Iyanla to know it. Rhonda was the part of me that simply refused to change, refused to grow. She was the part of me in need of healing. The part where all of my fears, foibles, and character flaws were hidden. I knew this was not about having a split personality. It was about history. Rhonda had a history; Iyanla was creating her own. Rhonda had a history of pain, abuse, and neglect. She had a history of doing things in a certain way, with certain expectations, based on those painful and abusive experiences. Her history and those experiences often allowed her to neglect herself in pursuit of the approval and acceptance of others. She also had a history of putting off the unpleasant, waiting until the last minute to do important things, and doing whatever was necessary to make other people like her.

I understood Rhonda's history and behavior. But I also understood that I had the power to change. I had the right to live in peace. I had the ability to transform my way of thinking and being, and to become a productive member of humanity. To do so, I would have to merge what I used to be with what I could be. Rhonda and Iyanla had to become one.

Who I am is not who I used to be. But who I am is all of who I used to be. It took a while, but that meditative insight, which I had received months ago, finally made sense. I understood that even when we change, our history does not. What you have learned through your experiences in life will influence, affect, and motivate everything you do. More important, if you are not careful and vigilant, the crap in your history will seep through and soil your present-day reality. I had been keeping a close watch on Rhonda, but somehow, here she was. Seeping through. Acting up. Rhonda had placed me in a situation that was familiar to her, but contradictory and repugnant to the new me. Here was a little more crap that I needed to clean up so that I would be able to celebrate what was about to happen in my life.

When I was at a very low point in my life, God sent an angel to watch over me. The low point resulted partly from Iyanla's stuff and partly from Rhonda's stuff. Back then, I had reached a point where, in seven days or less, I would be evicted from my home. I had no place to go. I had no money and none coming in the foreseeable future. My telephone had been disconnected. I had no male friend with whom to share my troubles. It was seventeen degrees outside, and I was standing in front of the 7-Eleven, using a pay telephone to transact business. It now seems absolutely amazing to me that when you really need help, the ego, your pride, will not allow you to ask for it. My career as a writer and speaker was just budding. I didn't want anyone to know the truth about my situation. (Rhonda's crap.) I had no agent, and the contract I had received that morning from a small independent publisher represented instant money. It was well below the money I had anticipated receiving for my book, but it was money nonetheless. God knows I needed it, but something about the contract just didn't feel right. (Iyanla's intuition.) I had been there before. Desperate for money. Making decisions in fear. Being evicted. And horny as all get out.

Shivering in my cheap—excuse me, economical—coat, I rested my head against the ice-cold telephone and uttered my favorite prayer: "HELP!" It always works for me. The prayer hadn't frozen in the cold air before the thought popped into my mind: *Call your editor, Darlene.* Obediently, I picked up the telephone and dialed. As if she knew why I was calling, Darlene told me about a manager she had lunched with the day before. "Give me her number," I said. I don't even remember saying good-bye or hanging up the phone. Two other people had mentioned the very same person to me under much less stressful conditions. I made the call. Karen, the manager I thought could fix my life and save me, greeted me as if she had known me all of my life.

It seems that people had been talking to her about me, too. With the preliminaries out of the way, I blurted out my story. The contract. The publisher. The back-and-forth negotiations. My verbal agreement with the publisher. My dream, my goal. The nature of the book. I acknowledged that, although I was a lawyer, I had practiced criminal law and knew little about contracts. I didn't have a clue, but I knew something didn't feel right about the deal. It takes a very focused person to absorb your life story in 3.3 minutes, then respond in a way that makes sense. Instinctively knowing that I had traumatized myself sufficiently and that I was now preparing to cry, Karen responded, "I'll take care of it." *Oh my God! I'm not going to be living in the park with the squirrels! The frozen squirrels! At least they have fur; all's I've got is K-Mart on sale!*

Although Iyanla had learned to expect a miracle and trust the process, Rhonda was into creating drama, panic, and the need to be rescued. Rhonda won that round. But within two weeks, the rent was paid, the telephone was on, I had a lucrative deal with a major publisher, and the angel named Karen was an integral part of my life.

Karen and I talked almost every day, about everything. Before I knew it, three years had passed. My career had soared. Karen and I were joined at the hip. She encouraged me to do more. She supported me in everything I did. She scolded me when it seemed that I was getting off track, and she fought for me tooth and nail. Rhonda needed that. She needed somebody to believe in her. She needed somebody to say the things she could not say for herself. Rhonda needed someone to take care of her and protect her, because Rhonda didn't believe that she could do those things for herself.

Iyanla had a completely different set of needs.

Rhonda's needs and patterns were on a collision course with Iyanla's sensibilities. Somebody had to take a stand. Eventually, there was a train wreck in my mind.

Often, when you are on the spiritual path, there is a war that goes on between the person you once were and the person you are becoming. Some call it "thought patterns." Others call it "habit." My experience was that there were two distinct personalities needing to be integrated. I discovered that the older you are, the more difficult it is to accomplish a smooth integration. The old you, the one who helped you survive, the one that was there for you in the rough times, is going to fight to stay alive. The old you knows your secrets and your history. The old you knows your defense mechanisms, what you will do when your buttons get pushed, and exactly where your weaknesses lie. The old you knows what works for you and is terrified by the thought of trying something new. The old you is comfortable with the way things were and are. The old you wants to stay in control. The old you has home-court advantage.

The new you, the spiritually conscious, spiritually grounded you, is fumbling around trying to figure out what works now. It is the part of you that has yet to be proven. You may believe strongly, you may want deeply to change, and for your newfound identity to emerge. But the new you is not quite sure it will work. It is there, in that glimmer of doubt, that the old you goes to work. It nags at you. It challenges you. It is called self-doubt and lame excuses. It looks like not having time to pray, to meditate, and not being able to figure out how praying and meditating are going to put food on the table. The new you views problems as challenges, knowing that with every problem comes the solution, the escape, the way out. The new you is willing to confront challenges and wants to do so in a spiritually grounded way. When, however, the new you is backed up to a wall, it will, out of habit, borrow from the old you. The instant the borrowing occurs, the new you is rendered dead—even if it is only for a moment. The challenge is that when the new you is brought back into focus, there is probably a pile of old-you crap that needs to be cleaned up.

Iyanla was determined to be born. I learned the hard way that you must be disciplined, vigilant, and obedient about the practices that will build your spiritual muscles and put the old you to rest. The truth is that you really are sleeping with the enemy, and the enemy knows that you are doubtful and fearful.

Over the years, I had fought with myself to move beyond the bad habits, the negative beliefs, and the consuming fear that I had lived with all my life. This was the identity that Rhonda nurtured in her bosom. These were the things that she knew so well. But these things did not work for Iyanla. Too many *I can'ts,* too many *don't knows,* too much fear and hesitation. Too much anger and shame that resulted in too much guilt. Iyanla did not doubt God or the process of life. I had no need to be rescued, no need to be taken care of, so why was I crying and feeling unworthy. *What was happening?*

There were things that I wanted to say, needed to say for myself, but for some reason the words were stuck in my throat. I was swallowing my truth because I was afraid to upset people. I was people pleasing because I was afraid to deal with confrontation. The most disturbing part of it all was the financial chaos and personal crisis that continued to rear their ugly heads at the most inopportune moments. It was annoying! I had exchanged a welfare check for a royalty check. I had exchanged gossip for self-judgment. It was getting tired! I thought I was finished with this stuff! And perhaps Iyanla was. But Rhonda wasn't.

The water had gotten cold again, and I hadn't even scratched the surface. It was truth-telling time, and I was more than willing. "Cleanse," I thought. "Cleanse and get clear. Get clear and grow." I was someplace else in my mind when my husband knocked at the door. "Are you okay in there?" He was used to me now and knew better than to open the door when I was processing. To put him at ease and to remind myself, I responded, "I'm blessed."

Even when it seems that your life is falling apart, there is divine restoration going on. Karen and I had built my dreams into a solid structure, brick by brick and book by book. Which was why this was so very, very hard. Something had happened along the way, things no longer felt good. We were arguing rather than celebrating. Things were being said that made me very uneasy. I had seen, and now felt, some things about Karen that let me know that the marriage between us was falling apart. Our time together was quickly coming to an end. The truth is that I had known it for about a year. But I owed her. But she saved me when I was down and out. But she took care of me. What would I do without her? How could I fire someone who had been so good to me? This was Rhonda's stuff!

Iyanla believed that Karen was her employee. She got paid to do a job, and that was all that was owed. Iyanla was grateful and loyal, but not beholding. Rhonda, however, had mixed business with friendship, and the business was going sour. Rhonda felt loyal to the patterns that she and Karen had established. Rhonda was also afraid. She was afraid of losing love and someone she loved. It was right there that the trains collided: Iyanla knew one thing; Rhonda believed another. Knowing and believing are not the same. When you know one thing and believe another, you experience conflict.

The water was just right. Hot enough to bring the crap to the surface and give me another hour of stillness. Rhonda needed healing. Healing takes place from the inside out. I had to go to the depths of my memory, the core of my soul, and make peace with what I had created. That's right, I created it. Whenever we don't do what we need to do, for whatever reason, we create crap. I once thought that if I prayed enough, meditated long enough, and demonstrated enough faith, things would work themselves out. I had thought I could live with the pangs of something being not quite right. Thank God I had grown enough to be unable to excuse away any level of dishonesty. Dishonesty was not a part of Iyanla's nature, the nature I had acquired with the name. Lying still in the water, I remembered how I had acquired my name.

There was a lot of activity at Balé's house when I arrived. A group of women were in one room, sitting on the floor, singing and pounding herbs in a large metal bowl. Several men were sitting in another room, laughing and talking. Balé was in his usual place, the kitchen. As always, he was glad to see me. He instructed me to take a seat in a room upstairs, while he continued his therapy. I sat listening for hours as the people on the first floor sang and talked and laughed. Each time I got up to go to the bathroom, I would peer over the railing, trying to see what was going on. I could hear. I could smell. But I could not see.

I had known Balé, my spiritual mentor and godfather, since I was nine years old. Sitting across the dinner table from him now, I felt as though I was seeing him for the first time. Although we had spoken occasionally, this was the first time I had seen Balé in fifteen years, and he had changed. So had I. Still, this man knew me. He knew my family; he knew my history. He knew Rhonda and he knew the person I was destined to be. He was my father figure. The father I had always wanted to love and approve of me. When I was a teenager, he had managed the dance troupe I belonged to. Many people, including my father, misread him. They thought he was an older guy taking advantage of a group of young girls. Nothing could have been further from the truth.

Throughout my life, Balé's had guided me through the critical periods. He kept me and my friends away from the "bad boys." He had taught us what it meant to be young African-American women. In fact, he bought the first piece of African cloth I owned. I made two skirts with it. One for myself, and one for Balé's younger sister. She was my best friend. She was the one who pawned her wedding ring to help me bail my husband out of jail. I had spent most of my teenage Thanksgivings at their house. When I was pregnant with my first child, Balé and his sister gave me a baby shower. Looking at him now, I realized how much I had missed him and how much he had influenced my life.

Balé is a Yoruba priest. He had been initiated when I was still a teenager. After his initiation, he left New York. He lived in Africa for a while and then relocated to Florida. I had recently discovered, purely by accident, that he was now living in New Jersey. When I called him, we were both thrilled to hear each other's voices. We wanted to celebrate our reunion. Now I was sitting in his house and trying to catch up on our individual histories. He had heard that I was living in Philadelphia, practicing law. He knew that my first husband and I were no longer together, that my second husband had died, and that I had been initiated as a Yoruba priestess. Now he wanted to know everything else.

I now remembered that the feeling I had sitting in Balé's house on that day had been just like being at Grandma's house. I had been banished to a room by myself. I could smell food being prepared, but I dared not ask for anything to eat. I was starving. I could hear people having a good time, but I was not being allowed to join in. The longer I sat, the angrier I became. The angrier I became, the more frustrated I became with my inability to express my anger. By the time my mind finished bouncing from anger to frustration, frustration to rejection, rejection to starvation, I had one doozie of a headache. I was just about to gather my things and head for the front door when Balé called me. Only then did I notice that the house was silent. All the people were gone.

"I know you must be hungry. Did you think I wasn't going to feed my baby? Come. Eat."

Balé had set the table just for me. He had placed an enormous portion of Brazilian chicken and rice on a china plate. He talked from the kitchen as I devoured the food.

"Don't be so fast to jump to conclusions. You have never seen this day. You have never seen the beauty this day holds. Just because it rained yesterday and the ground is flooded, that does not mean you are going to get wet today."

I dropped my fork in midair. *Damn! Damn! Damn! He had been in my head again.* My appetite disappeared.

"Do you know what I am talking about?" he asked.

"Yes."

"You have been through a lot. I know you have made some mistakes. But I also know that nothing you have done has been because you are a mean or malicious person. Most of what you have done has been what you were taught to do. Do you know that you are not a bad person?" The smell of the food on the table was making me sick.

"Sometimes I think I almost have myself convinced. Then I will do something, somebody will criticize me, and then I'm not so sure anymore."

"You are not a bad person, but you have placed yourself in bad situations. If you could be anything in the world—I mean any animal, food, fruit, mineral, or person—who or what would you be?"

I really had to think about it. At first I was trying to think of the "right" answer, the answer that would most impress Balé. Realizing how impossible that would be, I began to think of what would be most useful to the world: What would most people like or find useful? My criteria: useful, likable, and abundant. I did not want to be a rare thing or an unfamiliar thing.

"There is no right answer," Balé said. I had already figured that part of it out.

"A chicken. I'd like to be a chicken," I said. Of course he asked the reason.

"Everybody likes chicken. Chickens are very useful and they are abundant. They are rugged. And they can survive almost anywhere." I looked down at my plate and added, "Chickens give people the opportunity to be creative."

Balé stared at me for a second, then said, "Me, I want to be a cool, clear glass of water. I want to be able to see out into the world with no obstructions. And I want to live in such a way that nothing can be hidden."

I knew where he was going.

"You know, Adeyemi is a good man. He has always worked and done so much for the community. But he has already dragged your name through the mud once. I'm sure those were not his intentions, but that is what happened. Please do not allow that to happen to you again. You are a different person now than you were then."

This was getting to be pretty scary. I had just spent two days in Albany with Adeyemi. He worked in Albany during the week and went home to Brooklyn and his wife on the weekends. I knew something was wrong when he greeted me at the train station, but we made it through the weekend without incident. The morning I was to leave, he told me that we should not see each other anymore. He said he realized that he was not giving his marriage a fair try. Besides that, his wife was beginning to question him about me. I was furious. I told him that the marriage was not going to work because he had only gone back to ease his guilt. I told him that if he thought I was going to sit around and wait for him, he was crazy. And if he didn't want to be with me, that was fine by me! I left his apartment, vowing never to see him again. I called him the moment I got home. It was then that he told me he was moving his family to Atlanta.

I knew I had to stop seeing Adeyemi, but I couldn't seem to do it. He was, after all, the first man who ever held my hand. I tried to justify my actions by telling myself that he and his wife were separated and therefore he was fair game. That didn't explain away the fact that he was living with her in Brooklyn, and I was living in Philadelphia. It was wrong, and I knew it was wrong. But I was not ready to admit it. I didn't say a word to Balé. I stared into space, trying not to cry. Suddenly, I could see Nett as clearly as if she were sitting across the table from me. She picked up her cup, took a sip, and without blinking, said to me, "If a man is married and you are not, you are sleeping with a married man. It doesn't matter if he hasn't seen his wife in fifty years, or if he lives on one side of the world and she on another. If he is married and you are not, you are asking for trouble." Then she was gone. I swore to myself I was never coming back to this house.

Balé removed my plate from the table and told me to sit on the mat that he had spread out on the floor. Balé is a diviner. The process of divination for Yoruba people requires the use of sixteen cowrie shells. Once the shells have been consecrated with ceremony and prayer, a diviner will cast the shells to determine the answer to a question. The configuration of the shells when they fall reveals the answer. Balé blessed the cowries and began casting them. It's like rolling dice; you just have to know what the numbers mean in order to receive the answer to your question.

Balé never revealed the nature of his question. I watched him throw and pick up the shells for about ten minutes. Then he got up and left the room. When he returned, he carried a book. He consulted the book, then began throwing the shells again. Suddenly, he stopped. Closing his eyes and leaning his head back against the wall, he sat still for several minutes.

When his eyes flew open, I jumped. He picked up the shells again and cast them one last time. He was pleased. I could tell by the smile on his face.

"Are you ready for this?" he asked me. I had no idea what he was talking about.

"Yeah, I guess so."

"If you are not ready, just say so. We can come back to it at a later time."

Slightly pissed, I thought to myself, Why all the cloak and dagger? Either tell me what you are talking about, or don't ask me to respond.

"Balé, I have no idea what you are talking about. How could I know if I am ready or not?"

"If you would stop being so snippy and take a deep breath, you would know that you are ready." Now he was pissed. I did what he said.

"Yes, I am ready to pursue my destiny." That was an interesting response, I thought to myself.

"Iyanla. Your name is Iyanla. It is really not a name at all. It is a title. It is a title of greatness. The translation of Iyanla is 'great mother.' Back home in Nigeria, the Iyanla is the king's mother. She is a woman of great prominence and stature. She is the wise woman. She is the one all women look to and aspire to be, but cannot be. Iyanlas are ordained by birth. They come from God. It is God who has etched greatness into their souls. All of us want to be great. Iyanla is born that way. Her job in life is to remember her true identity. The 'great mother' teaches and guides the people. She heals the sick. It is even said in some circles that only the Iyanla can raise the living dead. Not *the dead,* but the living dead, because she knows the secrets of life and living. Iyanla is the proverbial Psalm 31 woman. I know you have not read Psalm 31, but you will.

"Iyanla is a woman of moral character and purity of heart. She is the one who is written about in Surah 19 of the Holy Qur'an. She is the essence of Ch'ien and the K'un of which the I Ching teaches. She is primal power. That which is light giving, active, and strong, because she is born of the Spirit. She is the receptivity of the earth that gives birth to all things new. Iyanla, the 'great mother,' is the grace, mercy, and goodness of God that resides in the hearts of all men. Her presence teaches about the goodness of God. She moves gracefully because she knows God. Those who know God do not pursue greatness. Those who know they are already great grow through the strength and grace of Iyanla. This is the potential, the purpose, that God has placed in your soul. My question is, Are you ready?"

My mouth was dry. My palms were sweating. My head was spinning. I could not open my mouth. Balé detected that I was about to throw up on his beautiful mat. "Put your head down. Breathe and put your head down." Then he continued. "Build your character, Iyanla. Seek the truth and speak the truth. Learn all that you can about teaching and healing. Learn all that you can about mercy and grace. Learn all that you can about God, because God and the high Spirits of God are the only friends you have. People are going to challenge you. Iyanla is welcomed by all, but feared and despised by many. When you know, do not be afraid to say you know. When you do not know, say so. You will be shown what to do. You will be told what to say. Only if you build yourself on the strength of good character will you be able to receive the answers you need. Know who you are. You are no longer Rhonda. She is dead. You can no longer live the way Rhonda lived. The questions you must answer now for yourself are: Who are you? and What to you want to do?"

Balé made us a cup of tea. I was completely overwhelmed. Excited, but overwhelmed. Never in my life had anyone given me such hope. I would never have connected myself to any of the things he had said. Whether I was right or wrong, good or bad—these ideas were about as close as I had ever come to his description of me.

"How?" I kept asking him. "How am I supposed to do that? To become that?"

"You are that already. Your name is your nature." Balé explained that he had asked for sixteen other names. He did not get a confirmation until he asked for Iyanla. Realizing that the excitement had made me bold, Balé listened patiently to my questions.

"Suppose you made a mistake? How do you know you didn't make a mistake?"

"That is your fear talking. That is self-doubt and fear. How many mistakes have I made in the past?" We both knew the answer.

Again, I felt overwhelmed. Balé had asked me such simple questions. They were simple, yet profound. They were questions for which I had no answers. Who are you? What do you want to do? Are you ready? I had never taken the time to ask myself those questions. Balé gave me a list of things I needed to figure out for myself: What is your favorite color? Food? Song? Most valued possession? What is your greatest strength? Greatest weakness? Greatest fear? Best skill? Greatest mistake? Greatest accomplishment?

"Ask yourself why," he said. "What is or was the energy behind each of these things in your life? What is the experience that brings you the greatest amount of joy? What is the one task that you are least fond of doing? Again, ask yourself why. If you were to die today, what is the one thing everyone who knows you would say about you? What would you want them to say? Why wouldn't or couldn't they say what you would want them to say?" I was taking notes.

"Once you have answered each of these questions, put your list away, then review it three months later, every three months for the rest of your life. That way you will always be in touch with yourself."

We spent the rest of the evening talking about the requirements for being a priest and a person of good character. Balé emphasized that the person always comes first.

"You may want to be as spiritual as all get out, but you are a human being, prone to making mistakes. When you do make a mistake, only a good, solid character will help you move through it."

That is what this day and this bath and these tears were about: building character and integrity. I was out of integrity. I was thinking things about someone without honestly sharing what I felt. I was talking to other people about the situation, which meant I mistrusted what I knew to be true. Somehow, I had forgotten that you must put your spiritual knowledge into practice all of the time. You have to tell the truth all of the time. You must declare your goal, state your intentions, ask for what you want, and remain true to yourself, all of the time. The minute you forget any one or all of those principles, the enemy will step in. When that happens, you have to work harder. The time had come for me to heal at a deeper level and get the lesson from another perspective. I may have simply scratched the surface. Or perhaps I had missed one tiny little detail. I did know enough to realize that what was showing up in my life was the answer. I now had to remember the question. I prayed.

> *Dear God:*
> *Please bring me this lesson gently and lovingly. Please let me see and understand what is really going on, and give me the courage to do whatever is necessary. Remind me of what I have forgotten. Inform me of your will for my own spiritual progress and the good of all others involved. I am ready and willing to know the truth.*

Don't ask if you really don't want to know. The minute I closed my eyes, I saw her. She was six. No, she was nine. No. She was twenty-one, bent over in pain, covering her swollen black-and-blue eyes. She was terrified. She was kicking and screaming. She was trying to get away. From whom? *What was she running from now?* No. She was fighting back. She was angry. I was having trouble breathing. No. She was having trouble breathing. She was dead. No. She was alive, fighting for her life. I was the object of her attack. I squeezed my eyes shut. My teeth were clenched. My fists were clenched. I was waiting for the blow. Before it came, I could feel the pain, the fear, and the terror. I could feel the scream rise up in my body. The memory of another bathtub at another time. Other blows, brutal blows, at other times. The reasons for the blows still a mystery. A history of not wanting to live. Rhonda's history.

Iyanla's heart was pounding, her mind racing. The crap was rushing to the surface. Oh God! This is too hard! Do it now! Do it right now! With that thought in mind, I buried my face in the warm wet washcloth and cried for Rhonda. I hoped it would be for the very last time. But I had to remember.

CHAPTER TWO

What's the Lesson When You Are an Unwanted, Neglected, and Abused Child?

When you meet anyone,
remember it is a holy encounter.
As you treat them you will treat yourself.
As you think of them you will think of yourself.
Never forget this,
for in them you will find yourself or lose your Self.

A Course in Miracles

LIKE EVERYONE ELSE'S IN THE NEIGHBORHOOD, Rhonda's house had a "front room." It didn't matter that the room was in the back of the house. The front room was the code name for where you kept the "good stuff." Having a house or an apartment that was big enough to contain a room full of good stuff was a good thing. Rhonda remembers the forbidden front room being full of plastic-covered furniture, knick-knacks and whatnots, and the Christmas candy (which also served as the Easter candy, the Thanksgiving candy, and the Halloween candy). On this particular day, the front room was full of people.

Everyone that Rhonda had to come to know as family, friends, or acquaintances from the neighborhood was in the front room. The mailman, milkman, and fish man were all there. It wasn't so much that they were in the room; it was that they were *eating* in the front room! No one ever ate in the front room, particularly not the children. Rhonda had learned from experience that when you entered the front room you walked stiffly, keeping both hands at your sides, allowing only your eyes to move around. This was the only way to keep from breaking something. But on this day, people were sitting on the plastic-covered furniture, eating mounds of food from paper plates. Rhonda knew that this was not a *normal* kind of celebration.

The doorbell rang constantly, announcing groups of people bearing covered platters of food. The men all wore suits, and most of the ladies wore hats. Everyone wore black, except the church mothers, who were also there. Some of the children from Sunday school were there, too. The people, the food, the excitement, and the suspense of not knowing what was *really* going on were somewhat overwhelming. As little Rhonda moved through the room, listening and watching, everyone she passed reached down or over to pat her on the head, almost sympathetically. She didn't know why they were patting her, and no one bothered to explain. Rhonda hoped that if she was gracious and smiled politely after each pat, she might be rewarded with a big piece of the big chocolate cake that was calling out to her from the kitchen. Unfortunately, between her and the cake stood Grandma. To Rhonda, Grandma always seemed larger than life. Today, she really was. Grandma was standing at the door, greeting a group of people who had just arrived. Grandma actually let the people hug her. Nobody ever hugged Grandma. Never! Except Rhonda's brother, Ray. And Grandma was wearing her pearls. The pearls she only wore to church. Hugging, pearls, eating in the front room! This was serious. Very serious.

"Grandma?" Rhonda called out in her sweetest voice. She looked right past Grandma to the chocolate cake that was now winking at her from the kitchen table.

"Go sit down, and don't get yourself dirty!" Grandma barked, before Rhonda could complete her question.

Rhonda knew by the tone of her voice that Grandma meant business. She also knew that Grandma wasn't about to risk letting Rhonda get icing all over her new clothes. Grandma had dressed her in a brand-new dress and a brand-new slip, brand-new panties and socks, with ruffles, of course. One look at Grandma's face, and Rhonda knew she had better turn on the heels of her new shoes before she got into trouble. Even though no one had told her so, Rhonda knew she had done really well so far that day. Before she could get back to the front room with all the grown-ups dressed in black and the plates of food, somebody yelled out, "The car is here!" Without warning, Rhonda was being buttoned into her good gray coat with the fur collar and the matching muff. Then she was whisked off, down four flights of stairs and onto the front steps of the building. There was a big black car waiting at the curb. Grandma, Rhonda, her brother, Ray, and Daddy got into the car. When the big black car pulled away from the curb, there was already a line of other cars waiting to follow it. Rhonda remembers playing with the handle on the inside of the rear door of the car. And she remembers getting slapped for it. That's where her memory of the events of that day ends.

It was many, many years later before someone had the decency to explain to Rhonda that the reason all the people had come to the house, eaten in the front room, and patted her on the head was because her mother had died. She didn't remember the funeral, barely remembered her mother; yet somehow, she'd kept a flower from her mother's casket. Her dead mother's casket. She kept it in a Bible that she had won at Sunday school for memorizing and reciting, in order, the sixty-six books of the Bible. She remembered winning the Bible more than the flower in the Bible, because the day she won it, Grandma almost smiled at her. Not quite, but almost.

Grandma, Rhonda, and Rhonda's brother, Ray, lived in a four-story walkup on a busy street in Brooklyn, New York. Although Daddy was supposed to be living there with them, he actually just stopped by every now and then. Daddy was a numbers runner. He was one of the biggest numbers runners in the neighborhood. Rhonda could count on seeing him at least twice a day; once when he came to figure up his morning numbers sheet, and again when he came to figure up his evening numbers sheet. The rest of the time, Daddy left Rhonda alone with Grandma.

Grandma, Daddy's mother, was a big lady, five feet, ten inches tall, with a large, solid frame. Grandma had a beautiful full head of salt-and-pepper hair and chiseled features and deepset eyes. Grandma never wore fancy or stylish clothes, but she would put on a little shiny pink lipstick when she was going to church. There was something about Grandma's face that was soft and strikingly beautiful in a cold and distant way. If you looked at her quickly, before she opened her mouth to speak, you would almost believe that Grandma was gentle, loving, and nurturing. It was this side of Grandma that Rhonda remembers only vaguely.

What Rhonda remembers clearly and will never forget about Grandma is her large breasts, big feet, and her huge, gnarled hands. On the days when she didn't appear strikingly beautiful, Grandma was wickedly mean. She'd squint those beady, intense little eyes as she hissed or screamed a command, letting Rhonda know it was time to get out of the way.

Rhonda used to run from Grandma, but she always came to a screeching halt at the door that led to the front room. Rather than run in there and risk breaking something, she would turn, head for the bedroom, and dive under the bed. Rhonda had enough sense to know that she had to do everything in her power to get away when Grandma was upset. She had to first tire her out. If she didn't, the power and strength of those huge hands would leave a lasting impression on some part of Rhonda's anatomy. If she could get away for just a few minutes, giving Grandma time to calm down, she would have a chance of surviving. As children, we learn a great deal about our ability to survive and get by in life by the way we are treated. It is ultimately our ability to withstand or understand the treatment we receive as children that determines what we think about ourselves as adults.

When Grandma wasn't being cruel, mean, angry, or violent, she was, at best, cool. Grandma never showed emotion, unless Rhonda's brother was somehow involved in the situation. She hardly ever smiled unless she was smiling at Rhonda's brother. She would laugh at Jack Benny or Amos and Andy on television, but that didn't really count. The only way for you to know that she was pleased, not angry with you, was when she would stare, poker-faced, in your direction and nod her head in the "yes" gesture. Grandma was Rhonda's primary caretaker after her mother's death. In a very cold and overt way, Grandma taught Rhonda her first lessons about mothers and mothering, as well as almost everything she believed to be true about herself.

Like most women of her era and race, Grandma earned her money as a domestic worker. Back then it was called "days work." It was hard, grueling work, for which Grandma was paid very little. She earned more as a cook than she did as a cleaning lady, but work as a cook required more hours away from home.

There were special days when Grandma would take Rhonda to work with her. On those days, Grandma taught Rhonda everything she knew about cooking, cleaning, and ironing. And although no one ever told her so, Rhonda knew she had learned very well. She knew it because if she ever made a mistake in the "Madam's" house, or with the "Madam's" clothes, the wrath of Grandma's hands or mouth would come crashing down on her.

When your primary caretaker is distant and aloof, it can be very confusing. You don't know whether to try and please her, or be desperately afraid of what will happen if you don't please her. When your primary caretaker is violent, you know that if you do the wrong thing, or say the wrong thing at the wrong time, in the wrong way, you could get slapped, pinched, screamed at, or punched. When your primary caretaker is violent, and you are confused, you live in fear. Many children learn to live in fear as a result of doing the wrong thing. It is a fear that they keep to themselves. They dare not tell anyone, because that would be the wrong thing to do—to say you are afraid, or to admit you have done a wrong thing. Few children learn to do the right thing on their own. Most children learn about doing the wrong thing, in confusing and violent ways. Rhonda was one of those children.

Grandma was not good at explaining to Rhonda how to do things the right way, the way that would please her. But she was very good at letting Rhonda know what would happen if she ever told what Grandma did to her when she was not pleased. Big lesson here: grin and bear your grief. Suffer in silence. Grandma said that silent suffering was good for the soul. Grandma would say, "You are not supposed to complain about the hand you are dealt by the Lord." Grandma loved the Lord, and she loved church. She was a church lady. A big-time church lady.

Every Sunday morning, Grandma would wake Rhonda up, scrub her clean, and dress her for church. After she was dressed, her hair combed, and her face smeared with Vaseline, Rhonda would sit on the edge of the bed and watch Grandma get ready for church. Rhonda loved watching Grandma get ready for church. It was a ritual. A womanhood ritual. By watching, Rhonda learned a great deal about the anatomy of a woman's body—and about the one thing strong enough to oppose Grandma.

After bathing and putting Vaseline on her body, Grandma had to put on her girdle. The girdle was a huge, stiff, white thing. It had shiny panels on either side of the lace panel that ran up the front. It also had legs. At the bottom of each leg were thick elastic bands with little hanging hooks for attaching stockings. Grandma didn't wear the pretty, sheer stockings Rhonda had seen on other ladies. Hers were heavy and coarse. Watching Grandma trying to get into the girdle was the most interesting thing about the ritual. It posed the greatest opposition to Grandma as she wiggled, twisted, pushed, and pulled her body into it. It was quite a sight. Grandma's breasts would swing from side to side, making a slapping sound against her skin. She would sweat, grunt, and struggle, but the girdle would hold firmly, refusing to cooperate. If she was rushing and hadn't dried herself completely, Grandma would have to jump up and down, pushing and pulling pieces of her flesh into the stubborn elastic compartment. There were days when it appeared as if the girdle would win. Rhonda always rooted for the girdle. But in the end, with the love of the Lord motivating her, Grandma always subdued her spandex opponent.

With the girdle defeated, she'd then put on her stiff, white uniform, hook her thick, white stockings to the girdle legs, put on her white shoes, and spray a little drugstore cologne on her neck. If Rhonda had been particularly still and quiet, Grandma would spray a little cologne on her, too. Together, they would walk stiffly down the block to the A train, then ride uptown to church.

Rhonda guessed that Grandma spent so much time in church because she was always so angry. Angry with Rhonda, angry with Daddy. Grandma was angry at the world. Sometimes she would even get angry at food and throw it around in the kitchen. Rhonda had seen her slamming a chicken into the sink and cursing to herself. Although church ladies weren't supposed to curse, Grandma had a pretty impressive vocabulary when the other church ladies weren't around. Her son, Rhonda's daddy, seemed to evoke the greatest anger in Grandma. "You and your daddy are cut from the same bolt of cloth. Ain't neither one of you ever gonna be s———t!" Whenever Grandma started down this path, Rhonda always knew where she would end up. "Neither one of you is worth the time it took to make you, and I am sick to death of both of you." It was like a daily mantra. Each time she heard it, Rhonda wondered if her daddy felt the same way about her that Grandma did. She also wondered if her daddy knew that she loved him no matter what Grandma said. Loving Daddy was an act of silent defiance. The only kind Rhonda could get away with.

Grandma was what they called a *prayer warrior* at church. For some reason, people believed that Grandma's prayers were stronger and got through to God quicker than their own. Whenever someone was in need of prayer, for their family, for a financial matter, a wayward husband, or any kind of illness, they would call on Grandma. She would sit with them at the kitchen window, listen to their story, and then write a "prescription" on a piece of brown paper. Even some family members who knew that Grandma was crazy would come to see her when they were desperate or in trouble. They all said that she had a gift. They also knew that she could pray for you or against you. It was the latter of which they were most afraid.

Praying was a skill that Grandma passed on to Rhonda. She put a great deal of time, energy, and effort into the prayer sessions she designed to teach Rhonda the mechanics of prayer, when to pray, what to pray for, how to pray for other people, and what to do while waiting for the evidence that a prayer had been answered. And with the same intensity she put into imparting the rigors of prayer, Grandma gave Rhonda a very good reason to pray.

There was hardly a morning that Rhonda didn't wake up to find Grandma sitting at the window, praying. Before sunrise, Grandma would sit with the open Bible in her lap, rocking back and forth on the kitchen chair, praying and singing hymns. Rhonda's memories of chicken frying in the pan and fresh rolls baking in the oven were colored with memories of Grandma singing "What a Friend We Have in Jesus," "Nearer, My God, to Thee," and "Jesus, Keep Me Near the Cross." Those were the same songs that Rhonda used to sing to herself when Grandma was angry and giving her a "healing" bath.

Grandma was the reason Rhonda learned to pray about soap. She prayed that God, or the appropriate saint in charge, would let Grandma know that using store-bought soap was not a sin. Grandma made her own soap. It was brown, odorless, and contained a variety of sticks, leaves, and pebbles that were quite abrasive to the skin. Rhonda prayed for the day she could use a bar of the sweet-smelling soap that she would see in the supermarket. The kind that left a scent on your body that you could smell as you moved around the house. "Buying soap when you can make your own is a waste of money. Wasting money," Grandma said, "is a sin!" Besides that, they both knew that Grandma's soap caused a lot more pain when Grandma gave Rhonda one of her special healing baths.

Healing requires a special approach to the problem presented before you. On the days when Grandma was particularly angry, and Rhonda had done something that particularly annoyed her, Grandma would resort to what she called "a healing." Rhonda would be stripped naked and made to stand in the tub. Grandma would take the special scrub brush from behind the bathroom sink, then douse Rhonda with a pot of cold water. Using the homemade soap, Grandma would scrub Rhonda's small body from head to toe, including her face. She would scrub and pray, scrub and sing. Grandma would scrub until she saw blood.

"I'm gonna scrub the devil out you!" she'd say. "I'm gonna wash this devil spirit away!" Then she'd begin to pray. The more she prayed, the harder she scrubbed. The harder she scrubbed, the more Rhonda whimpered. The more Rhonda whimpered, the louder Grandma sang. "Pleading the blood of Jesus! I'm pleading the blood to wash away your sins!" It was a ritual between Grandma and Rhonda, and it never stopped until Rhonda prayed out loud, "Please, God! Tell Grandma I'm sorry!" Sometimes, if Rhonda prayed loud enough or fast enough, Grandma would take pity on her. Most of the time, however, Grandma kept scrubbing and praying and singing until she saw the red of Rhonda's blood mixed in with the lather from the brown soap.

When the bath was over, Grandma would rub Rhonda down in mutton tallow, a thick yellow substance made from the inside of a lamb's skin. Over time, Rhonda figured out that using mutton tallow was Grandma's attempt to hide the scars and bruises from the brush. Grandma called it "waterproofing." "It's gonna rain today, and you don't want to catch a cold." She would then smear the tallow all over Rhonda's body while she hummed her favorite hymns. Though Rhonda would be sore and battered from the bath, she was glad to have somebody touch her in a somewhat gentle manner. The gentleness with which the foul smelling mutton tallow was applied to her battered body was an answer to at least one of Rhonda's prayers.

Dear God:
Please let the rain wash away the pain.

It is a fact of life that grandmothers know everything. And Rhonda's grandma was no exception. She was mean as hell, but she sure knew a lot. Grandma knew most about herbs. Over the years, Rhonda watched her use them in the most amazing ways. She knew how to mix them, how to cook them, how to rub them on various parts of the body, and which ones you could use or not use to make tea. At the time, Rhonda didn't know that Grandma was a Native American of Cherokee and Blackfoot heritage. But she learned more about Grandma and what she knew about herbs and healing when they went to Grandma's hometown of Smithfield, Virginia, to save Aunt Mattie's life.

Rhonda awoke one morning to find Grandma sitting in her chair at the kitchen window. This morning, there was something different. The sounds were different. There was the sound of the chair creaking as it struggled under Grandma's weight. That was different. Then there were the haunting grunting and moaning sounds spilling out of Grandma's mouth.

Grandma was so engrossed in what she was feeling and doing, she didn't even look at Rhonda when she passed by on the way to the bathroom. She didn't even ask Rhonda if she had her slippers on. Rhonda stood frozen in the doorway for a long time, watching her grandmother tremble, moan, and cry. In the early morning sunlight, Rhonda could see tears rolling down her grandmother's face. That, too, was different. Grandma's prayer time was usually her most peaceful time. Grandma crying? This was amazingly different! No. This was a problem! Grandma never cried. Never! Just as Rhonda was beginning to panic, Grandma's eyes flew open, and she turned to face the frightened child.

"Do you have your slippers on?" Rhonda's panic shifted into disbelief. A few minutes ago Grandma was in a trance of some kind, and now she was yelling! Her tears had seemed to dry instantly, though she never wiped her face. Now, Rhonda was crying. Her nose and eyes were running, but she managed to answer, "Yes." Grandma got up, closed her Bible, and moved her chair, all in one swift movement. "Hurry now, go on to the bathroom. We've got to catch the bus to Virginia."

Rhonda loved to go to Virginia, though she'd never mention it out loud. Grandma's oldest brother, Uncle Jimmy, lived in Smithfield. He and his wife, Aunt Mattie, ran a successful bootlegging operation from a small green house on a very dusty road. Aunt Mattie was a wonderful cook, and each time they went to visit, Rhonda knew she'd have hot rolls, grits, and steak and gravy for breakfast. She also knew that, with any kind of luck, Aunt Mattie would give her some sweet-smelling Avon soap and lotion to bring home.

Grandma packed the satchel in record time. Before Rhonda knew it, she and Grandma were on a Greyhound bus, holding greasy brown paper bags on their laps. The bags were filled with fried chicken parts and white bread wrapped in wax paper. The chicken was the sustenance that would take them from New York's Port Authority to the dank and dusty Smithfield, Virginia, bus depot. The chicken would be Rhonda's only source of company during the ten and a half hours of Grandma's silence.

Grandma and Rhonda stepped off the bus and into a yellow taxicab. Instinctively, Rhonda knew something was wrong. Grandma always said, "Taxicab riding is for rich folks, pregnant women, and sinners." Grandma sitting stoically silent in the back of a taxi meant that something was very wrong—or that Grandma had finally gone public about her own sinful ways.

When they arrived, Grandma pushed, pulled, and dragged Rhonda out of the taxi. The driver yelled at them for not shutting the car door, but Grandma was already on the porch and announcing her arrival. Uncle Jimmy was standing on the screened-in porch, staring at but not seeing them. His speech sounded mechanical. He said something about dying and a coma. He was talking about his wife, Aunt Mattie. She had suffered a diabetic stroke. Her doctor had insisted that she be taken to the white folks' hospital on the other side of the county. Colored people could only visit on Saturday. This was Tuesday.

Rhonda learned a great deal over the next four days, which proved to be very suspenseful. Later on in her life, what she learned would prove very helpful. Grandma began each day with a ritual of sorts. She would walk through every room in the house, lighting candles and incense. With that done, she would return to each room to pray and sing. Of Aunt Mattie, she said, "I've got to call her spirit back home." She said barely a word to Rhonda or Uncle Jimmy. And, much to Rhonda's dismay, she did very little cooking.

Uncle Jimmy stayed on the porch, rocking in his chair. If you didn't know any better, you would think that he was staring out into the woods that surrounded the house. But Rhonda knew that he was silently staring at Aunt Mattie's empty chair that sat directly across from his. Sometimes Rhonda would stand next to him and pat his shoulder in an effort to comfort him. He never responded. He just stared. Rhonda, a big-city kid left on her own in the Deep South, decided it best to keep company with the pigs and chickens.

When night fell, the suspense began. Just about the time it turned dark, Grandma would take Rhonda into the woods to pick herbs. When you're a big-city kid, walking in the woods at night can be a terrifying experience. When the grandmother with whom you are walking in the woods at night talks to the bushes before she picks their branches, terror is a more apt description. Rhonda hung onto Grandma's skirt every step of the way, but she knew that if one of those bushes answered Grandma's questions, Grandma would be on her own.

Rhonda was always relieved when she saw the porch lights that provided a beacon back to the house, where Grandma ritualistically prepared the collected herbs. Grandma carefully laid each bundle out before her on the porch. It was an unspoken signal for Uncle Jimmy to go inside. Silently, Grandma would pick up a bundle of herbs and pray over it. The prayers eventually gave way to the humming of a hymn, which continued until each leaf from every stem in the bunch had been picked and placed in a large metal washtub. Rhonda watched silently, resisting the urge to sing out loud when Grandma hummed her favorite hymns. When all of the leaves had been removed from the branches, Grandma covered the washtub with a white towel and motioned Rhonda into the house and to bed.

Grandma's pounding the leaves in the washtub with a large rock woke Rhonda before sunrise. Standing barefoot on the porch, Rhonda would watch Grandma pound, pray, and add water to the tub, transforming the dry leaves into a slimy green concoction. By the time Grandma saw Rhonda and ordered her into her slippers, she would have added a pile of Aunt Mattie's clothes to the concoction. Through the tiny screened window on the back porch, Grandma would watch Rhonda mount the milk crate in the bathroom, where she would stand to wash her face and the "tight places" on her body. On the back porch, Grandma put the clothes and the green concoction into the wringer washer. Eating biscuits and bacon, and drinking milk fresh from the cow, Rhonda watched out of the kitchen window as Grandma hung Aunt Mattie's clothes on the outdoor line. Rhonda knew that by noon the clothes would be dry and ready to be ironed.

It was "women's work," Grandma said. "You've got to know how to stay focused long enough, and how to pray hard enough, to bring healing into any place and any situation." Grandma said, "Women's work goes beyond faith. Faith is what you need when you don't have discipline, and when you don't know. When you know, you do the work, and you don't need faith."

During that trip to Virginia, Rhonda began to see Grandma in a completely different light. The cruel, violent, angry woman that Rhonda knew from back home had given way to a focused, disciplined, and compassionate human being. Rhonda didn't understand what was really going on, but she knew it was sacred. She had never before seen Grandma in this light. She liked it. She liked the way it felt. She prayed that it would last. Rhonda also learned something new about herself. She learned that she could do the right thing.

Saturday finally came. Grandma washed Rhonda's body with Aunt Mattie's Avon soap and let her put some sweet-smelling lotion on herself. After Rhonda was dressed, Grandma didn't even tell her where to sit, so she stood quietly on the porch. It was when she was in the backseat of Uncle Jimmy's big blue Caddy that Rhonda realized she had received the answer to another prayer. She could smell the scent of the store-bought soap and lotion rising off her body as Uncle Jimmy tore down the dusty country road, headed for the hospital. Rhonda fiddled with her patent-leather purse and the handle on the back door that controlled the car window. She knew she was pushing her luck, but there were moments when she sang, out loud. Neither Grandma nor Uncle Jimmy said a word to Rhonda or to each other for the entire ride.

When they arrived in Newport News, Grandma gave Rhonda a dollar and told her to get herself some ice cream. She asked the lady in the store if she would keep an eye on Rhonda for a little while. The man behind the counter gave Rhonda a big bowl of ice cream and a huge pile of napkins. He gave her a little extra when she told him she had come from New York. Before she could get herself situated in the seat and enjoy her treat, Rhonda looked up and saw Grandma, followed by Uncle Jimmy, and Uncle Jimmy, followed by Aunt Mattie, heading her way. Rhonda thought that Aunt Mattie was dead, or dying, or something, but looking at the slight smile on Grandma's face, she realized that the "women's work" that she and Grandma had done had been successful.

Things were back to normal. Every five words or so, Grandma would remind Rhonda, "Don't mess up your clothes"; "Take your time"; "Use your napkin." And on the ride back to the house, Grandma issued at least fifty don't-do-thats and leave-that-alones. Back in New York, Rhonda learned more details about the trip to Smithfield. Grandma told Daddy, the neighbors, and all the church ladies about how prayer had saved Aunt Mattie. She didn't tell them about the herbs or the washing and ironing of the clothes. And far be it from Rhonda to say anything to anybody about anything.

Grandma must have been really pleased with God for saving Aunt Mattie, because no matter what Rhonda did, she didn't get a healing bath for a very long time. They also spent much more time in church. The Sunday morning ritual spilled over into Wednesday and Friday nights. Grandma belonged to the Holiness church, complete with tambourines, drums, and people passing out on the floor. Grandma would spend her time with the other church ladies, cooking and praying, praising and shouting. Rhonda was never quite sure why people shouted, but once they did, they got to sit up front in the church.

After the time Grandma shouted, they always got to sit in the front row. It had happened so fast, Rhonda could hardly catch her breath or figure out what was going on. The Reverend was preaching, the organist and guitarist were playing, the choir was singing, and people were moaning and rocking. Then the Reverend started singing and swinging his tie over his head. People were up on their feet, waving their hands and slapping tambourines against their hips. The drums were beating out a ferocious tempo.

One minute Grandma was sitting there, her normal, cool self, and the next minute she was up on one foot, dancing, screaming, and waving her hands wildly in the air. As she shouted, she lost pieces of her clothing and her pearls. The church ladies in their white uniforms caught Grandma before she fell, convulsing, to the floor. Rhonda had seen it happen to other people, at other times, but to see it happen to Grandma was frightening. The church mothers came running from everywhere. They laid Grandma on the floor between the pews and covered her with a white blanket while her body calmed from spasmodic jerks to a mild trembling. According to every television program Rhonda had ever seen, a body on the floor, covered in white, meant death. Rhonda watched and waited for Grandma's body to stop moving, realizing that *once it did,* she would never have to take another healing bath. But also realizing that *if it did,* she might never have another decent meal.

Rhonda learned about spirituality and things of a spiritual nature under a cloud of suspense and fear. The same is true for so many children. Most children get religion. They are sent to church. They are told Bible stories. They learn the rudiments and regimens of religious practice. They are definitely taught that they are sinners. They are taught what not to do. They are also taught that if they commit the forbidden acts, God will get them. Children like Rhonda are taught about a cruel and punishing God. A God who is displeased with you and most of what you do unless you follow certain "prescriptions." Few children are taught that they are not separate from God, or that it is possible to develop an intimate relationship with God. They believe, like the adults who teach or do not teach them, that God is somewhere "out there," separate and apart from you, waiting for you to make the wrong move.

Rhonda couldn't seem to follow the prescriptions that would please God or Grandma. She wanted to. She really tried to. But the fact that she was always being punished, beaten, or bathed confirmed for her all that she had heard in church—she was a wretched sinner, destined to go to hell. Without an explanation from Grandma, or Daddy, or anyone else, she, like so many children, was left to her own perceptions and understandings.

Rhonda figured out very early in life that she was bad, and that something bad was going to happen to her. When Grandma started shouting in church, for a brief moment, Rhonda thought that something bad was happening to Grandma, too. But when Grandma didn't die, Rhonda remembered that Grandma was a saint, according to the church.

Grandma, who prayed just before she cursed, or as she scrubbed Rhonda until she was bloody. The same Grandma who berated her son, and who reserved lipstick wearing for Sundays, was not a sinner. She was a woman bound and determined to do God's work. And without any additional information, Rhonda thought it was Grandma's job to save her from hell.

Rhonda's family wasn't big, but they all got together on Thanksgiving and Christmas. They had birthday parties; they went together to Aunt Dora and Uncle Lowell's house in Atlantic City, and to Uncle Jimmy's farm in the summer. Rhonda figured that they all knew the family secret—that she was bad and destined for hell. Rhonda also concluded that was the reason no one ever came to her defense when she was being pinched, slapped, or beaten in their presence. Bad children expect bad things to happen to them. They expect to be punished. Instead of defending her, people winked conspiratorially, nodded knowingly, and secretly shoved money in Rhonda's pockets. Rhonda wondered if they knew about the baths. She wondered if they knew about the times when Grandma locked her in the closet when she went to work. Did they know that in Grandma's care, Rhonda's life was in danger? Did they know but were too afraid to care? Or did they know and just *not* care?

Where do children learn about God or love or life if not through the actions of those entrusted with their care? How do children learn to distinguish between loving acts, done to guide and protect the child, and those committed in mindless rage or misguided authority? From whom, and under what circumstances, do children learn to distinguish the difference between a loving hurt and hurts caused by lovelessness? And why do the adults raising children believe that love has to hurt in order to be love?

Rhonda, like so many children, learned about love through pain, abusive, negligently inflicted, and unnecessary pain. She learned about God in the midst of fear. She learned to expect pain as an ingredient of being loved. She learned that people who claim to love you can cause, and will ignore, your pain. Rhonda learned through the actions of her "loved ones" to expect that an act of love would be preceded by the imposition of pain. None of this was ever explained to her. She learned it all by watching and listening, and by experiencing the pain. Rhonda learned that if you do the wrong thing, those who love you will hurt you. And no matter how badly you hurt, or what you have done, if you bear the pain of love silently, you can hope against hope that someone will, one day, love you enough to hurt you again.

The water in the tub was beginning to feel a little cool against my body, but I couldn't stop, I couldn't move. There is no way to think about Grandma without thinking about Rhonda's Daddy, Grandma's son.

CHAPTER THREE

What's the Lesson When You Do Not Realize That You Are a Teacher?

A prophet is not without honour,
but in his own country,
and among his own kin,
and in his own house.

Mark 6:4

ALL LITTLE GIRLS WANT TO BE LOVED and protected and praised by their daddies. A daddy is a hero to his little girl even when the rest of the world thinks he is a bum. In a little girl's eyes, Daddy can do no wrong, unless he does something to hurt Mommy. But when there is no Mommy, Daddy can do no wrong, no matter how much wrong he does. No little girl wants to disappoint her daddy. She will find a way, something to do, that she hopes will make him smile. And perhaps, if she has done a really good job, he will swoop her up in his arms as a sign of how wonderful he thinks she is. I'm telling you, it would make a little girl's day and, possibly, a big difference in her life. Love, protection, praise, and swooping from a daddy are elements essential to the tender, budding psyche of all little girls.

All little girls wait for Daddy to come home, even when he doesn't. All little girls wait to tell Daddy about their day, or week, or month, depending on how long it takes him to show up. Even when he comes late, or doesn't come at all, there is a secret place in a little girl's heart where she waits for her daddy. No matter what is going on in a little girl's life, she believes that Daddy can fix it, save her, and make everything all better, even when he can't. In this respect, Rhonda was just like all little girls. Daddy was her hero. She needed his love, protection, and praise. She waited, although she never received them. She believed with all of her heart that Daddy could make everything better, even when he couldn't.

All the ladies agreed that Rhonda's father was really good-looking. Rhonda was always proud to walk down the street with him and watch them watch him out of the corners of their eyes. Like Grandma, he had finely chiseled features. A thick, bushy mustache covered his large lips. He had a deep, rumbling voice, and it was that voice that gave Daddy his way with the ladies. Daddy didn't sleep at Grandma's house. Rhonda didn't know where he slept, but he always came at lunchtime to have a sandwich and to calculate his numbers. The minute he hit the door, Grandma would start complaining about her lack of money, about Rhonda, and about Daddy in general. On a good day, Daddy would shove some money in her hand as soon as he walked in. That would shut her up. On a bad day, if Daddy hadn't hit a number or didn't have any money, Grandma would go on and on, cursing and screaming. But Daddy would never curse her back. He'd just look at her and say, "Ma, please. I've got to get this done."

Rhonda wasn't sure if she should interrupt Daddy to tell him about the dream.

"Daddy, the lady in my dream told me to tell you a number."

"That's nice, baby," Daddy said, as he continued his calculations.

"Do you want to know what the number is, Daddy?"

"Sure, baby. But not right now, though." And he took a bite of his sandwich.

Rhonda waited quietly by the kitchen door. She watched him work and eat. When he was done, he gathered his slips, shoving them in his pocket, grabbed his hat, and headed for the door. Rhonda knew he was trying to make it to the door before Grandma had a chance to open her mouth again. He almost made it.

"What time will you be back?" Grandma hollered from her room when she heard his keys jingling.

"'Bout six." He answered without slowing his pace. Just as he was about to open the apartment door, Rhonda ran over to him.

"Daddy, the lady told me to tell you the number. She made me promise not to forget."

"Baby, Daddy's got to go now," he said as he tried to shoo her away.

"But she made me promise." Daddy wasn't smiling. He was trying to get away.

"She told me to tell you 6-2-3." Rhonda was proud of herself. She had remembered.

"Okay. That's nice, baby. Thank you." And he slammed the door.

When 623 hit that evening, Daddy didn't make a dime. But from that day on, he would walk in and make it a point to ask Rhonda, even before he took off his hat or spoke to Grandma, "Did you have a dream last night?" Whenever she had a dream, Rhonda couldn't wait to tell Daddy. She would whisper the number in his ear so that Grandma couldn't hear it. It was their little secret. Daddy would smile, give her a big hug, and pat her on the head. Daddy never kissed Rhonda, not ever.

It never failed. If Rhonda gave Daddy a number, it played that day or, at the latest, the next evening. Daddy would be so happy that he'd stay a little longer at lunchtime. He'd call Rhonda baby and tickle her stomach. Before he left, he would give Grandma some money, and that night Rhonda wouldn't get a bath.

Daddy could always tell when Rhonda had gotten a bath. Maybe he could see the bruises on her arms and legs. Maybe he could see the sadness and the fear in her eyes. Maybe he became suspicious when Grandma would pray or sing just a tad bit louder and a little more off-key than usual. On those days, Daddy would quietly whisper to her, "You got another bath, yesterday, huh? Don't worry. You're tough like me. You can take it." It was *another* secret that Rhonda shared only with her daddy.

Sometimes, when Grandma had to go out to work at a particular "Madam's" house where she couldn't bring Rhonda, Daddy would take Rhonda with him to bars and pretty-women's houses, and to a variety of smoky haunts filled with loud and funny-acting people. There was Mr. Rootman. He was always nice and never failed to give Rhonda a stick of gum or some candy. There was Bubba John, who stuttered and spit when he talked. Then there were the ladies. They all wanted something from Daddy and didn't mind using Rhonda to get it. Rhonda didn't mind being used, because she always got a Popsicle or a lollipop in the process. Sometimes, one of the ladies would take her downtown and buy her new clothes. Grandma never liked the clothes that the ladies bought. She'd scream and holler about them being red or striped, too tight or too short.

"You look just like one of those whores you and your daddy hang out with," she'd yell. Rhonda thought she looked pretty nice. Grandma would fix Daddy with a mean stare, "Look at her. She looks just like a little floozy." But Rhonda thought her new clothes looked a lot better than the corduroy overalls Grandma made her wear. Then Daddy and Rhonda would be treated to another chorus of Grandma's favorite phrase: "Ain't neither one of you s——t! And you ain't never gonna be s——t!"

At home, Daddy was completely different from the daddy who hung out at bars and rode around with pretty ladies. Daddy never challenged Grandma. Whatever she did, whatever she said was okay. For Rhonda, the best times she spent with her daddy were on the days when Grandma had to go out and Daddy would stay home and cook and play games. Daddy grew up in the South, not far from Uncle Jimmy's farm. When he and Grandma moved up to New York City, Grandma went to work, and Daddy spent a lot of time home alone. Daddy was a good cook. He said that he learned how to cook when he was young and Grandma was away so much of the time. He also learned how to wash and iron and take care of himself.

Daddy told Rhonda everything he remembered about his own daddy, which wasn't much. It seemed that he died when Daddy was only two years old. Folks in the family used to say that Grandma had drowned him for beating her. Others said that he died in a fishing accident, but they never talked about the fact that Grandma's husband was half black and half white. Daddy used to tell Rhonda all about the army. He said he joined the army when he was nineteen years old to learn more about cooking. Rhonda thought he enlisted to get away from Grandma. When Rhonda was older, Daddy talked about how hard it was to be a

black man in a white man's army. He also told her about spending years
in Leavenworth for selling cigarettes on the black market, and how
they'd promised him his freedom if he'd go on a dangerous mission. He
survived the mission, and after that, they gave him his freedom and a dishonorable discharge.

That's why Daddy was a numbers runner. In 1950s America, as a
black man with a dishonorable discharge from the army, he couldn't get
a job. It was, he said, worse than being a black cat in the midst of the Holiness church. Daddy was bitter about his life. Perhaps because he grew
up without a daddy. Perhaps because his mother was so mean. Maybe it
was because he got dishonorably discharged from the army. Maybe it was
because, although he was a mathematical genius, he couldn't get work.
Maybe it was because his wife had died, or because he had two kids that
he couldn't take care of.

Rhonda was never sure what caused Daddy's bitterness, because nobody ever explained it to her. She only knew that her daddy wasn't there to
protect her. Her daddy wasn't there to look out for her. Her daddy knew
that *his* mother abused *his* daughter, and he never said a word. Her daddy
taught her many things about living and loving. He taught her that life
was hard and that you must do whatever is necessary to survive. He taught
her that it was all right for men to pass through your life, give you a little
money, say that they love you, and that you shouldn't ask for any more.

Rhonda knew that her daddy was bad, just like she was. The only
difference was that Daddy never went to church. Sometimes Rhonda
would ask him to go. She told him if he went they could pray together
and ask God to make them good and saints, like Grandma. Daddy
would laugh. "Who in the world told you that Grandma is a saint?"

"That's what they call her in church. Saint Harris and Sister Harris,"
Rhonda would explain to him.

"That doesn't mean that she is a *real* saint. That doesn't mean anything. It's just something they say in the church," Daddy explained.

"But Grandma said that you and I are going to hell and she and Ray
are going to heaven. Maybe if we pray real hard like Grandma showed
me, God won't send us to hell. It's very hot down there, and all the bad

people go there." By then Rhonda would be crying. She knew she was bad, but the thought of her hero, her daddy burning in hell was more than she could handle.

"Listen, baby," she loved it when he called her baby, even if it was only once in a while. "If you and I are going to hell, believe me, Grandma will be there when we get there." Daddy would wipe away Rhonda's tears and send her off to play. She wanted to believe him, but she had heard a lot more of Grandma's side of the story than she had her daddy's.

Daddy taught Rhonda that money is more important than personal honor, and that it is okay to do whatever is required of you to get the money you need to live. He taught her that family is nowhere near as important as your reputation among your peers. He also taught her that making do with what you have is more important than asking for what you want. More important still, he taught her never to tell the truth if it will make trouble, or get you in trouble. He taught these things to Rhonda in all that he said and did. He passed it on to her brother as well, by word and by deed.

Rhonda often wondered how her daddy felt. How he felt about her, how he felt about his mother, and most important, how he felt about himself. Perhaps, she thought, if someone knew how he really felt, they could help him. Perhaps if his mother knew how he felt, she would not have stomped all over his heart. It wasn't personal. It was about survival. Grandma was doing what she felt she needed to do to survive, and Daddy was doing the same thing. Rhonda was just trying to survive, too. Daddy and Grandma taught her to do whatever is necessary to get through the hard times, the difficult days, in order to survive.

Unfortunately, when you have a survivalist mentality, you become so caught up in surviving, you forget that there is another way of living. You forget about the joy and the gentleness and the softness. You forget about communication and intimacy. You forget that in the process of living you must remember to be gentle and kind. When you are a daddy, you may even forget that your little girl is watching you, waiting for you to make things better. Rhonda had a hard time learning all of the things that her daddy and the other adults in her life forgot.

CHAPTER FOUR

What's the Lesson When You Don't Realize That Life Is a School?

Today I am canceling mess!
Getting rid of confusion that's been hanging around like
cobwebs on my ceiling.
I am releasing my soul from tiredness and antiquated,
meaningless crap!
Stepping out of traps that have long been rusted.
I'm doing like some companies do when they reorganize,
forgiving debts, writing off losses, and establishing good credit
for myself.
There are simply some things that need to be written off.
Some people, too!

Reverend June Gatlin,
from *Spirit Speaks to Sisters*

I'M CONVINCED THAT expensive dogs are dumb. Mutts have good sense. They understand that they have to be good. They have to poop in appropriate places, they have to eat whatever they get, and they can't chase the resident seventeen-year-old cat. Unfortunately, I didn't have a mutt; I had an expensive dog. I could hear it outside the bathroom door, chasing and harassing the slow-moving cat. The fact that the water was cold and I had to rescue the old cat from the new dog provided an excellent opportunity to empty the cold, crappy water out of the Jacuzzi so that I could fill it up again. This time I would add a little peppermint and some rose oil to the water, a stimulating combination that takes the mind to the heart of the matter. After putting the dog in the basement and offering the stressed-out cat some Tender Vittles, I slipped back into the bathtub to continue my healing process.

Rhonda's father had a girlfriend and he also had a wife. His girlfriend, with whom he had two children, Rhonda and Ray, had died of breast cancer and leukemia. He married his wife two years before his girlfriend's illness was even diagnosed. It was a scandal. Daddy's wife was a very classy lady. So classy, in fact, that everybody hated her. Most people said if it had not been for her, Rhonda's mother probably wouldn't have died. How they figured the wife's presence gave the girlfriend breast cancer was a mystery to Rhonda. Perhaps they just needed a reason to hate her because she was so beautiful.

Daddy's wife could have been a model, except she was too short. Her fair complexion, shapely frame, keen facial features, and long black hair were quite acceptable to the world at large. And it was precisely these things that made everyone else in the family despise her.

"Who does she think she is?" one of the more endowed aunts would ask when Lynnette was not within earshot.

"She must think she's white!" was Grandma's pat answer. "She acts just like them highfalutin women uptown who ain't got nothin' but their looks to offer anybody."

Everyone, including Rhonda, called Daddy's wife Nett, and she had more than looks. She was beautiful. She was stylish. And she wore jewelry. As a matter of fact, one of the things about Nett that so endeared her to Rhonda was her jewelry, all of it gold. She wore a pear-shaped opal on a gold chain around her neck. It was her birthstone, she said. Nett also wore two beautiful gold rings, one on each of her ring fingers. One was her wedding band, she said. The other was a thin gold band that had a beautiful round stone called a diamond. Rhonda liked it when Lynnette made the diamond reflect light onto the wall. Nett also wore two bracelets, called bangles, on her left arm. They were made out of pink gold. "My mother gave these to me when I was a little girl," Nett told Rhonda. "One day they will be yours. I will give them to you, just like my mother gave them to me." What Lynnette didn't tell Rhonda was that on the day she would inherit the bangles, Nett would be dead.

Nett always wore a colored skirt, white blouse, and low-heeled pumps. The neck of her blouse was so heavily starched that it stood up on its own. There were times when Rhonda liked to sit and just stare at Lynnette because she was so beautiful. She was also kind, gentle, and very affectionate. Rhonda could tell that Daddy thought Lynnette was beautiful, too. She could tell by the look in his eyes whenever he was around her. Sometimes Rhonda wished that Daddy would look at her the way he looked at Nett, but he never did. But everything that Nett did made Rhonda *feel* beautiful for the first time in her life. And Nett was everything that Grandma wasn't.

It would be too mild to say that Grandma didn't like Nett. Hated would seem more appropriate. But it wasn't just that Grandma hated Nett, it was that she went out of her way to be mean to her and to say nasty things about her. Rhonda wasn't sure if it was a blessing or a curse. On the blessing side, it meant that Grandma spent so much time complaining about Nett, she'd go for days without complaining about Rhonda. From the curse perspective, her liking Nett made Rhonda a double enemy in Grandma's eyes and added new fuel to her repertoire of verbal abuse.

"She paints her fingernails! You like that, don't you?" Grandma would say, building up steam. "Only whores paint their fingernails. Guess you want to be a whore just like her. You want to be just like your daddy's whore, don't you? I don't know what that trash is she wears, but you can smell her coming a mile away. Bet you want to smell like that, too. Don't you? Homemade soap ain't good enough for you, huh? Want to smell like your daddy's whore, don't you."

At the time, Rhonda had no idea what being a whore meant, but if it was good enough for Nett, it was just fine by her. What really stuck in Grandma's throat had nothing to do with Nett's fingernails, nor the fragrance she wore. It had a whole lot to do with Nett's heritage. Nett's parents were Caribbean, she was a mixture of Jamaican and Cuban. Back then, black people from the South neither liked nor understood black people from the Islands.

"They eat monkeys, you know," Grandma would say smugly. "Keep them as pets, too! That bitch probably thinks you're her own little pet monkey." Rhonda must have heard Grandma's monkey-talk a thousand times. She didn't know most of the words that Grandma used to describe Nett, or whether she was even telling the truth. What she did know was that when you weighed Grandma's baths and abuse against Nett's bubble baths and pancakes, Rhonda would rather be a monkey in Nett's house any day.

On days when Rhonda went riding with Daddy, he would take her to Nett's house, and Nett would make her pancakes from scratch. It was absolutely amazing how she did it. Every pancake came out the same color and the same size. Occasionally, Nett and Rhonda would make tuna fish sandwiches together. Rhonda would peel the fragile shells off the hardboiled eggs, and Nett would finely chop the pickles and onions. Nett always toasted their bread just right, and she always gave Rhonda her own napkin.

As far as Rhonda could remember, Nett was the only person who ever really talked to her. She talked to Rhonda about important things like what the cartoon characters were doing and who was going to win the Miss America pageant. But most important was that Nett talked to Rhonda about Rhonda. She taught Rhonda how to polish her nails, and she taught her how to wash her panties out at night. And she never, ever yelled at her. A bath at Nett's house meant bubbles and sweet-smelling soap—a marked improvement from the baths Rhonda had taken at Grandma's house.

Nett also liked to do fun things like play war with aluminum foil spitballs and play tic-tac-toe on brown paper bags. She was the first person to take Rhonda anywhere fun. They'd go to the zoo or the botanical gardens. And, oh my God, did they ever go to the movies. A movie outing with Lynnette meant popcorn, soda, and a trip to the Horn & Hardart Automat. Nett was the first person to tell Rhonda that she was beautiful and who made Rhonda feel beautiful. "You know what, Ronnie," Nett would tell her, "one day you're going to be somebody." Nett was an angel, the first angel that Rhonda ever knew.

In the secret, most private place in her heart, Rhonda would pray that the day would come when she and Daddy and Ray and Nett could all live together. Grandma always said, "Be careful what you ask for 'cause you just might get it." And when the day finally came, the circumstances surrounding the move were far less joyous than Rhonda had expected.

Rhonda was five, and it was time for her to start to school. Grandma had had to take a full-time job cleaning and cooking, because Daddy's numbers-running business was slowing down. Rhonda hadn't seen the lady in the white dress in her dreams in a very long time. Nett volunteered to take Rhonda downtown to the big department store to shop for nice, and expensive, school clothes. Grandma left the house first, leaving Rhonda and her brother with the stern reminder that they were never to open the door for anyone. After Daddy left, Rhonda and Ray watched Mighty Mouse cartoons until they went off, indicating it was lunchtime and time for Nett to arrive. Rhonda could hardly wait.

Nett showed up, as promised, and let herself in with her key. Hugs and kisses, hugs and kisses. Nett was always good for hugs and kisses, though on this day, Rhonda didn't seem quite as eager to be hugged. "Come on," Nett told them, "let me bathe you so we can go shopping." Ray stripped in a matter of seconds. Rhonda lied and said that she had already had a bath. "Come on, now," Nett gently persisted. "You've got to take a bath and change your shirt. It looks dirty, and you smell kind of funny." Rhonda backed away. "Okay, we'll let Ray take his bath first, and then you'll take yours."

When Ray was done, Nett took Rhonda into the bathroom and ran her bath. "Take your clothes off, Ronnie," Nett said. When Rhonda hesitated, she added, "Hurry up, and I'll put bubbles in the water." Rhonda reluctantly took off her shoes, her socks, her overalls, and panties, then got into the bathtub and stood there with her undershirt still on. "You can't take a bath with your undershirt on." Nett smiled. "Come here and let me take it off." Instead, Rhonda sat down in the tub. Nett reached for her and stood her back up. She pulled Rhonda's undershirt over her head, and what she saw made her scream. "Oh my God! Oh my God!" All of the skin on Rhonda's back had come off with the shirt. "What happened to you?" Nett asked, her eyes mirroring the terror she felt in her heart.

"The dog did it," Rhonda said, her eyes were lowered to the bubbles in the tub.

"What dog?!" Nett asked. "What dog did this to you, Ronnie?"

"The dog downstairs in the backyard."

Nett carefully, gingerly, took Rhonda out of the tub. "Oh my God," she said over and over again to herself. Nett didn't want to wrap Rhonda in a towel, her back was so raw. "Oh, my poor baby," she said, "who did this to my poor baby?" And Nett began to cry.

Ray stood in the bathroom doorway and spoke up in support of Rhonda's story. "There's two of them, you know. One brown one and one black one. The black one barks all the time," Ray added.

"Just shut up about the damn dogs," Nett said. "I know didn't no dog do this to her back!" Now everybody was in a panic. Nett, Rhonda, and Ray.

"Tell me what happened to you, Ronnie," Lynnette spat out. Rhonda and Ray were wide-eyed and dumbfounded. Nett's voice sounded like Grandma's. The silence in the bathroom was heavy with fear. Rhonda was afraid to tell. Ray was afraid she *would* tell. Nett tried another tactic. "Tell me what happened, sweetie; tell Nett what happened to her baby, to her poor little baby." After a few minutes more of cajoling, Rhonda took a deep breath, lowered her little chin to her chest, and told Nett the truth.

"I opened the door for the man, and Grandma beat me with the ironing cord."

"What man? What cord?"

"Grandma always beats her with the ironing cord because she's bad," Ray said. Rhonda didn't know if Ray was trying to help, or trying to get her in trouble with Nett. But Nett's voice remained soothing, which let Rhonda know she could tell her everything. "When the insurance man came to bring Grandma mail, I opened the door so I could get the mail for Grandma." Rhonda had begun to cry.

"Don't cry, sweetie. It's all right. You opened the door for Mr. Cummings?" Rhonda couldn't speak, so she shook her head.

"Did you lock the door after he left?" Nett took another glance at Rhonda's back and closed her eyes.

"Yeah." Rhonda was gasping. "I did and I told Grandma I did, but she beat me anyway."

"Ooooo!" Ray thought it was about time he added another two cents. "Grandma told you that you better not tell anybody."

Nett shot him a quick shut-your-mouth glance, saying to him, "It's okay. You are supposed to tell when somebody hurts you." Then, to Rhonda, "It's okay that you opened the door, because you knew Mr. Cummings. But I want you to promise me that you won't ever do it again, okay?" Rhonda agreed.

It was two weeks since Grandma and the ironing cord had inflicted the damage on her back. The wounds had never been properly tended to, and Rhonda's back had become grossly infected. Nett was horrified as she wept for this frightened child with an infection that covered 75 percent of her back. Rhonda didn't get to go to kindergarten. Instead, she spent the next few weeks in the hospital. Nett came to visit her every day. Daddy came twice.

Nett told Daddy everything, which is what motivated him to do something that he had been putting off. He took Rhonda and her brother out of his mother's house. He packed up his kids and their belongings, and he and Nett stood facing a raging Grandma, who stood in front of the door, using her body to block their exit. She was screaming, begging, crying that Daddy not take *Ray* away. Daddy looked at her with disgust and said, "Ma, shut up and move." It was a glorious day that was etched in Rhonda's memory forever. Somebody had found the strength and the courage to tell mean, old Grandma to shut her mouth!

Dreams really do come true, and for the first time in her life, Rhonda was living a dream. She and Ray and Daddy and Nett were all living together like a real family. They had moved to a new apartment. It wasn't a big apartment, but it was a nice apartment. At Grandma's house, Ray always slept with Grandma, and Rhonda always slept by herself. Now there was enough space for Rhonda and Ray to share a room, complete with twin beds and crisp, new flower-patterned sheets to sleep on. Rhonda was comfortable, and for the first time in her young life, she felt safe.

Even though dreams may come true, there's no guarantee that they will last. Rhonda's family dream began to disintegrate the day the police kicked in their door.

In the community in which Rhonda grew up, every family fell on hard times sooner or later. Some father lost his job. Some mother got sick. Some family's car broke down when the rent was due. Hard times were nothing new to a working-class community. Back then, you learned to deal with it by helping the family out any way you could. But when hard times turned into tragedy, things got frightening for everyone. That's what happened to Rhonda the day her daddy got arrested.

It was one thing to have a daddy in jail. It was quite another thing to have your daddy arrested right in front of you, and in full view of everyone on the block. A few of the kids in the neighborhood had daddies, uncles, cousins, or older brothers who had been in jail or were in jail. People were okay about that. You didn't get a "rep" or stigmatized if someone in your family was in jail or had been to jail. But Rhonda's case was different. Her father got arrested right in front of everyone!

Nett was in the bathroom. Rhonda and Ray were watching television. Daddy and Mr. Johnny were sitting at the kitchen table, working on the morning's numbers pick up. They all heard the knock at the door. Daddy got up to get it. He half whispered and half hissed the *s* word as he ran back into the kitchen. The next knock was much louder.

"Get the door!" Nett hollered from the bathroom. Daddy and Mr. Johnny were frantically gathering the numbers slips from the table. The knocking became banging. Nett was coming up the hallway, mumbling to herself, when she collided with Mr. Johnny. At that very moment, the door to the apartment came crashing in. Daddy and Mr. Johnny were both trying to run up the hallway and away from the police officers who had crawled through the wreckage of the front door.

By the time Rhonda and Ray got to the kitchen, several white officers were rummaging through the garbage, the cabinets, and the refrigerator. Others were jumping over Nett, who was trying to get up off the floor. White men in the kitchen! They were big! They were white! They had guns, and they were tearing up the kitchen. It didn't matter that they were policemen. The only other white man who had ever been in the kitchen was the landlord. He came when the rent was late.

In a matter of minutes, things really got crazy. One of the policemen was holding Nett by her hair. In the struggle, either she slipped, or he slammed her into the wall. Two policemen were holding on to Mr. Johnny, who was halfway out the second-floor bathroom window. Rhonda was holding on and trying to bite the ankle of the policeman who had hurt Nett. Somebody swooped her up from behind, took her out of the apartment, and deposited her in the hallway, where Ray already stood.

Miss Brooks, their neighbor across the hall, took the children into her apartment. They could hear knocking and banging on the wall coming from their apartment. They could also hear Nett screaming and crying, "Please! Wait! Don't take him!" Miss Brooks made tea for the two terrorized children and gave them cookies. She patted them on their heads, hugged them, and ran back and forth to her front door to look out the peephole. On one of her trips back from the peephole, after what seemed like hours since they'd first sat down, Miss Brooks was accompanied into the kitchen by Nett.

Thanking Miss Brooks and hugging Rhonda and Ray, who clung to her for dear life, Nett tried to explain what had happened. Daddy and Mr. Johnny had been carted off to jail. She needed to pay some money so that they could come home. It was a mess. So embarrassing. For the time being, she said, she was taking the children home. It was a disaster. Broken wood and metal everywhere. Food all over the kitchen floor. Furniture piled up against the wall. Daddy would probably be in jail for a day or two, and they had no front door. The neighbors who had seen or heard about he episode were standing outside the apartment door-way. One by one, they began to come in and help Nett and the children clean up the mess. The superintendent, Mr. Ralph, found another door somewhere and was down on the floor, trying to screw on the hinges. Somebody they hardly knew stepped over him, carrying a plateful of sandwiches. It seemed that no matter how horrible a situation may be, people show you how much they love you with food! In a relatively short time, the house was back to normal.

When all of the neighbors were gone, Nett sat down, lit a cigarette, and counted the money they had shoved into her hand or stuck in her pocket.

"What's going to happen to Daddy?" Ray asked.

"He'll be okay," Nett told us, "and so will we." That's when they heard another knock at the door. The memory was too fresh; the association was traumatic. All three of them nearly jumped out of their skins. "Shhhh!" Nett cautioned. They were all frozen to their seats. Slowly, Nett got up and whispered to Rhonda and Ray to go hide in the bathroom. Ray immediately got up and turned to run. Rhonda refused to leave Nett's side. The knocking had become a persistent tapping. Nett pushed both children down the hallway and into the bathroom and slammed the door. Rhonda heard the apartment door open and close, muffled voices, then nothing. Her legs were trembling. When they heard footsteps coming down the hall, both children jumped into the bathtub. Before the bathroom door opened all the way, they heard Nett's voice reassuring them that it was okay to come out now. It was only Mr. Rootman, one of Daddy's "business partners." He had bags of potato chips and candy for the children and a huge wad of money for Nett. Mr. Rootman owned a candy store on the other side of town. The word, Mr. Rootman told Nett, was out on the street. Grandma had told on Daddy. It made no sense, and it made all the sense in the world.

Nett was cursing, calling Grandma all sorts of names. Nett hardly ever cursed. She said it gave you wrinkles. Nett was battered and shaken and didn't want to leave the children alone, so it was decided that Mr. Rootman should be the one to bail Daddy and Mr. Johnny out of jail.

Rhonda and Ray were so engrossed in their goodies, they barely said good-bye when Mr. Rootman left. After a soothing hot bath, they all went to bed. The next morning, Rhonda peeked into Nett's bedroom. She was excited and relieved to see that Daddy had come home from jail.

Bad times were when the rent is late and there is very little food. Rhonda, her brother, and Nett knew how to deal with bad times. But over time, bad times grew into progressively worse times. It was then that something had to be done. Daddy was more like a visitor than a resident in the house. He was writing and collecting his numbers at Mr. Rootman's store, which meant he only passed through home when he needed something to wear. Nett worked a lot of overtime, which meant she got home late almost every night. By the time she did get home, both children were too tired to care when she asked them about their day, too tired to care that they were hungry.

Rhonda and her brother had become latchkey kids. Worst of all, they were hungry latchkey kids, with far too much time on their hands. They started talking to people out the window, watching too much television, and ignoring their schoolwork. When Ray brought a letter home from school about his bad behavior, Nett knew that someone needed to be there to make sure they ate properly and did their homework. Grandma was available and delighted that she had found a way and an excuse to run Nett's household.

Grandma's meanness had become seasoned with age. With no one around to watch, Grandma was in rare form. If Rhonda's homework wasn't done fast enough, she got rapped on the side of her head. If she didn't get all the soap off the dishes, she got backhanded across the face. If Rhonda ate too fast, or asked for seconds, Grandma would scream at her. Ray, however, got to eat all the Oreo cookies he wanted, whenever he wanted, at whatever speed he wanted. By the time Grandma had been in the house for three weeks, Rhonda's nerves were frayed, her hair was falling out again, and Nett started getting sick. Somehow, Nett figured out that Grandma was the reason behind Rhonda's balding head and her own upset stomach. Knowing what the impact would be on her family, she refused overtime and started coming home on time. It was a signal to

Grandma that she was no longer needed or welcome. "I'd rather starve to death than have that old bat in my house," Nett told the children. It was her way of explaining their steady diet of potato soup.

Even during the worst of times, Friday night was the best night of the week. Nett got paid from her day job on Fridays, and that meant treats, treats, and more treats. It was a weekly celebration that both of the children looked forward to enjoying. Nett, as usual, would go out of her way to make Rhonda and Ray feel special for being good during the week. Sometimes she even thanked them for keeping the house clean and for not getting into trouble. She would bring home Rhonda's favorite treat, coffee ice cream. Ray liked butter pecan, even though he always picked the nuts out. Nett brought herself Oreo cookies, which she would dunk in milk until the bottom of the cup was filled with crumbs. The three of them would pile up on the sofa and watch television until they all fell asleep and somebody's foot ended up in somebody's mouth. Friday nights were good nights. Nights when Rhonda could hope that, in a little while, everything would be just fine.

Nett always let Rhonda play dress-up and try out her makeup. But on Halloween, Nett would make up Rhonda's face and let her wear something really pretty. By the time Nett finished with the eyeliner and lipstick, Rhonda felt beautiful. And falling off Nett's high heels was big fun. Rhonda and her brother would romp throughout the apartment building, collecting candy and other goodies. When they returned, they would divide everything equally between them, packing some things away in plastic bags for later in the week. One Halloween, just before the children went to bed, a real ghost appeared. Daddy came home for his weekly visit.

Daddy took one look at these children whom he had not seen in a week, and for whom he had barely provided all their lives, and asked his wife if she had lost her mind. "What the hell is wrong with her face? What did you do to her?" Daddy demanded of Nett.

"It's just a little makeup. They went trick-or-treating in the building." Nett shot Rhonda and her brother a get-to-bed glance, but neither child moved.

Daddy was ranting and raving about being sick and tired of Nett trying to influence his children against him, when Nett jumped up from the chair and snarled at him, "You know what you can do for me, don't you?" With that she snatched both children by their arms and stomped down the hallway.

While Nett removed the makeup, she told Rhonda that she really did look pretty and that she was glad they'd had a good time. She put Rhonda to bed, but Rhonda was too excited by the day's events to sleep. She remembered Nett putting the lipstick case on the edge of the sink in the bathroom. Intrigued by the golden wand that magically put color on your lips and made you pretty, Rhonda crept into the bathroom to retrieve it. Back in the bed, with the magic color wand, she realized she had no mirror, so she made another bathroom run to get Nett's two-sided mirror that was kept on a hook next to the medicine cabinet. An eight-year-old, standing in the dark on a toilet seat, trying to reach something that is too high up, is an accident waiting to happen. In this case, it was Rhonda knocking the bottle of Listerine to the floor. The big bottle crashed to the tiles and shattered into a thousand pieces. The crash made the already angry Daddy angrier.

Chances are Daddy wasn't mad about Rhonda getting out of bed or the Listerine bottle being broken or the lipstick on the sheets. Chances were better that Daddy was shamed by having to sneak into his own home at night to avoid the landlord. Or that Daddy was mad because he hadn't hit a number in months. Or that he was frustrated by having to be so careful writing numbers because he was on probation and didn't want to go back to jail. Whatever the underlying reason, Daddy was on his way down the hall, enraged, and needing to take it out on someone, anyone. Lipstick on the clean white sheets and broken glass on the black-and-white tile bathroom floor gave him an excellent excuse to take out all of his rage, his fury and frustration, on his eight-year-old daughter.

Rhonda tried to escape Daddy's grasp by running back to her bed and hiding under the covers. He came and got her.

There are spankings, there are whippings, and there are beatings. The beating Rhonda received that night at the hands of her father was the talk of the neighborhood for weeks. The beating Rhonda received that night resulted in her lying senseless in the bathtub.

It is not unusual for an angry adult to take their frustration and anger out on a child. It is not right, and the child is usually unaware that this is what is going on, but it happens all of the time. Adults who feel powerless, who feel they are at the end of their ropes, will strike out against the one thing or person they believe they can exercise power over. It doesn't make them feel better, and if they really hurt the child, it will make them feel worse. In the process, the child who is being used as a punching bag, or an ashtray, is trying to figure out just what they did to enrage the adult. There is no plausible explanation. The adult can profess to be sorry, promise never to do it again, but it doesn't matter. The child is wounded, sometimes physically. And in all cases emotionally and spiritually.

Rhonda's father became even angrier when his wife tried to pull the child he was beating—his child—away from him. He became angrier still when he saw his son standing in the closet, staring at him in horror, and knew he was powerless to change the image of himself he saw forming in his son's eyes. Daddy's sense of powerlessness led to such frustration that he continued to beat Rhonda until his unbelted pants fell down. Despite the fact that the pants around his ankles made it hard for him to move, he continued to beat the child until she had slumped to the floor unconscious.

Her eyes were shut. Her lips were swollen. Her nightgown was torn. Her arms, legs, back, and face were covered with large welts and streaks of blood. Somehow, as Daddy had become more and more exhausted, Nett had managed to pull Rhonda away from him. She dragged her into the bathroom and locked the door. Nett filled the tub and placed Rhonda in the warm water. She left her only for a moment to speak with the police, who had been called by a neighbor. When Nett returned to the bathroom, Rhonda was regaining consciousness. She didn't cry; she just grabbed on to Nett and held on for her life. Rhonda always felt that Nett was her only chance in life. Tonight, she knew it for sure. Nett rocked and rubbed and consoled the battered child, then whispered in her ear,

"Why don't you listen? Your Daddy loves you, but you must learn to listen!"

Rhonda learned a powerful lesson that night. Frustrated, angry people will hurt you. And if you don't do what angry people want you to do, then they will hurt you very badly, and it will be your fault.

Something had to be done. And when something has to be done about the way you are living, children must be the first consideration. The marshal was coming within the next seventy-two hours to put Rhonda's family out on the street. Nett hadn't seen her husband in three days. She needed help, and that evening, when she picked the children up from their afternoon caretaker, she decided to ask for that help.

Nadine was short and round like a pumpkin. Though the exact family line had never been explained to either of them, Rhonda and Ray called her Aunt Nadine. They spent every afternoon with her, after they had been dismissed from school. Rhonda thought she was nice enough, but not nice enough to live with. Nett explained to Nadine that she needed six to nine months to get back on track and that she was going to live with her sister in a small one-bedroom apartment. Nadine, who owned her home and kept children for a living, said she'd be more than happy to keep Rhonda and Ray. After all, she said, it was her own flesh and blood they were talking about.

Nett promised it would only be for a few weeks, two months at most. Although it ended up lasting five years, it wasn't all that bad. In fact, there were times when it was rather fascinating for Rhonda. It was the first time she'd lived in a house. As far as she knew, the only people who lived in real houses were rich people like the ones Grandma worked for. Nadine's was a two-story house with a finished basement. There were two televisions on the parlor floor and one in the basement, where there was also a bar with stools, a record player, and a complete set of living room furniture. It was called the family room. The most exciting thing was that the house also had a backyard. This meant that Rhonda did not have to go out front to play, nor explain to the other children on the block who she was and where she came from. It also meant less chance that she'd see her father driving by with women in his car. She wouldn't have to deal with the fact that her father was either ignoring her or had forgotten that she existed.

Aunt Nadine kept her house clean. The hardwood floors were always polished to a high shine. You could see your reflection in the linoleum tiles of the kitchen floor. Every surface, every nook and cranny in every room was dust-free. Even with all the children who were through the house each day, all the rooms were spotless. Rhonda and her brother each had their own room. His was on the second floor; Rhonda's was on the first floor, between Aunt Nadine's room and the bedroom of Aunt Nadine's only child, who was nicknamed "Beanie."

Rhonda was expected to keep her room as clean as the rest of the house, which she did to the best of her ability. She was also given a myriad of chores around the house for which she was paid a weekly allowance. She missed Nett, though. She missed her so much she ached with the missing. Unlike Nett, Aunt Nadine did not talk to Rhonda. She told her what to do and how to do it, but not much else. Rhonda did her best to help Aunt Nadine with the children she kept during the day. She helped feed them, she played with them, and it was her assigned duty to wash their hands and faces just before their parents came to pick them up. Aunt Nadine never thanked Rhonda nor told her she'd done a good job.

Rhonda had never seen anyone take her hair off until she went to live with Aunt Nadine. Aunt Nadine had a whole dresser drawer full of wigs. If she got up late and was in a hurry to leave the house, Aunt Nadine would reach in the drawer, pull out one of her hairy hats, and pat it into place on her half-bald head. At first, Rhonda was fascinated by Aunt Nadine's hair collection. But frequently, Aunt Nadine would put her wig on backwards. She'd brush it into place, *then* put on her glasses. Sometimes they'd be at the grocery store, or on their way to a PTA meeting, and one of their neighbors would lean in close enough to whisper, "Nadine, your wig's on backwards." Whenever and wherever this happened, Nadine would reach up, spin the wig around, and pat it into place. Rhonda would be mortified!

It was bad enough that the person who went to speak to the teacher on your behalf had a different last name from yours. But when she would adjust her hair, in full view of the public, moving her bangs from the nape of her neck to their proper place on her forehead, it was more than a child could bear! By age ten, Rhonda was ashamed of her own increasingly overweight body, and of the fact that her own father would drive past her on the street and not even speak. And on top of all that, she had to deal with the fact that her aunt, who really wasn't her aunt and purported to be her mother, walked around with her wig on backwards.

Rhonda missed Nett terribly. She felt she'd been ripped apart from the only person who had ever shown her love, the person she believed to be her real mother. As long as Nett maintained contact, Rhonda found ways to fill the moments of separation. But as the months and years passed, Nett's visits were less and less frequent. Rhonda had to work at getting the people she now lived with to notice her, to speak to her beyond the obligatory daily greetings. No one ever kissed her or hugged her. It was incredibly hard being in a place where she didn't feel she belonged, where she didn't feel loved or wanted or pretty. With Nett gone, there was no one to talk to her, to explain things to her. It was no wonder her hair started to fall out again.

Rhonda had gone bald at her temples and at the back of her head, so besides teasing her about her weight, the other children made fun of her hair loss. If Aunt Nadine had paid her any mind, she might have prepared Rhonda for the day she was sent to school wearing an auburn wig. She was teased, talked about, laughed at, and pushed around. Her teacher asked her, "Does your mother know your hair is red?" Several boys chased her halfway home, threatening to pull the wig off. Aunt Nadine's response was to put more hairpins in the wig to keep it in place in case someone actually did try to pull it off. "Stop your crying," Aunt Nadine told a weeping Rhonda. "It's better than nothing, and it's certainly better than being bald!"

Eventually, the kids at school got used to the wig, and so did Rhonda. Every week, Rhonda got 100 percent on the spelling test. She got an A on every book report. Rhonda was so smart in school the other children began to see her as potentially useful to them. Aunt Nadine's daughter, Beanie, had introduced Rhonda to African culture and African dance. Rhonda, in turn, shared all she learned from Beanie with her classmates. It made her popular in school, and she was no longer teased about the wig or the smell of the sulfur-based hair-growing concoction that emanated from beneath the wig.

Saturday nights were when other family members came to Aunt Nadine's to play cards, drink, and fight. For Rhonda, Saturdays were when she and her brother got money from total strangers who claimed to be their uncles or aunts. It was the day she and Ray got to drink all the leftover Coca-Cola and club soda. It was also the day when Rhonda got updates on Daddy and Nett, filtered through curse words and smoke and alcohol.

"She hasn't called in a week. Next time she does, I'm gonna tell her a thing or two!"

"Who does that yellow b———h think she is?"

"She thinks she's white, that's what she thinks! Why should she waste her time raising a dead woman's kids? She doesn't care about them one it, not one little bit."

"Well, neither does he, and they're his kids."

"Why should he care about them when he's busy making new ones on the other side of town!"

"He can't feed the ones he already has. What kind of fool woman would have children with a man who can't feed the kids he's already got?"

"Don't act like you don't know how some women are. They will do anything, I mean anything, to keep a man. Especially a good-looking man."

The grown-ups who came to the Saturday night basement parties always got drunk enough for their tongues to get loose enough to say things they wouldn't say when they were sober. In fact, they were drunk enough to forget that the children they were talking about were listening. Children and who they belonged to was not the only topic of conversation. They also talked about each other. One drunken person inevitably said something outrageous to another drunk in the group. By ten o'clock, somebody would slap, or threaten to slap, somebody else in the face.

Aunt Nadine, the shortest and smallest one in the group, usually started the fight. She would insult someone's husband, or call someone a nasty name. Before long, someone else would jump in to defend the offended party, and a free-for-all would start. Wigs flying. Bottles crashing. Rhonda thought it was funny, but sad, too. If it hadn't happened every weekend, she might have thought it was exciting. It was Rhonda's second lesson in domestic violence. She thought it was just the way things were and felt powerless to do anything about it.

Little girls learn a lot from the women they grow up around, whether they are related or not. Older women are like midwives who assist in the birth of a young woman's consciousness. It's not just what they do, it's who they are, and how they demonstrate who they are, that provides young women with "womanhood training." Young women and girls learn about themselves and what it means to be a woman by watching the older women in their lives. They watch how and what they cook. They watch how and what they use to clean. They watch what they wear and how they carry themselves, how they treat themselves and each other.

Whether they realize it or not, whether they intend to or not, older women, the "womanhood midwives," teach younger women what to expect from life. Some things are taught overtly, but the most important lessons are taught covertly. The words and actions of older women teach whether to expect life to be peaceful or stressful, hard or easy, honorable or dishonorable. Only a woman can teach another woman what it really means to be a woman.

The principal midwives in Rhonda's life—Grandma, Nett, and Nadine—had such a hard time learning, they had no idea they were also teaching.

Uncle Leroy was Aunt Nadine's husband. He was a thin, quiet man, a functional weekend alcoholic, and he was deeply involved with another woman. Uncle Leroy went to work at 5:30 A.M. every weekday morning and returned home at 5:30 P.M. on the dot. He would mumble a greeting when he came in, take a bath, eat his dinner, and go to bed. Once Uncle Leroy went to bed, everyone had to be quiet and creep around the house to avoid waking him up.

But on Friday nights, Uncle Leroy never came directly home. And on Saturdays, Uncle Leroy would show up after the basement partying was already in full swing. Rhonda knew why and so did Aunt Nadine. Uncle Leroy had another woman on the side. He knew that Aunt Nadine had a habit of driving by the other woman's house when he wasn't home on time. If she saw Uncle Leroy's car parked outside, she'd return home and start calling his girlfriend until the woman kicked him out and made him go home. Usually, he'd get off with just that smug look that Rhonda saw on Aunt Nadine's face when he came in, dragging his tail between his legs. Occasionally, if someone at the Saturday night party made a snide remark about his absence in front of Aunt Nadine, Uncle Leroy would wind up with a dented hood or a broken windshield on his new Lincoln.

Adults who talk about and in front of children as if they didn't exist were not the problem. Uncle Leroy getting drunk every single Friday night wasn't the problem, either. What happened when Rhonda was left at home with drunk Uncle Leroy while Aunt Nadine went to play bid whisk *was* a problem, one that was *impossible* to understand, accept, or live with.

CHAPTER FIVE

What's the Lesson When You Are Poor, Ugly, and Feeling Bad?

> Like all your brothers and sisters,
> you suffer from a basic sense of inadequacy
> and unworthiness.
> You feel you have made terrible mistakes
> which will sooner or later be punished
> by humans in authority or by some abstract
> spiritual authority like God, or karmic law.
> Paul Ferrini, in *Love Without Conditions*

BROTHERS AND SISTERS are expected to love one another. It is also expected that when life gets hard, siblings will hold onto each other and support one another through the rough times. Rhonda loved her brother, Ray. He was two years older than she was, and he was her hero. It was doubtful, however, whether he felt the same way about Rhonda. How Ray felt about himself, his life, or the life circumstances in which he and his sister found themselves was a mystery. Ray never spoke about how he felt except where his father was concerned.

Ray hated his father, and he was not shy about letting everyone know it. Ray would rant and rave so vehemently, he would bring himself to tears and sometimes to the brink of an asthma attack. Rhonda had not yet gotten to the point where she hated Daddy, but she would listen to

Ray just to be supportive. She didn't know for sure what Ray's reasons were for hating Daddy; he never told her.

Perhaps, she thought, he hates him because Daddy is so distant and angry. Maybe it's because he always criticizes and chastises Ray. Daddy's pet names for Ray were "punk" and "sissy." He would push and punch Ray just to "toughen him up," but this was never balanced with much needed guidance and support. Maybe it was the time he'd watched Daddy beat Rhonda into a state of unconsciousness. Or maybe it was the normal male rivalry that exists between boys of a certain age and their fathers. Rhonda knew that Ray was sick and tired of the war stories and the "white man's out to get you" stories.

Rhonda didn't understand having so much hate for one person. She never asked her brother why, and he never tried to explain. As far as Rhonda could see, her brother had absolutely nothing to complain about.

"You better stop talking about Daddy like that," Rhonda would caution her brother. But she was so glad to be having a conversation, she'd take advantage of Ray's anger just to keep the lines of communication open.

"Why? Why should I care about him? He doesn't give a damn about us!" Ray was vehement in his response.

"Yes he does. He's just busy."

"You are *so* stupid, Ronnie. You are as stupid as he is." Ray and Nett were the only two people who called Rhonda, "Ronnie." Grandma usually called her "a pain in the butt," and Daddy, when he was around, called her "lamb chop." But lately, "stupid" seemed to be Ray's favorite name for her.

"What are you complaining about? Didn't he buy you that bicycle for your birthday? He never buys me anything."

"That cheap piece of crap? He probably found it on the street or in the garbage. Probably got it from one of his women." That would always get Rhonda's attention.

"What women?" Were the rumors she heard at the Saturday night card parties true?

"See, stupid, you don't know anything. You see him driving up and down the streets with those women in his car. Who do you think they are? They're not our mother. She's dead!" Ray knew what effect his words would have.

"Our mother is not dead! Nett is our mother. She's out mother and you know it, Ray!" This was Ray's cue to back off.

"You are *so* stupid!" Ray would say as he headed toward the sanctuary of his room.

"She is too our mother!"

"Yeah, right, stupid. Get outta my face! You are so dumb it's unbelievable." With that, Ray would shut his bedroom door, leaving Rhonda fuming in the hall. Rhonda didn't know what Ray knew for sure, but she knew it was more than he was willing to share with her.

It wasn't Ray's fault that people liked him better than Rhonda, or that Grandma let him sleep in her big four-poster bed while Rhonda slept on the floor. He could hardly be held responsible for the fact that his sister was accused of asking too many questions, talking too much, and generally getting on people's nerves. What was he supposed to do when his sister was being beaten or punished for doing something that he had warned her not to do? So he ate the cookies Rhonda couldn't have because she was being punished or beaten, and he enjoyed his television programs while she had to sit on the floor, in the corner.

It wasn't his fault that his mother had died, or that his father was an angry, distant man who rarely had a kind word to say. Like his sister, there was little Ray could do about any of that. What he did do was stay out of everyone's way and keep his mouth shut. Besides, he had his own problems.

For the first twelve years of his life, Ray's biggest problems was staying alive. His silence was, in part, created by his history of having asthma. Whenever things got really bad, Ray's asthma attacks would render him speechless.

When Ray wasn't having an asthma attack, he simply had very little to say. He always said good morning and good night; he answered when called by name. But as far as general conversation was concerned, Ray was mute. It didn't matter to Rhonda; she loved him no matter what. But she also knew how to get a rise out of him. If she took his toys or stood in front of the television or pinched him while he was doing his homework, then he'd have something to say.

"Leave me alone, Ronnie!"

"You're such a baby! I wasn't bothering you!"

"Were too!"

"Was not! Baby! You're just a big crybaby. Crybaby, crybaby, crybaby!"

"I am not a crybaby!"

"Are too."

"I'm telling!" And Ray would scream at the top of his lungs. "Ronnie's bothering me! She won't leave me alone!"

Once Ray started hollering, some adult would come into the room and either slap Rhonda or order her to leave the room. The consequences of their sibling rivalry were consistent. Rhonda was always the one at fault. She didn't care. Once the adult had left the room, she would go right back to teasing Ray just for the sake of conversation. But she did understand that if she upset Ray too much, he might have an asthma attack.

Ray's asthma attacks were a source of devastating fear and turmoil for Rhonda. So far in her young life, Ray had been the only constant. When Ray was gasping for air, Rhonda tried not to bother him or ask too many questions. Ray's chest would swell to three or four times its normal size, his eyes would run, and the wheezing sound of his attempts to breathe would fill the entire room. Rhonda would sit as close as she could to him without causing him more discomfort. She would pass him clean tissues, and collect the dirty ones. If Ray was having a really bad attack, one of the adults would put a big lump of Vicks VapoRub in the humidifier, and Ray would sit as close to it as possible to let the soothing steam fill his chest. Because Rhonda was on tissue duty, she got to sit in the warm mist with her brother. If Ray needed something, like water or more orange juice, he would try to speak, but his words would come in painful gasps. So he and Rhonda developed a code. A flipping hand meant something to drink. Rubbing the nose or eye meant he needed a tissue. When he wanted to lie down, he would pat his lap, signaling for Rhonda to come sit next to him. When he reached out and grabbed Rhonda's hand, she knew it was time to go to the hospital. It made Rhonda feel good to know that even though it was never reciprocal, when her brother was feeling bad, he would reach out for her.

Poor people who couldn't pay for medical attention went to Kings County Hospital. It was the last place you wanted to be if you were sick, which is why people waited until they were in really bad shape before going there. As concerned as she was about Ray, Rhonda could barely contain her excitement about the prospect of having Tootsie Rolls drop out of the machine into her hot little hands. County was bad, but it had candy machines. They all knew there would be a minimum three-hour wait in the noisy, crowded, chaotic waiting room before Ray's name would be called. During that time, Rhonda would have to sit quietly and anxiously on a hard bench in a filthy room and listen to her brother wheeze and gasp for his every breath.

On one memorable trip to County, Ray almost died. When they arrived, Ray was barely conscious. Nett carried him into the waiting room and propped him up on a bench between two strangers: one drunk, one bleeding. Then Nett walked right past all of the people in line and asked the nurse at the reception desk to please take a look at her son. The nurse politely ignored Nett. When she persisted, the nurse told her to take a number. Nett, who was always as cool as a cucumber, began to scream at the woman, "I don't want a damn number! I want you to help my son! He's not breathing, he's dying!"

The drunk, who had been holding Ray's head in his lap, jumped for some unknown reason. Rhonda ran over and tried to catch her brother as he fell off of the bench. Before she could catch him, people started coming from everywhere. Hospital staff appeared from everywhere. The last thing Rhonda saw was Nett holding Ray's hand as she and the gurney disappeared through the swinging double doors. Rhonda stood alone in the middle of the crowded waiting room and wailed as if her heart were broken.

The strangers in the waiting room who weren't bleeding or totally uninterested tried to console her. A nurse gave her some water in a paper cup, but Rhonda would not stop crying. Not only was her brother gone, but she had not had a chance to get a quarter from Nett for the candy machine. After a two-hour wait, she looked up and thought she saw the cavalry coming to her rescue. It was Daddy! As he rushed through the emergency-room doors, Rhonda jumped up and ran toward him.

"Daddy, Daddy! Ray's gonna die!" she called to him. Rhonda couldn't believe her father had passed right by her in this strange place, with all these strange people, without so much as a word of consolation. By the time he reached the nurses' desk, Rhonda could almost grab the hem of his coat. But before she did, Daddy was on his way through the door that led to the treatment room. At that point, Rhonda lost it.

What Rhonda did on that day became a family story that was told and retold. She screamed, she bit people, she hit people and threw herself on the floor, howling, as Grandma would say, "like a child possessed." She wanted her brother! She wanted her parents! She wanted a Tootsie Roll! Someone went to get Nett, who found Rhonda thrashing around hysterically on the filthy emergency-room floor. Nett grabbed Rhonda, pulled her to her feet, and held Rhonda's face in both of her hands as she pulled her tightly to her body. Then she led Rhonda by the hand outside into the fresh air. Within moments, Daddy joined them.

"Ray's going to be okay, baby. But he's got to stay here for a little while."

"Are you going to stay with him?" Rhonda was prepared to have another fit if necessary.

"No, I'm going home with you."

After Nett reassured her that the nurses and doctors would take good care of Ray, Rhonda reluctantly went home without a Tootsie Roll and without her brother.

It was the longest two days of her life. The empty bed in their room frightened her. Though if Ray had been there with her, he probably would not have been speaking to her or playing with her. He would have been his usual quiet and withdrawn self. His *not being there* was very much like his *being there*. Still, Rhonda did not want to lose him. He never did anything to help her, but, he never did anything to hurt her, either. A time would come, however, when her fear of losing Ray would become a reality.

Though most of the adults in Rhonda's life had betrayed her in one way or another, Ray was the first person to betray her publicly. The betrayal came in the form of a lie when Rhonda was five years old.

Every summer, the family went to Uncle Lowell and Aunt Dora's house in Atlantic City. Just how Uncle Lowell and Aunt Dora were related to Rhonda was never explained. They were joined by more unexplained aunts, uncles, and cousins who came from all over the country every Memorial Day and Labor Day to party at the beach. The younger children spent their days on the beach or the steeplechase under the watchful eyes of the older children. The adults spent their days resting and their nights drinking, smoking, playing cards, and eating crab.

The day of the betrayal was gloomy. It rained, and the children were forced to stay in the house, fighting over the television set and playing games they made up on the spur of the moment. The grown-ups, anticipating that the rain would stop by nightfall, bought a bushel of crabs. The children from the South knew all about crabs. They were familiar with how the crabs were prepared. The water was seasoned, and the live crabs were put in the boiling water to cook so they could be eaten. Rhonda and the other children from the North, however, saw the process of putting living, feeling, defenseless creatures into scalding hot water and killing them as a barbaric act.

The grown-ups prepared the crabs, seasoned the boiling water, and dropped the crabs into the big crab pot. They turned the knob on top of the pot that locked the cover in place and left the crabs and the children in the kitchen. The northern children decided to help the crabs escape.

Much to the joy of the not-yet-dead crabs, one of the children—it was never discovered who—unlocked the pot. The crabs leaped out of the pot and ran for their lives.

Crabs were everywhere! They scrambled all over the kitchen floor and all over the northern children. The southern children knew better; they watched and laughed as the northern children tried to get the crabs back into the pot. The crabs latched onto anything they could, including the children's hands, arms, and faces. The kitchen was in total chaos! Crabs clutching, clawing, and hanging on the children; children running, screaming, and stepping on the crabs that tried to get away. Rhonda was one of the youngest, and in her effort to save the crabs, she had gotten more crabs on her than anyone else.

When the grown-ups heard the commotion, they came running. Grandma was the first adult to enter the kitchen. Two unexplained aunts and one unexplained uncle followed her. Daddy was the next adult to arrive and the first to ask the question, "Who opened the pot?"

Had everyone stuck together, they could have gotten away with a unified "I don't know," but the North and the South still had issues to resolve. The southern children immediately blamed the northern children. The northern children were too busy yelling and trying to shake the crabs off to deny the accusation.

"Shut up! Everybody just shut up! It serves you right." Grandma's jarring voice cut through the room, and everyone fell silent. It was in that moment of utter silence that Ray spoke up.

"Ronnie did it."

Rhonda couldn't believe her ears and neither could anyone else, since Rhonda was one of the youngest and shortest of the children. She couldn't deny it, or defend herself, because she still had crabs hanging off of her T-shirt. The other children were so relieved not to be blamed, they didn't say a word. Before any of the adults could volunteer a more plausible explanation, Grandma backhanded Rhonda, sending her flying across the kitchen floor onto a pile of half-cooked, half-dead crabs.

"Oh, Ma. Please!" Daddy said weakly. "You don't have to slap her like that."

"You know she did it. She's always doing something she's got no business doing!"

Daddy was taking a big chance by challenging Grandma publicly. He approached Rhonda tentatively, but by the time he reached her, Grandma had grabbed her and slapped her again.

One of the aunts tried to help by offering, "She didn't mean it. You know how kids are." Grandma shot her a glance that shut her mouth for the next two days. Everyone knew Grandma was crazy. Everyone knew that she abused Rhonda. Unfortunately, no one in the room was brave enough to attempt to put Grandma in her place—on her broom, headed for the sunset. They were all afraid of what Grandma might do to them. Everyone, that is, except Nett. She had announced to everyone that she would "go to her grave willingly rather than stand by and allow her to abuse that child." But by the time Nett made her way through the crowd into the kitchen, Ray was standing in the corner, Daddy was arguing with Grandma, and Rhonda had been slapped three more times.

Lessons in life come in a variety of ways. Children are so observant, sensitive, and impressionable that their most powerful lessons come from what they see and hear others do around them and what others do to them. They learn early in their lives that adults place value on perceived beauty. Children who are not valued and protected feel that they are not beautiful or worthy of protection. Ray was honored, valued, and protected for the most part. But he witnessed his sister being beaten, neglected, and ignored. He had to ask himself the question, "What is so good about me?" and conversely, "What is wrong with my sister?" In his circumstances in life, he was left to answer those questions for himself.

When they moved to Aunt Nadine's, the silence between Rhonda and her brother turned to distance. They still ate every meal together. They still walked to and attended the same school together. Ray would protect his sister when the kids at school were teasing or chasing her. He would walk behind her and in front of the gang of boys or girls, daring them to touch Rhonda. They never did.

But at home, something was different. Ray had begun to physically push Rhonda away whenever she came near him. He had started calling her names like "fatty" and "blackie." When Rhonda's hair started to fall out, Ray seemed to get a big kick out of calling her "wiggy" and "baldy," just like the kids in school. Rhonda knew he was just teasing her, but it was disturbing that her brother, who once had nothing to say, now had so many mean things to say.

The worst thing he called her was "ugly." Ray told Rhonda that she was ugly to the point of being "oogly," which he said was a cross between ugly and a disaster waiting to happen. Ray was her older brother, whom she loved. And she believed him.

Rhonda began spending a great deal of time in the bathroom, sitting on the edge of the sink, and eyeing her ugliness in the mirror. She would pinch her nose, tuck in her lips, and pretend she was pretty like the women she had seen on television. She was particularly fond of the character Penny on *Sky King*. After her hair started falling out, Rhonda would bobby-pin yellow or red knee socks to her hair, pretending they were pigtails like Penny's. She would twist her head back and forth so that the socks would swing across her face. In the mirror, Rhonda didn't look so bad, but according to Ray, most ugly people didn't know they were ugly. Rhonda believed that, too, until the day the woman showed up in the mirror.

Rhonda was sitting on the edge of the sink, just staring at herself, wondering what it would be like to be beautiful. Suddenly, as if she had come through the door, there was the image of a beautiful woman in the mirror. Rhonda couldn't move. She stared at the woman, who was smiling at her. She seemed to walk right up behind Rhonda until their faces were side by side in the mirror. Watching intently, Rhonda wanted to speak. She could not, but the woman did.

"Your beauty is on the inside," the woman said, and smiled. "Look inside for your beauty." The words were melodic and seemed to linger in the air after the woman had spoken them. Suddenly, there was a banging on the bathroom door. Startled, Rhonda jumped, her foot slipped, and she went tumbling onto the hard, cold bathroom floor, bumping her head and mouth on the cold toilet on the way down.

"What are you doing in there?" It was Ray. He needed to use the bathroom. Rhonda quickly scrambled back to her feet and hoisted herself back on the edge of the sink. But the woman was gone. The only image in the mirror was Rhonda's "ugly" face that was now swollen and bruised.

Every now and then, Ray was good for a laugh. He would either do something or say something that would be totally hysterical.

Aunt Nadine and Uncle Leroy, like everyone else, seemed to like Ray more than Rhonda. He was a lot less trouble, and when he got in trouble with either one of them, he went to his room, not to be heard from for hours, sometimes days. Aunt Nadine and Ray tangled only once, but it was an encounter that Rhonda would never forget. Aunt Nadine was not in a good mood. You could tell by the way she was slamming things around the house. Ray obviously hadn't noticed, nor had he learned that when some adult is in a bad mood, you stay away from them. Rhonda knew a lot about grown-ups being in bad moods. Ray was about to learn.

Ray asked Aunt Nadine if he could go to the park. She said no. Then he asked if he could go around the corner to his friend's house. Again, Aunt Nadine barked, "No!" Ray was in rare form that day. He asked, "Why?" Aunt Nadine told him to get out of her face, not to question her, and to go to his room. Ray turned to walk out of the kitchen. On his way out, he started mumbling under his breath. Aunt Nadine hated mumbling. By the time Ray got to the staircase leading upstairs, he had a little chant going:

"Going to Uncle Eli's, you can't go! Going downtown, you can't go! Going here, you can't go! Going there, you can't go!"

Rhonda heard what her brother was chanting, and so did Aunt Nadine. Ray, who had never talked back before, didn't seem to care whether everyone heard him or not. This was obviously an act of rebellion and totally out of character for Ray. Either he didn't hear her or he chose not to respond when Aunt Nadine told him to shut up. Ray started stomping up the stairs, chanting loudly. Aunt Nadine called out to him again. Once again, he failed or refused to respond. Furious, Aunt Nadine looked around the kitchen for something to hit him with. She grabbed Baby, the cat.

Aunt Nadine ran out of the kitchen and up the stairs, holding the cat by the hind legs. By the time Ray realized what was happening, Aunt Nadine was swinging the poor cat in his direction. Ray ducked and tried to ward off the blow, but Baby's protruding front claws connected with Ray's back. The cat started screeching, Ray was screaming, Aunt Nadine was furious, and Rhonda thought it was the funniest thing she had ever seen. Rhonda had been beaten with a lot of things, for a lot of reasons, but never with a cat! Ray stayed in his room for days, refusing to let Rhonda see him. The cat stayed under the bed for days, refusing even to eat or to curl up at the foot of Rhonda's bed.

As Ray got older and began to hang out with boys his own age, the distance between him and Rhonda increased, but when he became interested in girls, the distance became incalculable. When Aunt Nadine got sick and had to stop taking care of children, Ray got a part-time job. So, in addition to being silent, he was hardly ever home. When Ray *was* home, he and his friends hung out in his room, a place Rhonda dared not go for fear of Ray intentionally embarrassing her again. In front of all those cute boys, he'd say, "What do you want, ugly?" or "Take your ugly self on out of here." His friends found it all very amusing. Rhonda was mortified.

Somehow, without her knowledge, Rhonda had become offensive to the brother she loved so much. With Nett gone and Aunt Nadine sick and sleeping most of the time, Rhonda felt very alone. Sometimes she tried to figure out what had happened to change Ray. Other times, she ate. She'd sneak sandwiches into her room and eat them all alone. The food helped to fill the hole in her heart left by her big brother.

Ray was distant and aloof and, at times, oblivious to everyone and everything in his life that should have been important to him. He confirmed the lesson Rhonda was taught by her father. Men are emotionally, and often physically, unavailable. Ray, through his asthma attacks, taught Rhonda that you must put other people's interests ahead of your own. When he got older and his asthma attacks began to subside, he taught her how to love people despite their mistreatment of you. The one thing Rhonda wanted was to have a normal, loving relationship with her brother, but Ray taught her that it is painful at best, and impossible under most circumstances, to have what you want. Rhonda learned that people close to you could betray you and that they didn't care what happens to you. At Kings County Hospital, Rhonda learned that being poor was synonymous with being treated like less than nothing. And Ray taught her that, unlike him, she was neither valued nor beautiful. She was, in fact, ugly.

CHAPTER SIX

What's the Lesson When You Are Raped as a Child?

Every situation with which we are confronted,
whether it be in our body or in our outer affairs—
every situation—
contains somewhere within it
the seed of our good.

Richard Jafolla, in *Soul Surgery*

I HAD BEEN SOAKING in a bathtub of warm water for one hour and thirty-three minutes. My toes and fingers were gray and wrinkled. It was amazing to me how much of my life I had remembered. It was equally amazing how much pain I had remembered without experiencing the pain again. You can feel bad and recover without it being hard. I really had healed so many wounds. What I had not done was acknowledge and celebrate my healing. I still panic when things go well. When we do not remember to celebrate our progress, the day-to-day revelations that led to our feeling better, what we do remember is the pain. It is the pain that keeps us stuck in our patterns. The pair is familiar.

I still panic when things don't go well. I still beat up on myself when I make mistakes. I automatically believe that I am the one at fault, the one who is wrong, when people get upset with me. I still doubt myself when I am criticized or challenged by other people. I allow them to say too much about what I do, how I do it, and when I do it. And I use what they say as the foundation for why I do it.

I had to fire Karen. Period! I had to figure out why I had not or could not seem to honor my own personal boundaries when dealing with her. Hell! I knew this was not about Karen, it was about me. It was about new levels of the same old wounds. It was about uncovering them, understanding the influence, and healing them.

I had to continue, but I could not take another minute in the tub. It was time to get down. And that's just what I did. I placed four big bath sheets on the floor and lowered my wrinkled body onto three of them, covering myself with the fourth. It was time to "get naked in front of God," as Grandma used to say. It is hard to believe that as mean as she was and as badly as she had treated me, I could still find some of the things she said to me useful. I guess there really is some good in everything and everyone.

Uncle Leroy was a mystery to Rhonda. When he was sober, he was silent and brooding. He rarely spoke when he came home from work. He ate in silence, made little comment on his activities of the day, and refused to answer the telephone. He never asked about the children, even when one of them was sick. Rhonda had never heard him mention his family, his job, or even the weather. She did know, however, that Uncle Leroy had a girlfriend.

But with a few drinks to loosen his tongue and his temperament, Uncle Leroy was a totally different man. He'd tell funny, risqué stories to the children when Aunt Nadine wasn't listening. He'd pretend to be a wild stallion and let Ray, Rhonda, and Beanie ride around the room on his back while he bucked and tried to throw them off. Sometimes Uncle Leroy would grab Aunt Nadine and dance her around the house, singing off-key love songs loudly in her ear. The children loved it when he'd do his James Brown imitation. He'd use the broom or mop for his microphone while he did outrageous dance steps across the kitchen. When Aunt Nadine told him he was acting like an old fool and scuffing up her newly waxed floor, Uncle Leroy would sing his promise to lay down more wax and paint the whole kitchen to boot. When he was drunk, Uncle Leroy had a need to paint. He painted the kitchen every other month. First it was pink, then yellow. Once he pained it a dark, almost navy, blue. Rhonda, Ray, and Cousin Beanie had to cover it with three coats of paint when sober Uncle Leroy went back to work on Monday morning. The best thing about Uncle Leroy when he was drunk was that he'd leave his money lying around as he slumbered through intoxication to sobriety.

Rhonda learned how to rob Uncle Leroy early on. The first time, she was scared to death. How would she explain having money? You get an allowance, stupid! How would she hide the things she bought with the stolen loot? Buy things to eat, fool! Ray robbed him, too, but Rhonda never knew how often or how much he took. Rhonda stuck to coins. Fifty cents here. Thirty cents there. As long a she did it when he was drunk, Uncle Leroy never seemed to miss it.

Aunt Nadine had started having high-blood-pressure problems. She had neither the strength nor the energy to keep children, and she seldom left the house now. One Saturday, Aunt Dora insisted that Aunt Nadine come along to a bid whist card party that was held regularly at a friend's house. Aunt Nadine loved it. She even won a little pocket money her first time out. After that, Aunt Nadine became a regular. If she won, they'd have pizza for dinner, and Rhonda would get new clothes. Aunt Nadine didn't shop at the big, expensive stores that Nett patronized, but at least Rhonda would get blouses that matched her skirts and socks that matched the blouses.

Saturdays became an even lonelier time for Rhonda with Aunt Nadine off playing bid whist and Beanie at dance classes all day. Ray would be at football practice most of the day, and Uncle Leroy—drunk or sober—was no company at all. Rhonda would fill the empty hours sewing, reading, watching television, or playing with her dolls while she waited for someone, anyone, to come home.

On one rainy Saturday afternoon, Rhonda found herself home and virtually alone with Ray, who had banished her from his room twice already, and Uncle Leroy, who had gotten drunk and passed out in the basement hours ago. Rhonda wanted to sew something, an apron, perhaps, but couldn't find any material. She had already gotten into trouble with Aunt Nadine for cutting up one of her good sheets. She quickly became bored with television, then with reading a Nancy Drew mystery, and had no new comics to read. Rhonda decided she would go down to the basement and play some records and dance, but the music disturbed Uncle Leroy, and he told her to get back upstairs. He rolled over on his side, drooling on the sofa cushions and snoring loudly. Rhonda saw a wad of bills sticking out of his back pants pocket. She crept over to the sofa and slowly pulled a five-dollar bill from the roll. She backed away from the sofa, then tiptoed back up the stairs.

An hour later, Rhonda was drying off her rain gear and convincing herself that it was okay to take Uncle Leroy's money. After all, he'd give her money anyway when he was drunk. She sat on the floor of her bedroom, surveying her loot: a long-necked bottle of Pepsi, five new Archie comics, five candy bars, and a half-gallon bottle of Nett's favorite bubble bath. Rhonda lined her comics up in a neat row on the floor near her bed. She put the Pepsi and the bubble bath on either end of the row and placed a candy bar beside each comic book. Her plan was to first drink the Pepsi, then read a comic, then eat a candy bar, and so on until she got to the bubble bath; then she'd take a nice long soak in the tub. By then, Beanie or Aunt Nadine should be home.

She had barely savored the last sweet swallow of soda, when she heard a loud crashing noise from the kitchen. Quickly, she shoved her comics, candy, and bubble bath under the bed and went to see what all the commotion was about. Uncle Leroy was falling down drunk. He had tripped over a chair and lay spread-eagle on the floor, against the refrigerator. He was trying desperately to right himself and the chair, when Rhonda came running into the kitchen. She placed the chair back at the table and pulled Uncle Leroy to his unsteady feet.

"Where's everybody?" Uncle Leroy slurred, holding onto the wall.

"Aunt Nadine's gone to play cards," Rhonda said. Uncle Leroy was trying to focus his gaze and figure out why he was in the kitchen.

"Your brother home?" he asked.

"He's watching TV upstairs," Rhonda answered, anxious to get back to her own room.

"You doin' some reading?"

"Yes, Uncle Leroy." There was a long pause while Uncle Leroy tried to think of something else to ask. Rhonda fidgeted with the buttons on her blouse and waited politely for an opportunity to escape back to her comics and candy. Finally, Uncle Leroy mumbled something under his breath, then turned and left the kitchen.

Halfway through her first comic, Rhonda heard Uncle Leroy calling her name. Exasperated, she went to the top of the steps leading down to the basement and saw Uncle Leroy sprawled across the bottom steps, unable either to get back up the stairs or back to the sofa. He looked pitiful, and Rhonda wondered whether he was lonely, too. "Yes, Uncle Leroy? I'm here."

"C'mon down here and talk to me, baby," Uncle Leroy slurred. "And bring me some of them pig feet, I'm hongry."

He knows! He knows I took his money. I should have just taken coins. No, I shouldn't have taken anything. He wants to talk to me about all the times his money's been missing. How come Ray's never the one to get caught? What am I going to say?

Rhonda always tried to avoid looking at the big glass jar of pickled pig's feet when she opened the refrigerator. Just the sight of the dismembered feet lying in the bottom of the jar in the murky juice made her sick to her stomach. It reminded her of horror movies and mad scientists doing weird experiments in their dungeon laboratories. Maybe she'd make him a salami sandwich instead. No. She was already in enough trouble; she'd better fix him just what he asked for. It might help her case.

Rhonda removed the huge jar from the back of the top shelf of the refrigerator and placed it on the kitchen table. She got down a plate from the cabinet and put it next to the jar. She got a fork and a knife from the silverware drawer, wrapped them in three paper napkins, and placed them on a wooden tray. Aunt Nadine had made a large bowl of potato salad that morning, and Rhonda put a heaping scoop on the plate. Next, she filled a plastic tumbler with cold water and put it and a bottle of hot sauce on the tray. She saved the worst for last. Holding her breath, she opened the jar and took out two of the smelly pig's feet and placed them on the plate next to the potato salad. She tried not to breathe until she had replaced the lid and put the jar back behind the milk bottles in the refrigerator.

Rhonda stood with the tray at the top of the steps, squeezed her eyes shut, and said a silent prayer. She asked God to please not let Uncle Leroy be too mad at her, to please forgive her sin, and to please let her keep the bubble bath. Then she carefully descended the stairs to the basement.

Uncle Leroy was sitting up on the sofa, leaning hard to the left. He motioned her to put the tray down on the coffee table in front of him. Rhonda did as he indicated, but avoided looking directly at him so he couldn't see the guilt in her eyes.

"That's nice, baby. Real nice," Uncle Leroy said. He patted the seat cushion next to him. "Sit next to me while I eat. We can talk and maybe have us a little fun, too."

Even from across the coffee table, Rhonda could smell the stale liquor on his breath. The last thing she wanted to do was get closer to Uncle Leroy and watch him eat pig's feet. This was not her idea of fun. But what could she do? She had stolen his money and now she had to pay.

"C'mon, baby," Uncle Leroy said, "I won't bite you. I just want to talk to you."

Rhonda walked around the coffee table and sat stiffly on the far end of the sofa. Uncle Leroy picked up a pig's foot and took a big, juicy bite, letting the juice roll down his chin and onto his shirt. Rhonda was disgusted. The stench of the alcohol plus the strong vinegar smell of the pickled pig's feet was overwhelming, and Uncle Leroy was making loud, smacking noises as he chewed and talked at the same time.

"Why don't you have the other one?" he asked. He shook the pig's foot in her direction, and it slipped from his greasy fingers and fell to the floor between his feet. "Get that for me, baby. My head hurts too bad to bend down that far."

Rhonda slid down the sofa toward Uncle Leroy and retrieved the offensive foot. When she offered it to him, he grabbed her wrist instead, and pulled her to him. The meat fell onto the sofa between his legs. Rhonda instinctively pushed him away with her free hand, but he grabbed that wrist as well and forced her onto his lap. Rhonda tried to free herself from his grasp, but drunk as he was, Uncle Leroy held on fast.

"You gonna get that for me, baby?" Uncle Leroy's mouth was at Rhonda's ear. Her stomach was churning from the foul, sour odor. Uncle Leroy was smiling a drunken, seductive smile. Was he trying to punish her for taking his money by scaring her? The more she twisted her wrists to get away from him, the tighter his hold and the closer he pulled her to him.

"I can't pick it up while you're holding my hands," she said. Uncle Leroy released one of her hands, and when she reached for the pig's foot, he pushed her hand into his crotch and held it there. He stuck his tongue in her ear, then gave her a sloppy, wet kiss on the mouth, pushing his tongue against her tightly clenched teeth.

"Don't fight me, baby. We gonna have us a little fun, that's all. Don't it feel good? Take it easy. Your old uncle can make you feel real good, if you just relax a little." He let go of her hands and pulled her face to his, but she turned away before he could kiss her again. He stuck his tongue deep into her ear and slid his hands under her blouse, fondling the nipples on her flat chest.

Rhonda was rigid. She couldn't breathe and she couldn't move. What was he doing? He told her she could call him Daddy; after all, he provided for her and her brother, he gave her piggyback rides and told her funny stories. Was he so drunk that he thought she was Aunt Nadine? He wasn't supposed to be doing these things to her. She was sure of that. Did he think he could do the nasty to her because she stole his money?

Did he think she wouldn't tell on him because then he would tell on her? He had torn her blouse and now he was ripping off her panties. He was mumbling about fun and how beautiful she was. He was unzipping his pants. He was forcing her down onto her back and climbing on top of her. She was sorry for what she did. She had told God how sorry she was. His weight was crushing her, his rough, callused hands were scratching and bruising her private parts. She'd willingly give up the bubble bath if only he'd stop pushing his thing into her. He was hurting her. He was making her pay. There was nothing she could do but lie there while he grunted obscenities in her ear and told her he loved her.

The chill of the bathroom floor was coming right up through the towels and penetrating my spine. How many times? How many times do I have to live through that? As many times as necessary, until it no longer makes you sick to your stomach. I was freezing. Get in the tub. Get back in the tub and wash this crap away. Naked, I crawled over to the tub. The bathroom seemed to be filled with the stench of stale liquor on an old man's breath. I turned on the hot water full blast. This time, I even put the Jacuzzi jets on. Reaching for the lavender oil, I fought the urge to vomit. Just breathe!

But I could hear Rhonda crying in my mind. I could see her lying there, mute, numb, violated, frightened, and guilty. I forgive myself! I forgive myself! I forgive myself! Why does it take so long for the tub to get full? I could feel Rhonda's eyes piercing my heart. I could feel her pain in the pit of my stomach. She was waiting to see what I was going to do. Rhonda wanted to know if someone, anyone, was going to help her. To save her. To protect her. I am not a victim. I am not his victim! Not today. Not ever again! The words didn't help. I was about to have a combination-tear experience. As my shoulders slumped and I lowered my butt onto the freezing tile floor, big, hot salty tears fell from my eyes, streamed down my face, and rolled down my breasts. I felt so bad for her. He had taken her innocence before she even had breasts.

When a little girl is being violated, her mind will escape from her body and wander randomly. She won't smell the stench of liquor on her violator's foul breath, she won't feel his callused palms on her flat chest, nor will she suffer the pain of his grown-man's penis ripping the virginal tissue of her vagina. Instead, she might wonder if her mother is really dead; she might wonder why her father didn't have the time or desire to provide for her and her brother; or she might wonder how she would explain the grease stains on the sofa from the pig's foot she still held in her hand.

When Rhonda's mind returned, she found herself upstairs, sitting in a bathtub of warm water. She was bleeding, and her head ached. Her eyes stung, and her face felt hot and flushed. Her legs and feet, her hands and fingers, were sore and tender. Her mind was numb. Her heart was cold. How did she get upstairs? Had she really tried to call Nett? Did Ray actually kick her out of his room when she tried to tell him what happened? Her torn blouse was in the bathroom sink and smelled of vomit and vinegar. She vaguely remembered crawling under the kitchen table, then throwing up and having to clean the kitchen floor. She must have let Baby in the house, because the cat now sat beside the tub, peering up at her.

She was still bleeding when she put on fresh clothes and sat on the edge of the bed, holding the cat. Rhonda was in a state of shock and oblivious to the hot tears that fell from the outside corners of her eyes as she sat and stared and waited for Aunt Nadine to come home.

If people don't ask you how you feel, what you think, what you want, or what you know, there is no way they can know who you are. When people don't know who you are, they mistakenly believe they can do anything they want to you. And they *will* do it, if they don't know. When that happens, it is up to you to take a stand for yourself. It is up to you to let them know what you need. It is up to you to tell them what you think. It is up to you to let them know that you don't know what they think you know. At all times, under all circumstances, every individual must shoulder full responsibility for telling other people exactly how they feel, what they need, what they know, and who they are. If, however, you are an eleven-year-old child, chances are you haven't learned how to do that yet.

If you haven't, and the people around you don't realize it, you are in grave danger of being misunderstood. Rhonda was learning the dangers of being misunderstood.

Rhonda had no idea how much time had passed when the front door opened and Aunt Nadine strolled into the house and announced that she had won $250. Still clutching Baby to her chest, Rhonda somehow found the words to tell Aunt Nadine exactly what had happened. Aunt Nadine stared at her in disbelief for a very long time. Then she turned on her heel and headed for the basement. Rhonda, with Baby, moved into the kitchen and sat down until Aunt Nadine called her. She put Baby down and descended the stairs slowly, painfully.

"Tell him what you told me," Aunt Nadine demanded. Uncle Leroy was sitting precariously on one of the bar stools, trying to maintain some semblance of sobriety, but he looked guilty as hell under Aunt Nadine's angry stare. A greasy piece of pork clung to the front of his shirt. Rhonda looked from Aunt Nadine to the empty liquor bottles on the bar. She couldn't bring herself to look at him looking at her. She stared at the floor between his shoeless feet, then at her own shoes before finding the courage to repeat the accusation.

"That's a bold-faced lie!" Uncle Leroy jumped to his feet and pointed an intimidating finger in Rhonda's direction. "I didn't hurt her," he slurred. "I didn't even penetrate her." Aunt Nadine never took her eyes off Uncle Leroy. She listened to Rhonda's tearful declaration that she didn't know what "penetrate" meant, but that, yes, he had definitely hurt her. Aunt Nadine's stony glare reflected her anger and disgust. She didn't say a word, and shards of silence hung in the space between her and Uncle Leroy. Rhonda waited for the blow that was surely about to be dealt. The piece of pig's foot left an oily stain as it slid down Uncle Leroy's shirt and fell quietly to the floor.

"Go to your room, Rhonda," Aunt Nadine said without altering her gaze. "You go on and go to bed now." Aunt Nadine's voice was cold as ice.

Rhonda lay on her bed and listened to the silence that shouldn't have been there. Yet there was a silence and stillness throughout the house.

There was silence where there should have been yelling. There was silence where there should have been the sound of the front door slamming shut. There was silence where the sound of Uncle Leroy's Lincoln driving off forever should have been. There was silence where there should have been comforting words and healing hands. There was silence where there should have been an apology and a promise. And there was silence where there should have been an acknowledgment of the wrong and a declaration of the truth.

Silence teaches you many things. It teaches you how to listen and how to hear. It teaches you how to feel and how to translate into words what you are feeling. When you can't translate what you are feeling, silence allows you to go deeper into yourself and find the peace that surpasses understanding. A peace that enables you to move forward, even when you don't understand. Most of the time, silence is a good thing. But there are those times and circumstances when silence will kill you. A killing silence can destroy your identity and your spirit. It can kill your heart and your soul. When silence is used as a means of avoiding something you know you must deal with, it will murder your sense of worth. When you use silence to hide the truth, to avoid the truth, or to color the truth, it is the same as saying that the truth doesn't matter. It demonstrates your belief that people who tell the truth don't matter.

But they do.

CHAPTER SEVEN

What's the Lesson When You've Been Taught That You Are Unlovable?

Conflict is simply a result of something getting in the way of the forward flow of life. This happens when you see yourself as being incomplete in some way, and so you are trying to add something to help you feel more complete. Those who are always using others to satisfy their needs or purpose are always filled with conflict.

Tom Johnson, in *You Are Always Your Own Experience*

SOMETIMES YOU NEED SOMETHING to bring you back to reality. Like a bucket of ice-cold water dumped on your head. I heard pounding on the bathroom door. It was the dog, again. I was convinced that she was crazy. I needed to get rid of her and get myself an honest, God-fearing mutt. Now she was banging on the door. If I had to get out of the tub, I was going to kill that dog! Okay, she's dead! Dripping wet, I yanked the door open to find my very expensive, very dumb dog eating my brand-new red suede shoes. I hadn't even taken the paper out of them yet. She had. There were tiny pieces of white tissue paper strewn all over the bedroom floor. China, the dog, was lying at the entrance of the bathroom with the tip of my shoe in her mouth and her hind legs inside the shoe. I knew that if I reached down, I was going to strangle this dog. If I wasn't such a shoe diva, I might have thought she looked cute. But I was, and right now she didn't look cute, she looked like dead meat!

Just as I bent down and extended my arms in her direction, my husband appeared. "Oh, oh, China! You're gonna get yourself in trouble." He didn't even seem to notice that I was buck naked and dripping wet.

"I thought you were working or bathing or something," he said.

"I was remembering," I said. He took the shoe from the dog.

"You go on and finish up. I'll put her away." He always knows just what to say. God! He is such a blessing.

Heading back to the bathtub, I noticed that the lump in my throat was gone. I was beginning to feel better. My boundaries were getting clearer. But I still had a ways to go, and the water was still warm.

Beanie was devastated when her mother died. Aunt Nadine had been in and out of the hospital for over a year before she passed on, and Rhonda had become used to her absence. She felt little compassion for Beanie and no grief whatsoever. She watched the aunts and uncles and cousins cry their eyes out at the funeral; then watched as they returned to Aunt Nadine's immaculate house, got drunk, and started fighting as though it were just another Saturday night.

Rhonda retreated to her room with Baby, the cat. Suddenly, she saw Grandma and Daddy standing in front of her. Only they weren't really there. The platters of food and the big black car weren't really there either. Rhonda sat very still as her heart raced and she held her breath, praying for the images to disappear. Then the lady in the white dress appeared. Her eyes were closed as she stepped out of a large casket and stood before Rhonda. She was the lady from Rhonda's dreams, but Rhonda was awake. Rhonda screamed when the lady's eyes opened wide just before her image vanished and the real Grandma rushed into the room.

Nett came in right behind Grandma and tried to calm Rhonda down. Before Grandma could say something cruel and nasty, Nett sent Rhonda up to Ray's room, where all the boy cousins and Ray's friends from school were hanging out. Nett thought she was sparing Rhonda, but Ray sensed

Rhonda's vulnerability and took advantage of the opportunity to exercise some Grandma-like cruelty himself.

"Hey, Ronnie. Guess what?" Ray said loud enough for all the boys in the room to hear. Rhonda had laid her head down on the pillow on Ray's bed and was trying to be as inconspicuous as possible when suddenly all eyes were on her.

"You know Junior, here?" Ray nodded his head toward Uncle Lowell and Aunt Dora's twelve-year-old son who sat on the floor between two of Ray's football buddies. "Hey, Cousin Junior," Rhonda said weakly, not knowing where Ray was going with this. Junior knew exactly what Ray was about to do and averted his eyes without answering Rhonda's greeting.

"It ain't *Cousin* Junior, stupid. Junior is our younger brother."

Why Ray felt the need in that moment to disclose this information, Rhonda did not understand, nor question. She had too many other things to think about. With Aunt Nadine dead, it could be that she and Ray would have to move again. Where would they go now? Who would not want to be bothered with them this time? And now her brother, who seldom had anything to say to her, was announcing in front of everyone that their cousin was actually their brother. It was information that Rhonda neither needed nor wanted, but that didn't stop Ray. He went on to explain that when Junior was born he was so messed up that their mother, Sarah, gave him away because she couldn't take care of him and their daddy wouldn't take care of him. Junior had been only two months old when Sarah died. "Why," Ray said angrily, "didn't he just give all of us away? At least that way we could have all been together!"

Before Ray could say another word, Rhonda sat straight up in the bed and told him, "He did give all of us away!" Rhonda looked over at Junior and realized that they were spitting images of one another. She bolted from the room, stepping on the cutest boy in the bunch on her way out. She found a relatively quiet corner in the kitchen amidst the drunken relatives, and sat down near the door leading to the backyard, humming to herself. "What a friend we have in Jesus. All our sins and grief to bear . . . " Rhonda really needed a friend.

♥

Something magical happened to Rhonda when she danced. She forgot to remember that she was overweight. She forgot to remember that rainy Saturday night. She didn't think about her daddy and she didn't think about Grandma. When Rhonda was dancing, she was free. She was beautiful. And she was at peace. Rhonda had started dancing after Aunt Nadine died. Sometimes she went to dance practice with Beanie; sometimes she went to the after-school center. When she couldn't think or feel, dancing made it all better. Dancing had helped her body to develop, and, finally, she could fill a bra cup. Her bottom, which had been just round, was now shapely, and her stomach was flat as a board. The boys in school started calling her "foxy," instead of "wiggy." Dancing kept her alive.

Nett called more frequently now, and Rhonda's dancing gave them something positive to talk about. One Saturday, as they sat at a table in Nett's favorite diner, she asked Rhonda, "Am I your friend?" Rhonda felt pangs of guilt. Nett had always been good to her, but after the stories she'd heard at Aunt Nadine's drunken parties, she wasn't sure if she could still trust Nett. She didn't have the nerve to tell Nett about her misgivings, so she looked up from her almost empty plate and answered, "Yes."

"Do you trust me? I would understand if you didn't. I know it has been hard for you to understand why I left you at Aunt Nadine's for so long, so that's why I would understand if you didn't trust me anymore." Nett's question and the aftertaste of the greasy french fries gave way to a sour taste in Rhonda's mouth. Somehow she knew where Nett was headed, and it was making her sick to her stomach. Rhonda simply said she understood; she didn't like it, but she did understand.

"Since we are friends, and since you do trust me, will you tell me the truth if I ask you something?" Rhonda was beginning to squirm. Then she thought, "Maybe she's going to ask me about stealing money." That wasn't the question, but what Nett asked was directly related. "Has your uncle ever touched you? Has he ever put his hands under your clothes or anything like that?" Rhonda stared at her across the table. She knew she'd throw up if she opened her mouth.

"I've seen the way he looks at you, and I don't like it." All of a sudden, Rhonda was burning hot. Then she began to shiver as if the temperature in the diner had suddenly dropped to subzero. Bloody underwear flashed in her mind, and she could smell the stench of stale liquor. It started as a murmur, but by the time it spilled out of her mouth, Rhonda was screaming, "Stop it! Stop it!" When she realized she was talking to her friend in a public place, she changed the statement, but not the volume. "Don't ask me that! Don't ever ask me that!"

People at nearby tables were staring. Nett must have realized what was about to happen, but she couldn't get out of her seat and around the table fast enough. Rhonda was now wailing so loudly that one of the waitresses came over and asked if everything was all right. Oh sure, Rhonda thought, people always have breakdowns in diners. Nett waved the woman away as she tried to slide off the diner bench, pulling Rhonda along with her.

Rhonda was trembling and wailing. Nett tried to help her stand, then walk. They made it through the diner and through the maze of people trying not to stare. Nett guided Rhonda into the ladies' room, where Rhonda fell to her hands and knees and crawled to the nearest corner. By then, Nett was crying too. She walked over to where Rhonda was cowering and sat down next to her. They sat crying and rocking for a long while. A few ladies who entered offered them tissues. Others just stared. Nett didn't say a word all the way home, or the next day when she arrived to help Rhonda load her belongings into the back of a taxicab. It took Ray about two weeks before he decided to join them.

With school, homework, three dance classes a week, drill team practice, and household chores, it was a wonder Rhonda had any free time at all. Let alone time to get pregnant.

She and Reggie talked about sex for a long time. Eventually the talking gave way to the doing. They started going to "hooky" parties with other kids from the community band they both played with. They'd skip school and spend the day partying. When Ray would become suspicious because he hadn't seen her in school, Rhonda would skip the hooky parties and attend classes for at least the next few days. It was purely accidental that Rhonda discovered that on days she was at school, Reggie was spending his time at the hooky parties locked in a room with a girl named Beverly. Reggie admitted that he and Beverly had been "together." Rhonda was crushed. Her silence around the house alerted Nett, and it wasn't long before Rhonda told Nett everything. It precipitated their first "womanhood" talk. Unfortunately, the talk came too late.

There are things that young girls with budding breasts and plump round bottoms need to know about becoming a woman. Unfortunately, at the time they need to know these things, their circumstances may be transitional. Their families may be unsettled or dysfunctional. The women in their lives may be busy, ill, or absent. Or the women may be too uncomfortable to talk about the things that perhaps no one talked to them about. Young girls still need to know, and they have questions that need to be answered. All young girls need training, *womanhood training,* in the sacred art and science of becoming a woman. This training includes having information and examples that will enable the young girl to take care of herself and her "womanness" as it grows within her and through her.

At the time Rhonda needed to be taught about being a woman, her circumstances were very transitional. Aunt Nadine was in and out of the hospital, Beanie was always distraught, and Nett was an infrequent visitor. No one had told Rhonda about menstruation, first love, or sex. None of the women in her life ever mentioned or exemplified self-nurturing, self-respect, or self-honor. Rhonda had no one to giggle with about the sacred, secret, innocent "girly things." She saw no pictures or examples that would help her understand what would happen to her body, what to expect once it happened, or what to do about it when it happened. Most of what Rhonda learned came from the walls of the girls' restroom at school and from what boys saw fit to say when they wanted to educate you fast. By the time someone noticed that Rhonda was becoming a woman, it was too late for training. Her innocence had been stolen, and she had received all the information she could handle "on the job."

Teddy hung around with the other boys in front of Nett's apartment building. He lived on the top floor with his mother, his brother, and his mother's boyfriend. Nett had her eye on Teddy because she had noticed that Teddy had his eye on Rhonda.

"Stay away from that man! He's not a boy, he's a man, and I don't like the way he looks at you." Rhonda didn't say a word. She had absolutely no intention of staying away from him. In fact, she'd been waiting for a time when she could speak to him when Nett wasn't looking. She didn't have to wait long.

When you need to be loved, you take love wherever you can find it. When you are desperate to be loved, feel love, know love, you seek out what you think love should look like. When you find love, or what you think love is, you will lie, kill, and steal to keep it. But learning about real love comes from within. It cannot be given. It cannot be taken away. It grows from your sense of self. It grows from your ability to re-create within yourself, and for yourself, the essence of loving experiences you have had in your life. When you have not had loving experiences, or when you do not have a sense of self, the true essence of love eludes you. Instead, you hold onto, reach out to, and find yourself embroiled in, your mistaken beliefs about yourself and love.

"Hi!" Teddy said, catching up to Rhonda as she walked to the bus stop. "I was wondering what happened to you." Teddy was charming; his Southern drawl was smooth as silk.

"What do you mean?" Rhonda asked.

"I used to see you and your brother leaving for school every morning, but I haven't seen you for a while," Rhonda was flattered. He had been watching her!

Over the next several months, Reggie and Rhonda were on again, off again, but things with Teddy were heating up. Rhonda was thirteen, Teddy was nineteen. He had come to New York from Mississippi to find work after he finished high school. He had been raised by his grandmother and wanted to make some money to send back home to her. Teddy said he had six aunts and uncles who kept having children and dropping them off for his grandmother to raise. His grandmother was old, tired, and poor. Rhonda told Teddy about Grandma, who showed no signs of aging, could still move fast, and was mean as hell.

Whenever Teddy saw Nett, he tried his best to be extra nice to her. He would hold the door for her, offer to carry her bags, and always had a friendly and respectful greeting when she passed. But Nett wouldn't give him the time of day. She didn't like him and made no effort to hide her feelings. It didn't matter; Teddy persisted in his pursuit of Rhonda. One morning as Rhonda was leaving for school she found Teddy waiting for her in the hallway.

"Can I walk you to the bus stop, Miss Lady?"

"No!" she almost screamed at him. "If somebody sees us . . . I mean if somebody tells my mother . . . I mean no, I'm in a hurry."

Teddy snatched Rhonda's book bag from her and headed down the stairs. "I can walk fast, too, you know."

They walked together to the bus stop, laughing and talking like boyfriend and girlfriend. When the bus rolled to a stop in front of them, Teddy leaned over and kissed Rhonda squarely on the mouth. It was a nice, warm, friendly kiss.

When Rhonda got home that afternoon, Teddy was sitting on the stairs waiting for her. He smiled. She smiled. She moved toward the door to her apartment, and Teddy followed her. As Rhonda fumbled nervously for her door keys, Teddy gently maneuvered himself in front of her and kissed her again. This time, thrusting his tongue inside her mouth. Rhonda was stunned. She panicked. But then Teddy spoke and asked if he could come inside. The request had the same effect as cold water being thrown into Rhonda's face.

"Are you crazy!" she screamed. "You can't do that!"

"Then why don't you come upstairs with me?"

"My brother will be here any minute. I can't."

"I promise. You don't have to stay long. You can watch for your brother out my window."

Teddy's house was very different from Rhonda's. There was a lot of furniture in his living room and lots of dirty dishes in the sink. There was a dirt ring around the bathtub and a pile of clothes on his bed. Reggie and Rhonda usually "did it" standing up, fully clothed, with their underwear down around their ankles. Teddy pushed the pile of clothes onto the floor, and the next thing Rhonda knew, she was lying nude on Teddy's bed.

Rhonda was thirteen and a half years old, naked in bed with a grown man. She couldn't think of anything to say. Teddy kissed her from head to toe. She didn't know how to respond. He asked her if she loved him. She kept her mouth shut. He told her that he loved her. She closed her eyes and forgot that she could even talk. Seven and a half minutes later, she was back up, getting dressed. She was speechless.

Rhonda couldn't believe that an attractive, handsome man-child would be the least bit interested in her. Her father wasn't. Her brother wasn't. Reggie was, but he was a boy, not a man. She couldn't believe that a grown man would want to have sex with her. It was only when she danced that she felt beautiful. Otherwise, Rhonda felt she had never stopped being ugly. She was going to make the most of every opportunity she had to be beautiful and feel loved. But Rhonda hadn't learned that men will say anything and do anything to get you to have sex with them. She had yet to learn how to distinguish between a lie and the truth. And it never dawned on her that Teddy could be lying through his teeth.

When Rhonda told Teddy that she thought she was pregnant, he disappeared. He didn't move. He just disappeared. Rhonda had continued to see Reggie, but far less frequently. She had spent every stolen moment she could find with Teddy. Rhonda and Beverly had become friends again, and Rhonda confided in her. Beverly told her sister, Sandra, who took Rhonda to a doctor. Much to their chagrin, the doctor confirmed that Rhonda was indeed pregnant. Four months pregnant to be exact. Sandra kept saying how sorry she was for Rhonda; Beverly was too freaked out to say anything at all. Rhonda had no idea what to do next.

That night, Rhonda called Reggie and told him she was pregnant. Reggie was shocked, but he was a decent boy who cared about Rhonda and the predicament she was in. Reggie didn't disappear. He told his mother, who then called Nett. There was a meeting with all the parents and thirteen-year-old Rhonda and fifteen-year-old Reggie. It was decided that the children were too young to get married and that Rhonda would have the baby, then put it up for adoption. Then it was decided that Rhonda would have the baby and Reggie's mother would raise the baby until Rhonda finished school. Then they decided that Rhonda would stay at home and attend a school for pregnant teenagers. In the end, Rhonda was sent to a foster home for pregnant girls in Jamaica, Queens. It was there that Rhonda realized no one had ever asked her who the baby's father was.

Three weeks after Martin Luther King was assassinated, Rhonda gave birth to a baby girl. Little Tracey, named after Teddy's sister, was five pounds thirteen ounces, and seventeen inches long. Tracey looked just like her father. Same eyes, same color, same everything. Tracey went directly from the hospital into foster care. Rhonda went back home to Nett's disappointed sadness, Ray's indifference, Grandma's predictable "I told you sos," and to begin living with her own shame.

One day, soon after she returned home, Teddy reappeared. She was walking home from the store when she saw him.

"Was it a boy or a girl?" Teddy knew where Rhonda had been because his mother and all the other mothers in the building had been gossiping about why Rhonda had disappeared right in the middle of the school year.

"A girl." Rhonda said and never stopped walking. She refused to even look at Teddy. When they got to the front of the apartment building, Teddy said a quick "see ya" and ran across the street to the park. For the rest of that day and for several days after that, Rhonda sat in the window and watched Teddy.

The train ride uptown usually took about twenty minutes, but on this day it seemed to take forever. Every time the train stopped, every time the doors opened, every time one person got up and another sat next to her, Rhonda would break down and cry again. By the time the train reached the Seventy-second Street stop, she was weeping inconsolably. Some of the women on the train, sensing her pain, offered her tissues and cough drops. At the Eighty-sixth Street station, one of the women helped Rhonda off the train and asked her what was the matter. Rhonda explained that her six-month-old-baby, who had been in foster care, had died that morning, and she didn't know why. Her mother was at work and couldn't leave, and she didn't know where her father was, and the baby's father had disappeared—again. The only thing the woman could think of to say was, "You're so young." She gave Rhonda some extra tissues, wished her well, and went on her way. Rhonda was alone and on her way to identify her baby's body.

Reggie and his entire family came to the funeral. The social worker and the foster parents also came. Nett, Daddy, and Ray refused to attend. Surprisingly, Grandma wanted to come, but Nett lied to her about the day and the time. Tracey lay in a small white casket and wore a little white dress. She looked so tiny. Rhonda sat still in the pew and wondered why she felt no grief for her dead child. She felt no sadness, no loss, no pain. She waited all through the funeral, hoping that she'd feel something. She waited as they placed the tiny casket in yet another big black car, and even as Tracey was lowered into the ground. It wasn't until Rhonda looked up and saw the lady in the white dress standing in front of the grave that she felt anything at all. And what she felt was closure. Finally, it was all over.

With all that behind her, things returned to normal pretty quickly. In a matter of weeks, Rhonda was back to her schoolwork, hanging out with her friends, and her dance classes. It took several months before she got up the courage to share her experience with her dance buddies. And to her surprise, most of them already knew or at least had some idea. Things at home had changed, however. The only time she and Nett talked was when Nett was questioning her about where she was going, where she had been, and whether she was "messing around again." Whenever Daddy showed up, he looked over her, around her, but never directly at her. At sixteen years old, Ray was becoming a full-fledged alcoholic. He could care less that his sister had been pregnant and buried a baby.

Rhonda had learned a great deal in the past year. Everything had happened so fast that the lessons has come in fragments. One fragment of what she learned led her to believe that when you don't matter to the people in your life, the things that happen to you don't matter. Another piece of the lesson was that once people get what they want from you, they leave. Another small portion of the lesson that life was teaching Rhonda was that when you don't have anything that people want to begin with, they will leave. The biggest, and most difficult piece of the lesson that Rhonda had learned was that when you really need someone, the people that you expect to be there will not be there. Nothing in this lesson was new. These were all things that Rhonda had learned a long time ago at Grandma's house and at Aunt Nadine's. She had learned how to cry and keep on moving. It was painful and sometimes hard, but Rhonda had learned her lesson well.

Things were not going so well for Nett. She was working two jobs, trying to make ends meet. But the ends were not connecting, were, in fact, miles apart. Each payday, Nett had to decide whether they'd have food in the house, a telephone, or have the lights on. There was never enough money to pay for the necessities, let alone little extras for herself, Ray, or Rhonda. Rhonda never complained, though she wanted so many of the things that her friends had. She understood that Nett was doing the best she could for them and seldom asked Nett for anything that cost money. Rhonda would faithfully wash and wear her two skirts and two blouses, week in and week out. Nett would sit at the kitchen table late at night, eating her warmed-over dinner and watching Rhonda iron her clothes, carefully avoiding the spots that were threadbare or shiny from being ironed so often. Sometimes, Nett would get angry and pick a fight with Rhonda. She'd interrogate her about her whereabouts that day and ask her who she was taking such care ironing for. Other times, Nett would push her plate aside and put her head down on the table. When Rhonda asked her what was wrong, Nett would just say she was tired, but Rhonda knew she was hiding her tears. No matter how hard she tried, no matter how she skimped on her own needs, Nett rarely had two nickels to rub together.

To make matters worse, Nett had found out that Daddy was spending his money on another woman. Nett, who had always prided herself on her looks, could no longer afford nail polish or expensive perfume or trips to the beauty parlor to get her hair done. Nett, who had given up so much just for the reflection of love she saw in Daddy's eyes, was at first uncontrollably angry then sullen and depressed when she smelled the perfume she could no longer afford on one of Daddy's shirts. The thought of him impressing some brazen hussy in Mr. Rootman's bar with the money she and his own children so desperately needed and deserved sent Nett over the edge.

Ray, like Daddy, was seldom home, and Rhonda usually took the brunt of Nett's erratic and moody behavior. Rhonda did her best to stay out of Nett's path, but the slightest infringement would bring Nett's misplaced wrath down on her head. If Rhonda's chores weren't done on time or done properly, Nett would go into a rage and deny whatever minor privileges Rhonda had. Most nights, Nett came home tired, defeated, and mad at the world. If she was more tired and defeated than mad, she'd eat her meager dinner and go right to bed. If anger prevailed, she'd burst into Rhonda's room, accuse her of sleeping around with some unnamed boy, and threaten to kick her out of the house if she ever got pregnant again.

The physical and emotional space between Rhonda and Nett grew wider each day. They denied each other the love, compassion, and understanding that they both yearned for. Rhonda felt that she was losing Nett's love and that she would never regain Nett's trust. But the money problems and the problems with Daddy were not her fault. She was doing her best not to ask Nett for anything, and Nett didn't even seem to realize that Rhonda wanted nice things too. She wanted new clothes, new shoes, a few dollars now and then for the movies or romance magazines.

Nett came home in a particularly bad mood one night and found Rhonda in her room, painting her toenails.

"Nail polish? Where in the hell did you get money to buy nail polish?" Nett was furious, her tone accusatory.

"Aunt 'Nita gave me the money," Rhonda said meekly.

"Oh, really? And just how much money did she give you?" Rhonda didn't answer. "Fifty cents? Two dollars? Twenty dollars? Enough to pay the gas bill? The phone bill? How much, Ronnie?" Nett stood with her arms crossed, daring Rhonda to tell a lie.

"Forty dollars." Rhonda's voice was barely audible.

"I know I didn't hear you correctly. How much did you say?" Nett stepped closer to where Rhonda now stood trembling.

"Forty dollars," she repeated.

"Where's the rest of the money? I know you didn't bring forty dollars into this raggedy-ass house and spend it all on yourself." Nett looked into Rhonda's guilty face and already knew the answer. "You mean after all I've done for you, all the sacrifices I've made for you and your brother, all the hours I've worked just to put a lousy piece of salt pork in a pot of beans and keep a roof over your selfish, ungrateful head; you mean after all I've done to provide for you when your own whore of a father wasn't giving me a dime, you went out and bought forty dollars' worth of what? What could you possibly have needed so badly that you became a liar and a thief? Just like a rat leaving a sinking ship. Everyone for themselves. Is that the way I brought you up? Haven't I always told you that you take care of the people who take care of you? You're hopeless, you know that, Ronnie? You're pathetic. You don't appreciate anything I've done for you. All you think about is your own sorry self. I work my ass off, and this is the thanks I get? Well, you know what, Ronnie? Let me tell you something—" Nett hesitated for a split second, but not long enough to stop the words. "You and your Daddy are just alike. Neither one of you is s——t, and you never will be s——t!"

An avalanche of hurt and despair and deep sadness rolled across the room, filling every corner, sucking the very air from Rhonda's lungs, blocking the light from her vision, killing her wounded spirit.

Nett had turned and stormed out of the room and was halfway to the kitchen when she realized what she'd done. Somehow, Grandma's venomous words had come from her own mouth. She had used them as weapons to vent her anger and frustration. Nett slumped down heavily onto a kitchen chair. The meanness of her spirit and the viciousness of her words shocked and frightened her. What had she become that she could purposely inflict such pain on someone she loved so dearly? She had to apologize. Immediately. She had to hold Rhonda in her arms and tell her how sorry she was and that she hadn't meant to say those terrible words. She had to explain that she was just upset about not being able to provide for her family, and that she was angry, not with Rhonda, but with Rhonda's father. She had to tell Rhonda how much she loved her, how she would never stop loving her.

It was too late. Rhonda had gone into the bathroom and taken all the pills she could find, including Ray's asthma medication. Then she had walked quietly past the kitchen into the living room and laid down on the sofa. She did not expect to wake up in the morning.

CHAPTER EIGHT

What's the Lesson When You Don't Reconcile Your Past Before Moving Ahead?

Trials are but lessons that you failed to learn
presented once again, so where you made a faulty
  choice before
you can now make a better one, and thus escape
all pain that what you chose before has brought to you.
In every difficulty, all distress, and each perplexity,
Christ calls to you and gently says,
"My brother, choose again."

A Course in Miracles

IT WAS TIME FOR ME to get out of the bathtub. The water shooting through the jets no longer felt soothing. It was beginning to hurt. Maybe it was because I was remembering so much, so fast, and this had made me sensitive. When you start to remember who you were, you become sensitive about who you are. You may begin to doubt your ability to go any further. You may even doubt whether you have the right to go any further.

I have, at one time or another, doubted myself. Doubt is a common side effect of remembering. It is human nature to assess what we can do according to what we have done. When I didn't do so well yesterday, I have been afraid of making the same mistake again. At this point in my life, however, I realize that if I don't remember what I did, I cannot do anything differently. If I don't pay attention to the details of my actions, I will do the same thing over and over out of habit. I don't want to do that anymore. If that means that I must search every little corner of my life until I understand what I do that gets me into places I don't want to be, then I am willing to stay in the tub and remember and cry and be wrinkled and cry some more. I also believe that if I get any more wrinkled right now, my brain will shrivel and I won't remember anything.

I decided to take a walk. Walking helps you remember. I got out of the tub, put on my favorite high-water dusty pink sweats, and hit the nature trail. The woods are a beautiful place to go to find yourself. At the beginning of this trail, there are giant weeping willow trees that hang over the path. They sometimes look like people, so I am never alone. I have talked to the weeping willows. I admit it. Thank God, they have never answered me. The willows know all of my secrets, and all of Rhonda's, too. I have told them about her, and they have helped me remember.

There are several paths that lead into the woods. The one I chose was not straight. It snaked through the sun-dappled willows and poplars, winding sometimes to the east, then curving off toward the west. Some portions of the path were smooth and flat, offering an easy, casual stroll. Other times the road was rocky, with steep inclines that made your heart race and your breathing deeper. There were places where tall branches seemed to reach for the sky, inviting the bright sunlight to splash through to the wildflowers that bordered the path. Some stretches were thick with foliage that dared the light to pass and made you walk just a little bit faster. Rhonda and I stepped onto the path, took a deep breath, and headed for the clear, blue pond at the end of the trail.

By the time Rhonda realized that she was pregnant with Gary's baby, he was trying his best to make himself invisible. Especially to Rhonda. She was only sixteen but had squeezed forty-five years of living into her short life. Rhonda was fragile, needy, and the therapist who treated her after the suicide attempt told her she was also "emotionally damaged." Sometimes we learn things about ourselves that we would never know unless somebody told us. Sometimes people tell us things about ourselves that we really need to know. Other times, people would serve us better by keeping their thoughts and opinions to themselves. The lesson is in determining which is which. Rhonda had not yet learned that lesson.

Gary was an attractive, hormone-driven, nineteen-year-old track star. He had a fierce reputation as a ladies' man. But Rhonda was new to Jefferson High School, and she had no way of knowing that. She had never been on a date, not a real high school date with a real high school boyfriend. Gary was hot stuff. He was from a stable home and destined to go to college. And he was clear. Rhonda was still bouncing around from one relative's home to another's, wondering where she could receive her subscription to *Teen Life* magazine. She felt unwanted and unsettled. She was not clear at all.

After the suicide attempt, she had stayed with Nett for a while, but the threat of eviction meant that she and Ray had to go live with Beanie. When Beanie's boyfriend expressed too much interest in Rhonda, she went back to live with Nett. It was at that point that Ray decided to get off the "family-go-round." He stayed with Beanie and was high most of the time.

The high school that Rhonda attended was a two-hour commute from Nett's house, so she transferred to nearby Jefferson High School. Rhonda started dancing again and soon became the captain of the Jefferson High Dance Club. Gary first noticed Rhonda at a school assembly, where the Dance Club performed. Gary was focused on athletics and had not been exposed to African dance. He was intrigued by Rhonda the dancer and by what she could do with her body. Rhonda was flattered to have the attention of a handsome track star. She was easily seduced by his hormone-motivated overtures, the sly winks in the hallway, the late-night telephone calls, the secret meetings. It all happened very quickly. Nett figured it out before Rhonda had the courage to tell her.

Rhonda and Nett had developed a morning routine. Nett would get up every morning, put on the coffee, and take her shower. When she came out of the bathroom, Rhonda would take her shower. By the time Rhonda was dressed, the coffee would be poured and waiting. She and Nett would sit at the kitchen table and talk and laugh together before they went off to work and school. They used this time to discuss everything and everybody. Nett shared what was going on at her job, and Rhonda told Nett about school. They prepared the grocery list and decided who would pick up what. They talked about boys and clothes and what they'd seen on television.

One morning over coffee, Nett set her cup down on the table and looked Rhonda squarely in the eyes.

"You're pregnant again, aren't you?" Nett said. "I can see it in your eyes; I can see it all over you." Rhonda's eyes started to well up with tears, but she held them back, refusing to cry. "Who is it?" Nett asked. "Is it that guy that calls here so late?"

"If I am, he is," Rhonda said, the tears beginning to fall.

Nett took a sip of her coffee and continued.

"Ronnie, Ronnie. You can't keep having babies. I know you want a family and somebody to love you. I know how hard it's been for you growing up, but having a baby is only going to make it harder. You have to finish school. You are going to be somebody one day, and having a baby is going to make that harder, too."

This was their private talking time, so Rhonda spoke up. She told Nett that Gary hardly spoke to her anymore, that he was avoiding her at school and not calling her at home anymore. Nett was furious. First with Rhonda, but mostly with Gary.

"Does he have a father? Does he have a mother? Does he have a telephone number?" Nett took the number and called Gary's house. When Gary's father answered, Nett informed him that her daughter was pregnant by his son. She suggested a meeting to discuss plans for support of the child. Gary's father said he would discuss the matter with his son and get back to her. (It was three weeks after the baby was born when he called back.)

The next day at school, Gary materialized long enough to tell Rhonda he was mad at her for telling. For the remaining months of her pregnancy, Rhonda was angry. She was angry with herself and angry with Gary. She felt alone, unwanted, and ashamed. Gary would ignore her if their paths crossed at school, but one day when no one was around, he winked at her, then tried to touch her swollen belly. Rhonda spit in his face and ran away.

Damon was a beautiful baby boy. He had a tendency to choke but was otherwise normal and healthy. He offered Nett and Rhonda a new lease on life. "Babies take your mind off the things that don't matter," Nett said. "They give you something more to live for." Nett liked being called Nana. She was delighted with Damon and overly protective. Rhonda was happy, but confused and afraid. The day that Damon turned three weeks old, Rhonda was standing over the crib, staring at her baby son, trying to figure out whether she was happy, confused, or afraid, when she noticed that Damon's little body was turning blue. When she touched him, he was cold and rigid. She snatched him out of the crib and held him to her breast. "Please, God!" she screamed. "Not again! Please!" Nett's reaction to Rhonda's screaming was to run. She ran out of the apartment, down the stairs, and out onto the street. The superintendent of the apartment building also heard the scream and called an ambulance.

As Rhonda sat in the emergency room, waiting for Damon's test results, she had an overwhelming urge to call Gary. She needed to tell him that the son he had never seen had almost died. Damon was fine, but Rhonda felt his father needed to see him anyway. Gary did come to see Damon that day, then again when he was three months old. When Damon was nine months old, Gary came to see him on the eve of his wedding day. After that, the visits virtually stopped.

Rhonda had to get up at 5:30 in the morning. She'd dress herself, dress the baby, walk five blocks to the subway station, and board the train for a forty-five minute ride with Damon on her hip. She worked from 7:00 A.M. until 7:00 P.M. taking care of other people's children, and then she'd take the train back home. She'd leave Damon with Nett and take a thirty-minute bus ride to night school. By the time classes were over at 10:00 P.M., Rhonda was exhausted. She'd return home by 11:00, eat dinner, do her housework, wash diapers, and do her homework. If she was lucky, Nett would stay up and help her so she could get to bed by 1:00 A.M. If she wasn't so lucky, she'd get to bed at 2:00, sleep for a few hours, and then be back up at 5:30 A.M. to do it all over again.

Rhonda was a teenage unwed mother. Her weekends did not include parties or dates or hanging out with her girlfriends and shooting the breeze. She spent part of the weekend washing clothes, shopping, and caring for Damon. The other part of the weekend was spent studying at the library, or reading at home so she didn't fall behind in her schoolwork. Rarely did Rhonda indulge in any luxuries, but occasionally she would squeeze a few dollars out of her paycheck and go to the hairdresser. Her life was difficult, but Rhonda did what she had to do. Nett wouldn't let her *not* do it.

Damon had just turned a year old when Beanie introduced Rhonda to Curtis. He was the cousin of Beanie's boyfriend. His *real* cousin. Curtis was handsome, very shy, and on his way to Vietnam. Rhonda thought he was nice enough, and meeting him was the closest thing she'd had to a date in a long time. Nett took one look at him and decided he was a nut. He was looking for someone to correspond with while he was overseas, and as if she didn't have enough to do, Rhonda agreed to keep in touch.

He wrote. She wrote. They had been writing back and forth for about a year before Curtis asked Rhonda to marry him. She was flattered, but after Curtis proposed to her, Rhonda stopped writing altogether. He continued to write for a while, but then the letters stopped. Then one beautiful Sunday afternoon, Rhonda was at home reading, and Nett was playing with fifteen-month-old Damon, who was now walking and talking, when the doorbell rang. Nett said it was probably Daddy, who no longer had a key to Nett's apartment. She had taken it from him the day she discovered he had five children by another woman. Rhonda went to answer the door. A neighbor who was going out had let Curtis in. When Rhonda got downstairs, he was standing there with a bouquet of roses, wearing a big grin on his face.

Somewhere between dinner and the good-night kiss, Curtis presented Rhonda with an engagement ring. She was stunned. Nett sucked her teeth and stomped out of the room. Yes, Curtis had said, he was very serious about marrying Rhonda. He was ready to settle down. He loved her and was very fond of Damon. He'd always wanted a son. Rhonda said she was sure she could put together the wedding in two months' time, before Curtis was assigned his next tour of duty. Rhonda was so excited. She started making lists of places, food, and, of course, guests. Curtis immediately called his mother, who had a reaction similar to Nett's. She was not at all pleased that her only child wanted to marry a girl that he hardly knew.

Had Rhonda been paying attention, she would have understood what Nett kept telling her: "He must be some kind of nut!" But Rhonda couldn't see it. She was too busy looking at the fact that a man wanted to marry her. He was willing to take care of her and her child. He was prepared to take her away from the place where she had known so much pain and rejection. He was making a commitment not to leave her, not to disappear, not to break her heart. Once she got married, she would no · longer be "an unwed mother," she would be someone's wife. Curtis was in the army, and one day he'd have a pension and they could buy a house. He represented an end to the shame, the hard work, an end to being alone.

I sat down to rest on the granite bench beside the pond and listened to the gentle sound of the water lapping at the shore. It gave me clarity. How long did it take Rhonda to learn that you cannot fix a broken something simply by replacing it with something else? A replaced thing is still a broken thing! When you discover that something is broken, you must determine the cause of the break. In order to do that, you must open the thing, examine it, and find the origin of the break or malfunction. Once that is done, you must make a determination as to whether or not the thing is worth fixing. If you determine that the fixing is worth your effort, it must be done carefully. If, on the other hand, you decide that the thing is not worth fixing, you must get rid of it. You must throw it away, clean the place it once occupied, and when you are ready, find a suitable replacement. This is called "closure." It is a prerequisite for healing.

When the thing that is broken is your life or your mind, your heart or your spirit, you must follow the same process. Determine what is broken and how it got broken and decide whether to fix it or not. You must dismantle whatever isn't working piece by piece, find the broken part, fix it, reassemble the whole thing, and give it a test run. Everything in life must have at least one test run.

When you decide to fix something, it is important that you fix only what is actually broken. Not what you think is broken. If you fix the top when it is the bottom that is broken, the thing is not going to work. If you fix the left side, and leave the right side hanging and broken, the thing will fall apart again. If you fix the outside when there is something broken on the inside, there is no way the broken thing can work to its full potential. Rhonda was trying to fix the outside. She did not understand the relationship between what was going on inside and what was happening outside.

The day after the wedding, Rhonda, Curtis, and Damon moved to Fort Benning, Georgia. They rented a house and filled it with rented furniture, using the money they'd received as wedding gifts. While Curtis was in Vietnam, he had started using drugs. Heroin, speed, and psychedelics. Rhonda discovered he was a heroin addict when he started slapping her around and burglarizing their neighbors' homes. Eventually he was arrested and pled guilty to the burglary charges against him. The army informed Rhonda that she could no longer live in the subsidized housing complex and that she would no longer receive her monthly allotment checks. She called Nett and asked her to send the money for them to fly back home. By the time she got back to Brooklyn, she'd found the courage to tell Nett that she was four months pregnant.

Rhonda named her baby daughter Gemmia. Damon was thrilled to have a baby sister and fascinated that something so tiny could make so much noise. Gemmia would cry all night. The walls in the two-bedroom apartment were thin, and neither Rhonda nor Nett was getting much sleep. It made Rhonda so nervous, she was down to wearing a size 8. The crying drove Nett absolutely crazy, and it made her uncharacteristically evil.

Being a young mother with one child and working and going to school was hard. But being a young mother with two children and frazzled nerves made work an impossibility for Rhonda. She was forced to go on public assistance. Nett went from being evil, to being disgraced and ashamed.

"I never thought I would live to see the day when my own child would stand in line for peanut butter and cheese!"

"I won't go get the cheese," Rhonda said. "I hate the cheese."

"Well, you still have to stand in line with the rest of the trash to cash your check. Your welfare check!" Nett said.

"People don't know what kind of check I'm cashing, Nett. They just know I'm standing in line at the bank."

"They can figure it out. They'll assume you are just like the rest of the trash in line."

Rhonda admitted she was a very young, very nervous wife and mother with a husband who was in jail. She refused to add "trash" to the list. To avoid being mistaken for such, Rhonda would wait a day or two after she got her check before she went to the bank.

Curtis came home nine months after he went to jail and went to live in his mother's house in an upscale neighborhood. Rhonda and the children stayed with Nett. It took Rhonda five months to find an apartment that she could afford. Curtis still had a flaming addiction to heroin and couldn't work. She and the children were only in their new home six weeks when Curtis burglarized his own mother's house. He took her silverware, television, cameras, and her jewelry. He ransacked the house to make it look like a stranger had committed the burglary. Curtis was not a rocket scientist. He was arrested when he tried to pawn his mother's diamond earrings.

Rhonda was devastated, but Curtis was her husband. She and a girlfriend pawned their engagement and wedding rings to bail him out of jail. On Tuesday, he was out. On Thursday, the day before he was scheduled to appear in court, Curtis disappeared.

Nothing and no one in Rhonda's life seemed to work well for any length of time. She had wanted so much for her marriage—and her life—to work out. Ray had gotten married, had a son, separated from his wife, and was now drunk or high most of the time. Ray couldn't work. The State of New York had legalized off-track betting, which had seriously infringed on Daddy's street gambling operation. So Daddy wasn't working. Grandma had gotten old. She was still mean as hell, but she could no longer work. Nett had a new boyfriend, and their relationship was working, but her relationship with Rhonda had gone downhill.

Rhonda was thin, she had hair, but nothing else in her life was working. She started going to dance classes at the community center to make herself feel better and met a new friend, Charlene. Charlene offered her a job teaching dance and told her about another job, working as a counselor for young women in a twenty-four hour rehabilitation center. That's where Rhonda met John.

CHAPTER NINE

What's the Lesson When You Engage in Self-Destructive Behavior?

You are free to believe what you choose,
and what you do attests to what you believe.
Let us be glad that you will see what you believe
and that it has been given to you to change
what you believe.

A Course in Miracles

I KNEELED DOWN AT THE EDGE of the pond and dipped my hands into the cool, swirling water, letting it flow through my fingers. Though the water was clear, my reflection was distorted. It was Rhonda's shadow. There was still so much of Rhonda in me and around me. What she did and how she did it. What she felt and how I responded. The branches of the weeping willows that encircled the pond seemed to hang a little lower, to bend a bit more. Still, they were beautiful and very soothing. Nestled among the poplars, surrounded by the summer flowers that were dying to make room for the fall blossoms, they formed a type of symmetry that was not present in Rhonda's life, but which Iyanla desperately needed to see.

I had remembered Gary and Curtis, a marriage gone bad, a husband in jail, and the birth of two children. I had refreshed my memory of the heaviness of Rhonda's first nineteen years.

I could see how and why Rhonda thought she was a victim. I could see how she ran from one place to another, trying to get away from some place else where she had been victimized. I could see why she thought she was ugly, unlovable, destined to hurt and be hurt forever. I felt sad for her. I was not as sad about what had happened to her as I was about the fact that she could not see what was happening. I was sad that she could not see her pattern, and that there was no one available to point it out to her. She was embroiled in a destructive pattern of being hurt and moving on without healing the hurt, only to find herself in a situation in which she would be hurt again.

I could see clearly that Rhonda was living her own interpretation of what she had been taught by Grandma and Daddy. It was a pattern that had emerged in her childhood. She was young, wounded, and confused. Wounds and confusion beget wounds and confusion. Abuse and betrayal beget abuse and betrayal. Rhonda was attracting what she was because she had no idea that anything else existed. She had a pattern of running from what was without a clear understanding of what could be. I wanted to sing for her. I wanted to open my mouth and sing along with a chorus of weeping willow and poplar trees, blooming chrysanthemums and begonias. I wanted to sing a song for the abused, abandoned, confused little girl who was crying in my soul. The song that came to mind was Patti LaBelle's "Somebody Loves You, Baby." I was afraid that someone would wander up the trail and hear me, so I hummed as I turned around and headed back toward home.

It was an annual ritual that Rhonda and the children had been looking forward to all week. It was Sunday. Cartoons and pancakes for the children. Coffee and girl talk for Rhonda and Nett. It was also Nett's birthday, so all of them bore presents under their arms. The children had made their own cards. Rhonda had saved for months to buy Nett her favorite perfume and two books that Nett had threatened to buy for herself. Rhonda was sure that she had beaten Nett to the bookstore. She was excited about that, and she was excited that she could drive up to Nett's house in the car Daddy had given her for her birthday. Rhonda was also glad to have a few hours away from John, who had been in a foul mood all week.

She was in front of Nett's apartment building, trying to lock the car door, when she looked up and saw John approaching her.

"Give me the keys," John said. Rhonda was sure it was a demand.

"For what?" she asked. John didn't like the tone of her voice, nor did he like the fact that she was questioning him.

"What do you mean 'for what'? Because I asked for them, that's for what. I've got to go by my mother's, too." Rhonda knew that John's mood had not improved.

"I'll only be here for a few hours. I'll drop you off when I'm done here."

"Look b——h, give me the keys!" John had never spoken to her like that before, and she did not quite know how to take it. She locked the car door and turned to walk away, ordering the children to hurry up.

"You'd better not walk away from me." John was walking directly behind her. Something just didn't feel right. Rhonda turned to face him, prepared to ask what was wrong with him. Had she been facing him all along, she would have seen it coming. His hand reaching back, then coming forward against her face. Had she not turned around, he would have hit her in the head, but it might not have hurt as much.

When John pulled Rhonda up from the ground, she didn't realize he was trying to help her, so she started screaming. Rhonda didn't realize that John was trying to kiss her, so she pushed him away, gathered the children, and ran before he could hit her again.

When Nett saw her face, she was furious. John knocked on the door, and Nett informed him that he was never again welcome in her house. After the door was slammed in his face, Rhonda and Nett stood with their ears plastered against it, trying to detect if he was really gone. When the telephone rang, they almost jumped out of their skins.

"I'm sorry. I am so sorry. I will never do that again. I'm sorry. Do you believe me? Please believe me," John sounded desperate.

"I'll talk to you later" was the only thing Rhonda could say. The second call was an insincere attempt at begging. By the fifth call, John sounded as if he were crying. Two hours into the calling marathon, Rhonda didn't care that he was crying, she just wanted him to stop calling.

The children each told Nana how their daddy had hit their mommy, then they ate their pancakes as if the incident had never happened. Nett was in favor of calling the police and having John arrested. She was also in favor of poisoning him. That evening, after they had eaten dinner, Rhonda decided that she would go to work and that she would figure out what to do about John at a later date. The last thing Nett said to Rhonda before she left the house that night was, "Once they hit you, they never stop." For a very long time, it seemed that Nett would be proven wrong.

Rhonda and John worked together at the rehabilitation center. Rhonda was the only female counselor on the staff. John was a recovered heroin addict and the assistant director of the program. Rhonda knew nothing about the culture of drug addiction and even less about the process of recovery. John was her teacher. He had been on the other side of the table for eight years and on this side for the past five. He was a good teacher and quite protective of Rhonda during the first few months of her employment. They both worked the night shift and often ate dinner together. They ran support groups together. They spent many nights talking about clients and other things. John made Rhonda laugh. She helped him with his reports. It seemed very romantic. When the program director gave Rhonda a glowing review after her first nine months, Rhonda gave John a key to her house. That was one year before he hit her the first time.

When Rhonda got to work that night after he hit her, John insisted that he was sorry. "You made me mad," he said. "You made me hit you." That was his apology. He explained that he didn't like it when Rhonda didn't answer him. He didn't like it when she turned her back on him. That, he said, was disrespectful and unnecessary. Rhonda peered at John over the rims of the sunglasses Nett had loaned her to hide her bruised eye. She thought she must be hearing things. Then she understood.

"You're blaming me for making you hit me?" John didn't like the sound of that.

"It *is* your fault. Every time you get around your mother, you act like you're too good to talk to me." He had a point. Rhonda was aware that Nett didn't like John, and it probably did influence her behavior when Nett was around. But that was not the case this time.

"My mother was in her house when you hit me for not giving you the keys to my car." John didn't like the way that sounded, either. He stood up at his desk, towering over Rhonda. When she instinctively put her hands up to cover her face, John became sorry again and sat down.

"Please go home. Your eye looks so bad. I don't want anybody to see you like this." He sounded genuinely concerned, but Rhonda knew the truth. John did not want the clients or staff to see the results of his outburst. Eventually, John's pleas got the best of Rhonda. "I promise I'll never hit you again. Do you believe me? Please believe me." John was still pleading when the taxicab pulled off to take Rhonda home.

When you think you love someone, you try your best to overlook their shortcomings. John had many shortcomings, some of which were glaring, most of which made him extremely insecure. Although he had been to college, he could barely read or write. John was six feet two inches tall and weighed two hundred pounds. That was not the reason he had one overdeveloped breast. The breast was the result of a glandular dysfunction that also altered his moods. It was the same dysfunction that caused his asthma. It was the asthma that incapacitated him when he became angry or upset. It was the frequent periods of incapacitation that led to the excessive machismo when he was feeling good.

Rhonda was grateful to John for all he had done for her. He had paid attention to her when no one else had. He had taught her a great deal about the profession of counseling and the process of recovery. He'd helped her through the difficult time she was experiencing after Curtis disappeared. John knew all about Curtis and Gary; and he still treated *their* children like they were *his* children. Damon and Gemmia called John "Daddy." It takes a real man, Rhonda thought, to raise another man's children and let them call him Daddy. John was also the first man who had ever given Rhonda money to help her provide for her children. In the beginning, he had no problem turning over most of his paycheck to Rhonda for household expenses, child-care costs, and anything else that she needed.

Only a man who loves you gives you his money. Rhonda was so grateful to be loved that she was willing to do her best to return the favor. So grateful, in fact, she decided to have John's child. And it wasn't until she became pregnant that John started accusing her of being with other men. It wasn't until after Rhonda told John that she was pregnant that someone had started calling the house, and when she answered, hanging up. One night, after several such calls, she decided to stop answering for the rest of the evening. When John came home, he went crazy, even though Rhonda explained to him why she wasn't answering the phone.

"How am I supposed to know where you are? I thought something happened to you and the kids. Are you crazy?"

"John, it's late. Leave me alone," Rhonda answered. She pulled the covers over her head and tried to turn over onto her pregnant belly. John grabbed her up out of the bed and slapped her so hard she hit the floor. He snatched her up and slapped her again. Rhonda tried to get away. He straddled her. She screamed. He slapped her again, this time telling her to "Shut your f——g mouth!" Then he began his interrogation. "Where have you been? Who have you been with?" Each time she didn't respond, he would slap her. When she did respond, he'd slap her and call her a liar.

The noise of furniture crashing and Rhonda crying woke the children. John ordered them back to bed and ordered Rhonda to shut up. Perhaps if he'd stopped throwing her onto the bed, picking her up from the bed and slapping her, she would have been absolutely quiet. When John felt the onset of an asthma attack, he slapped Rhonda one final time before retreating into the bathroom for his medication. Rhonda picked herself up, took her children back to their beds, and stayed with them until they fell asleep. Then she crawled into bed with the man who had just beaten her pregnant body and had sex with him. It made her sick to her stomach.

The afternoon breeze felt good against my face. It was refreshing, and I certainly needed to be refreshed. The walk back home always seemed shorter than the walk to the pond. When I opened the door, the dog greeted me. She is cute. A pain in the butt, but cute nonetheless. My husband was doing his favorite Sunday chore. Watching television. When he turned and saw my face, he tried to think of something to say. He couldn't find the words, so he stood up, walked over, and gave me a hug. Feeling the strength of his arms around me, I started to cry. "This is so hard. I hate it!"

"You can do it. I know you can," he whispered. "You have to do it. You won't feel right until you do. Take your time. Just take your time."

I had been at it almost four hours and I still hadn't figured out why I needed to fire Karen. He made us some tea, turned off the television, and I shared with him some of what I was remembering.

Rhonda was staring at her battered face in the bathroom mirror when, suddenly, a woman appeared in the mirror behind her. Rhonda jumped! She spun around, but no one was there. Her face was a mess. Each time the children saw her, they cried. Her eyes, lips, and nose were swollen out of all proportion. John was so disgusted with himself, he didn't come home for four days. On the third night of his absence, Rhonda had a dream about the woman that she had seen in the mirror. Her name, she said, was Carmen. She introduced herself as Rhonda's friend, who had "always been there." Her message was clear: "Leave this place! Leave the man with whom you are now living. I will tell you where to go and what to do. As soon as your baby girl is born, you must leave. If you do not leave, he will kill you. Do you trust me?"

For Rhonda, it was unusual to remember a dream. But she remembered this one. She remembered, but she didn't listen.

Rhonda believed that John was reconfirming his love for her when he bought her a new washing machine. This was after he fractured three of her ribs and her jawbone when she was eight months' pregnant. That, she told herself, was the reason she never fought back. You can't hit a man who loves you.

"If a man is beating your brains out," Nett screamed at her, "you can't love him, and he can't love you!" Nett had known for a long time that John was beating Rhonda, but nothing she said would convince Rhonda to leave him.

"I've got three children by three different men," Rhonda argued. "Where am I going to go? I have no money and no education. The only things I can do are sew and dance. Who's going to want me?"

"When he's finished with you, no one will want you!" Nett yelled at her. "You'll be a stark raving lunatic!"

Nett was afraid, disgusted, and angry. Rhonda was tired and confused and beat up. Everyone asked her the same question: "Why do you stay with him?" Gary's mother lived next door to Rhonda. She, too, asked her why she stayed. She could hear the beatings through the walls and said she was furious with her son for not helping Rhonda get away. Gary's mother thought he should at least take his son away. All of Rhonda's friends asked her why she stayed. They would listen to her story, offer her advice on what to do to John while he was sleeping, and insist that she leave him. But no one ever went so far as to offer her a place to stay if she did leave. Rhonda guessed it was because everyone was afraid of John. It was Grandma all over again.

Baby Nisa was the spitting image of her father. That was the only reason John's mother started being nice to Rhonda. By the time the baby was six weeks old, she'd begun calling Rhonda her "daughter-in-law," which was a whole lot better than "my grandbaby's mother." The birth of Nisa seemed to calm John down as well. He didn't come home more frequently, but when he did, he was at least civil.

Things will get better when we move, Rhonda told herself. John was busy trying to find them a new apartment, which she attributed to his new improved attitude. Rhonda had her hands full watching the children and packing up all their belongings for the move. It seemed that she had finally convinced John that she was not fooling around on him, so Rhonda allowed herself to believe that things really could get better. When John came home and announced that he had found an apartment and that they could move in the following Saturday, Rhonda was definitely convinced that things were going to work out.

John did not come home the Friday night before the move. Nett agreed to watch the children while Rhonda finished packing. On Saturday, when the moving van had not shown up by late afternoon, Rhonda realized that she didn't know the name of the moving company. Late afternoon turned into evening, and she still refused to believe what she knew was happening. The telephone had already been disconnected, so Rhonda walked to the pay phone at the corner and called Nett to bring the children back. When Nett arrived, she took one look at all the boxes that Rhonda had packed for the move and began to cry.

After Nett left, Rhonda went back to the pay phone at the corner, children in tow. She called the landlord at the new apartment, who informed her that "her husband" had never made the deposit on the apartment. The landlord had already rented the apartment to someone else.

Somewhere in the back of Rhonda's mind, a voice kept saying, *Breathe! Just keep breathing!* Rhonda could feel her tired body going numb. Back at home, she fed the children and put them to bed. She laid baby Nisa on the mattress on the floor and was trying her best to keep breathing. It finally hit her: This is not going to work. *Breathe! Just keep breathing!* Rhonda found a box marked BATHROOM, and opened it. She retrieved all of the medications she could find. Phenobarbital. Nytol, Tylenol, aspirin, and even vitamins. She pulled out bottles that were so old she could no longer read the prescription or the directions. She brought the pills into the kitchen and put them in a pile on the floor. She swallowed them slowly, one pill at a time. Rhonda did not want to breathe any longer.

Acceptance or rejection of how you are treated by others is a function of how you feel about yourself. When you are wounded, you bleed. It is the bleeding that makes you feel bad. The way in which the wounds are inflicted determines how long and how badly you bleed. Superficial cuts will cause the blood to rise quickly, and though they are painful, it is easy to stop them from bleeding. When there is a deep gash, the blood takes a minute or two to surface. In the case of a deep wound, it often takes a while to recognize how much damage has been inflicted. If the wounds are deep enough, and the bleeding continues over an extended period of time, you can learn not to like yourself at all.

Rhonda had had some superficial wounds, but most of her life had been a series of deep, penetrating gashes that had never healed and were continually bleeding. She tried to stop the bleeding with food, cigarettes, and even sex. The blood continued to flow. It was oozing out of her mind, out of her heart, and spilling over into her life. She did not like herself. She did not feel good about herself. How could she? She was not even aware that she was wounded. Rhonda was just trying to survive. She had no idea that the only way to heal her wounds was to acknowledge them. She needed to remember how she had been wounded. She needed to look into her heart and make peace with those who had inflicted the wounds. But this was a pretty tall order for a twenty-one-year-old mother of three who only wanted a father for her children and someone to love her.

She heard the baby crying, but she could not get up. She couldn't tell if the light in her face was daylight, the kitchen light, or some mysterious light that was making her feel warm and peaceful. *Oh, my God, I can't breathe!* Rhonda saw people standing all around her. Sarah was there. The beautiful woman she'd seen in the bathroom mirror when she was a girl was there. Carmen was there. And a very large, very black man who was not wearing a shirt was straddling her body. The baby's cry was becoming faint. *Oh God, please help me!* The next person Rhonda saw was herself. She looked absolutely beautiful. The woman from the mirror identified herself as Mary, and reached out to the beautiful Rhonda. Mary kissed Rhonda's head and face. Then everything went black.

When Rhonda awoke, her throat was sore and her eyes felt like they had been glued shut. She wanted to ask where her children were, but she couldn't speak. The next time she woke up, she was able to ask the woman standing over her what day it was. It was Tuesday. When Rhonda asked where she was, the woman responded, "Snapper Five. The psychiatric ward of Brookdale Hospital."

Rhonda knew it was exactly where she needed to be at this moment in her life.

CHAPTER TEN

What's the Lesson When You Are a Motherless Child Raising Children?

Remember this: Every decision you make
stems from what you think you are,
and represents the value that
you put upon yourself.

A Course in Miracles

WHO WOULD THINK THAT LIFE on a mental ward could be such a thrilling experience? Who would consider coming to a mental ward when one is desperately in need of rest, clarity, and peace of mind? Rhonda had never once considered the possibility, but now she was convinced. Everything around her had been painted the color of pea soup. There was a pungent aroma in the air that was making Rhonda's head spin. There were thick cuffs of some kind attached to her wrists and just above her. And the drugs that were flowing into her arms from the glass bottle hanging over her head were making her sick to her stomach. But that was not the thrilling part. It was absolutely thrilling, though, to see herself floating above her self on the ceiling of the pea-green room. Rhonda kept trying to get down from the ceiling, but since she couldn't get her lips to work, she went back to sleep. When she woke up again, there was a man standing beside her bed, and the room had changed colors. Now it was battleship gray.

"Do you know where you are?" he asked.

"Yes." Rhonda's lips were working now.

"Do you know why you're here?" She knew, but she was too embarrassed to respond. She ignored him and the question. "Do you know that you tried to hurt yourself?" There was no way to avoid this one.

"Yes. I think so. I mean, yes. I tried to kill myself."

"Do you know why?" he snapped. He was being persistent. This was no longer wonderful. It was becoming painful and annoying, embarrassing and difficult. Keep it simple, she thought.

"Yes. Because my husband, I mean my boyfriend, told me we were going to move, but he lied, and the baby was crying."

"You want to tell me about it? About moving. About the baby crying."

"Babies cry when they are hungry or scared or cold," Rhonda said. "They cry when they think they are alone, or when they think someone is about to harm them. If you make loud noises when they are asleep, they will wake up crying. If you don't kiss them before you put them to bed, they will cry themselves to sleep." Rhonda wasn't sure she was making sense, but she continued anyway.

"Babies cry when their mothers die and when their fathers leave them. They cry when you lock them in closets and when you beat them. A baby will cry when it believes that you love all the other babies more than you love them. And if you do something mean to a baby, but tell it not to cry, then the baby will . . ." Rhonda's voice trailed off. She was headed toward the ceiling again.

"What happens when you tell a baby not to cry?" The doctor's voice anchored her back in the bed.

"Then the baby will end up in a mental institution."

"Like you?" The doctor was following her.

"Yeah. Just like me," Rhonda answered.

Once you scratch the surface, everything you know will spill forth. Rhonda was talking fast, just in case her lips stopped working before she could get it all out. She told the doctor about Ray and his asthma, about Nett having to work overtime. She told him about wearing a wig and about dancing. Just to impress the doctor, she threw in the fact that she worked all day and went to school at night. Then she started to cry and told him that she was ugly and fat and that she ate too much all the time.

She did not tell him about the rainy Saturday in the basement with Uncle Leroy, or that he had raped her because she stole his money. Or that at that very moment, a part of her was floating on the ceiling. She did not tell the inquisitive doctor about the beating Daddy gave her on Halloween night, or that he would ignore her when he drove by with a woman in his car. Why bother mentioning anything about the woman in the mirror—Carmen? Or the woman in the white dress who had been following her all of her life. When Rhonda had told the doctor everything she thought he needed to know, she looked him dead in the eye and asked, "Who in the hell are you? Where exactly am I?" The doctor paused a moment and considered his response before he spoke.

"I think you'll be staying with us for a while."

She had already figured that one out on her own. And she was grateful. When the doctor stood up to leave, she indicated the straps and asked meekly, "Can you please take these things off?"

As if every fiber in his body had to be readjusted in order for him to answer, the doctor took at least three minutes to ask, "Are you going to hurt yourself again?"

Rhonda was insulted. "No! Of course not!" she said curtly. "What do you think? You think I'm crazy?" This time, the doctor didn't respond. He turned and walked away.

Several minutes later, another wonderful person entered the room and gave Rhonda another shot of the thrill-inducing narcotics. When she awoke, her hands and feet were free, and she remembered where she was.

The first telephone call she made was not to find out about her children. It was not to Nett, nor to her father. It was not to John. The first telephone call Rhonda made was to Gary, her son's father. She told him where she was and asked if he would come to see her. Within three hours, Gary was walking across the day room toward the woman he had not seen or spoken to in a year. The woman who lived right next door to his mother. The woman who had given birth to his son.

Rhonda and Gary talked more that day than they had since they met in high school. He went so far as to say that he was sorry to see her in this place, although the other inhabitants of the day room looked quite normal. He asked what had happened, and then he admitted he already knew. He knew that Rhonda felt like she had nowhere to go. He didn't quite say he was sorry, but he did say that when she got out, he would do what he could to help her. Gary talked about his new job and explained why he and his wife were no longer together.

When he stood up to leave, he bent over and kissed Rhonda on the forehead. As she walked him to the door, he held her hand and told her that he knew she would be all right. "You can do it. I know you can." Rhonda did not see him again for five years.

Nett declared that she could not and would not visit Rhonda in "a place like that." Every time they spoke, Nett cried, so Rhonda stopped calling her. It took Daddy three weeks to get there. When he came, he told Rhonda that he and his "wife" were looking after Damon and Gemmia, and that John had taken the baby.

"You look fine," Daddy said as he peered around the room.

"You mean I don't look crazy?" Rhonda shot back at him.

"Nobody here *looks* crazy, but people have problems." Daddy knew he had better quit while he was ahead.

"Nett sent you some clothes and other things." Daddy handed Rhonda a plastic bag. "Do you need money in this place?" he asked.

"No." Rhonda was peering into the bag. "My friend Ruth Carlos cashed my checks and brought me the money yesterday."

"How much money?"

"I don't even know. I didn't count it. As a matter of fact, I don't want to keep it here. Would you hold on to it for me?" Rhonda asked her father, not remembering his financial situation.

"Yeah." Daddy was trying to hide his excitement. "Do you need me to pay anything for you?"

"No. Just hold on to it. I'll need it to try to get another place when I get out of here." Rhonda excused herself to go back to her room. When she returned, she handed Daddy a paper bag full of dollar bills. He promised he'd be back to visit her on Friday. The next time Rhonda saw Daddy was six weeks later, after she'd been released from the hospital. She *never* saw the money again.

Often, we fear solitude. We mistake it for loneliness and attempt to fill the emptiness, the silence with activity and noise and people. But the solitude of Snapper Five provided Rhonda with the silence she needed to hear herself think. She was able to become still and allow her feelings about herself to surface. Through the silence, she became aware of her fears as well as her strengths. She learned that she possessed faith, and she learned to trust the power of that faith. The solitude of Snapper Five also brought Rhonda much-needed clarity. She became clear about what it was she specifically wanted in her life and what she did not want.

Rhonda was a model mental patient. She always took her medication. Actually, she would hide it under her tongue and then take a nap so that the nurses would know it was working. She also made an earnest effort to answer the dumb questions Dr. Miller asked about her life. When the medical staff wasn't bothering her, she sat by the window and remembered. What she remembered, she wrote down.

She remembered the adults in her life who had taught her to be afraid; afraid of them and afraid of what they could do to her. She wrote about the pain of what they had and had not done. She remembered all the ways they had hurt her body and her feelings. She wrote it all down. Then she wrote about the things they said and the lies they had told to her, on her, and about her. She remembered how she had trusted them to take care of her and protect her. She wrote about how they had not done that. She decided that she could no longer trust people. "People," she wrote, "do not care about you." She also decided that she was not going to be like any of the adults who had raised her. She wrote that down, too. Then, she wrote about herself and how she wanted to be.

Rhonda remembered many of the things she had done and said and felt. She was trying to remember the reasons. She remembered being scared most of the time. She remembered feeling sad that she was always so scared. She remembered being angry a great deal of the time. She figured out that it was the anger that led her to lie to people and to steal things from them. She tried to remember all the lies she had told and all the things she had stolen, but she stopped when she realized that it would take her all day. She had done those things, she concluded, not because she wanted to, but because of something she wanted. She couldn't remember what it was, but she knew she wanted it badly.

Maybe, she thought, what she wanted was to be loved and to be pretty and to be acknowledged by Daddy. Perhaps she just wanted to be more than the s—— her grandmother had condemned her to be. What she really wanted was for Nett to be her mother and for Ray to stop drinking. She wanted money and a nice place to live. She wanted to know the truth, the real truth about her real mother. It's hard to be a person when you don't know the truth about your mother. And Rhonda wanted very badly to be a person, not a punching bag. She wanted to live a normal life. The way she was living, and had lived, was not normal by any stretch of the imagination. People thought she was normal, and she knew that was what made her situation so dangerous.

If you do the things people think you should do, the way they think you should do them, they mistakenly believe that you are okay. Rhonda knew that she was not okay. She wasn't crazy, but she was neither normal nor okay. What she did not know was who cared about her. She did not know what was wrong with her or why it mattered. Rhonda really wanted to matter to somebody.

Then she remembered that she mattered to her children, her precious babies. It was only by the grace of God that she found the strength to take care of them. It was only by his mercy that she was able to give them something she had never had. Love. But did she really love them? Yes. Rhonda knew without a shadow of a doubt that she loved her children. Admittedly, she did not want them at first, but she loved them. If you have never been loved, have never known real love, how can you love? Rhonda pondered the question for a moment, then decided that unlike the adults in her own life, she loved who her children were.

They were three unique personalities who possessed qualities she could love.

She loved their beautiful faces and the warmth of their little hands in hers. She loved the way they smelled after she had bathed them and put them to bed. She loved to comb Gemmia's hair and kiss her neck. She loved the way Damon always made her laugh. He was such a little joke-ster. A real showman. They were smart, too. Damon could count to one hundred by the time he went to kindergarten. He didn't like to do it, but he could do it. Gemmia was an artist. She would draw with anything, on anything. Gemmia was fragile and delicate, just like Nett. Rhonda's eyes filled with tears when she thought about her baby, Nisa. She was only six weeks old, and they hadn't gotten to know each other yet. She wouldn't even let herself consider that Nisa was not being cared for, or that she might be wet or hungry or missing her mother. She decided that she would know and believe that Nisa was just fine and knew her mother loved her.

She didn't cry until she allowed herself to remember the frightened faces of her children when John was beating her. When she was crying about John not being there, it frightened them. When she remembered their faces, she also remembered her own fear, and that made her cry. When you are a patient in a mental ward, you cannot be seen crying in the common areas. If you are, it is believed that you are having an "episode." Mental patients who have episodes get drugged. Rhonda did not want to be drugged. She felt as if she was getting clear for the first time. So she learned how to cry on the inside, without shedding tears. She taught herself how to remember and feel and cry in her heart, main-taining a perfectly normal appearance for the outside world. As a matter of fact, she thought, that's what she'd been doing all of her life. She thought they called it "acting."

Every day, Rhonda would write a letter to her children. Most of the letters were apologies for all the things she had not done, all the places she had not taken them. She apologized for never telling them that she loved them. She explained that no one, not even Nett, had ever looked her directly in the eyes and said "I love you." She apologized for yelling at them when she was angry, and for not always having dinner ready on time. She made big promises to her children in those letters. They were promises she wanted to keep. They were promises she didn't know how to keep.

She had to do better, just like Gary said. But how? How was she going to learn how to do better? Who was going to teach her? The people who had had the opportunity to teach her, to tell her what she needed to know, had not done a very good job. She had to learn how to be better by herself. She had to learn how to be a better mother, but first she had to learn how to be a better person. Rhonda believed that she was not a whole person. She was something else. Something broken and battered and hopeless. She felt she was hideous and ugly and dirty. She had to figure out a way to get whole and clean and beautiful. Gary had said that she was too beautiful, too smart. The smart part was easy. But beautiful? She would have to think about that for a while.

She could only think of herself as beautiful and brilliant for brief moments. What did that mean? Beautiful like who? As brilliant as what? She didn't feel beautiful. She had never seen brilliancy demonstrated. How can you be beautiful when you are angry and confused and afraid? Rhonda admitted that she was afraid of what her anger, confusion, and fear would do to her children. They might turn out to be just like her. Oh my God! What a horrible thought! She knew she had to do something quickly. Dr. Miller and his colleagues thought they were treating her because she had lost her mind. Rhonda knew she was really there to find it. She was on a quest to find her beautiful self and her brilliant mind. Sitting in the window, in the day-room window of the Brookdale psychiatric ward, Rhonda remembered how to pray.

"Prayer can do things that you can't do," Grandma always told the other mothers at the church. "It can fix things that you didn't even realize were broken." There is little you can do when you are in a state of mental fatigue and exhaustion. There is little you can do when you feel that no one loves you or cares about you. It renders you incapable. When you believe that you do not matter, you may be tempted to stop even trying to do better. But somehow, Rhonda remembered that when you can't do anything else, you can pray. It started as a mantra: *Please, God, please help me. Please, God, please help me.* It became a bit more definite over time: *Please, God, please help me raise my children. Please, God, please help me understand who I am. Please, God, please help me get away from John. Please, God, please help me feel better.*

Rhonda would pray all day. She would pray while she was bathing and getting dressed. She prayed while she was eating. She would pray while she helped the other patients find invisible things and dead things they told her were hidden in their rooms. She prayed while she was talking to Dr. Miller. Once while he was counseling her, she prayed out loud.

"Do you see Jesus or some other religious figure?" he asked.

It was true. They really did think she was a nut! Rhonda knew she was a little off, but she wasn't crazy enough to answer that question. With all the sincerity she could muster, and without laughing in his face, she said, "Dr. Miller, you can't see Jesus. He's in heaven with God!" Dr. Miller wasn't convinced.

"Do you hear voices? Do the voices tell you to hurt yourself?" Rhonda lied. She did hear voices, just not the kind he was talking about.

"No, Dr. Miller. I do not hear voices or see lights or eat invisible bugs."

"Are you angry?"

"No! And I am not crazy, either." The old feisty Rhonda was back.

"What do you want to do when you leave here, Rhonda?"

"Why? Does it matter?" she shot back at him.

"Of course it matters. You are young and beautiful. You have three children to raise. *You* matter, Rhonda, and don't allow anyone to tell you that you don't." His words were so gentle and sincere, Rhonda knew that he meant what he was saying.

"I want to find myself, my real self. And I want to raise my children in a better way than I was raised."

"Both of these things matter," Dr. Miller said, "they matter a lot."

Rhonda didn't know how she knew, but she knew that Dr. Miller had just given her the answer to her prayers. *Find your real self and raise your children in a different way. Not just different. Better.* When she stood up, Dr. Miller was in the middle of a sentence. She stared at him for several seconds before saying calmly, "Thank you, Dr. Miller," and leaving the room. Three days later, he discharged her from the hospital.

Thank goodness for people who change their minds. Gary had paid the rent on Rhonda's old apartment, preventing the landlord from throwing her belongings out on the curb. When she arrived at her apartment, she found Lady, the dog, standing at the door. You could see her ribs through the matted, gray coat. It looked as if she had not eaten since Rhonda left. The apartment had a foul odor. All of the utility services had been disconnected. There was no sign that John had been there. The sight, the smell, the awesomeness of the task before her, weakened Rhonda's knees. Her mind felt cloudy again. Before the first tear rolled down her cheek, a voice filled her mind and the room. *Stop! Do not be afraid. Do not panic. You will be shown what to do. You will be told what to say.* Rhonda froze. She had already lost her mind, then found a piece of it again. Was she losing it again? *Feed Lady and go to your mother-in-law's house. John and your baby will be there.* Without questioning what she was hearing, she left the apartment.

It seemed like only a matter of minutes had passed before Rhonda found herself standing ten miles away on the other side of town, ringing Mildred's doorbell. When she opened the door, Rhonda stepped inside quickly, just in case Mildred tried to keep her out. "When did you get out of the loony bin?" Mildred said snidely. Rhonda walked inside the house without responding. She went directly into the living room. Neither John nor Nisa was there, but she knew her spirit had not misled her. Mildred followed her, mumbling about b———s and crazy people. There was no sign of John or the baby. When Rhonda spun around without saying a word, Mildred jumped. She really must have thought Rhonda was crazy. Rhonda knew she wasn't. For the first time in her life, she was standing up for herself. She would not cry or run away. She meant business, and somehow, Mildred knew it, too.

"He ain't here," Mildred said before Rhonda could ask the question.

Rhonda stared directly into Mildred's eyes and spoke so calmly it was frightening.

"Call him. Tell him I'm here and I want to see my baby." Mildred could sense Rhonda's new resolve and moved quickly to the telephone to make the call. Rhonda's eyes never left her as she talked. Once she hung up, Rhonda left her standing there, walked into the living room, and sat down in a ragged, overstuffed chair.

Rhonda sat without moving a muscle, her back erect. She never opened her mouth. She stared at the wall and remembered the promises she had made to her children in the letters she wrote. She sat there for thirty minutes, waiting for John to arrive. It made Mildred very nervous.

In the middle of a thought, Rhonda felt something move through her body. It seemed as if a light were covering her. Again she heard the voice. Dr. Miller would not like this, she thought. The voice said, *You have left me for darkness. Why?* Rhonda closed her eyes, remembering her Snapper Five prayer/mantra: "Please, God. Please help me." She could feel her body start to vibrate. She wondered—but didn't really care—if Mildred were watching her. Then a buzzing started in her head. Even with her eyes closed, Rhonda could see. She saw herself falling from a cliff. Her stomach did a quick flip. Her body felt a jolt as though she had been electrocuted. When she heard the doorbell ring, she jumped to her feet.

John walked in holding Nisa, who was hidden within the folds of her blanket. When their eyes met, Rhonda stood and extended her arms to receive her baby. John backed away from her. She sat down in a chair on the opposite side of the room, facing her. Rhonda diverted her eyes momentarily to make sure Mildred wasn't getting ready to attack her from behind. Mildred always got bolder and more aggressive when John was around. When she turned back to face John, she noticed a young woman standing in the doorway, holding the baby's bag. The room was still and silent. Each second seemed to take an hour to pass. Rhonda calmly returned her gaze to John.

"Can I please have my baby?"

John ignored her. He began to unwrap the blanket from around the baby. Rhonda could hear her heart pounding in her head. She could feel it pounding in her feet. The blanket was one that Nett had crocheted for Damon five years earlier.

Finally John looked over at Rhonda. He began to shout obscenities at her, telling her what he would and would not do.

Rhonda remained calm. The voice guided her: *Do not panic. You will be told what to say. Speak your words with power and authority.* When Rhonda spoke, she felt the calmness beginning to dissipate.

"Please, John. Give me the baby. Let me hold her. I'm not going anywhere with her." Too many words, too fast. It sounded like the plea of an anguished mother crying out for her child. John was not moved. Mildred was.

"Give her the baby, Johnnie," she ordered. "Don't be stupid." The baby was now fully exposed. John clutched Nisa to his chest and raised his voice.

"You don't know her. She's crazy. Don't tell me what to do! I ain't givin' that b—— my baby!" The voice guided. *Be still!* Suddenly, John jumped to his feet and lunged at Rhonda, screaming, "Who you lookin' at? Who are you lookin' at?"

Rhonda didn't move. She was praying. "Yea, though I walk through the valley of the shadow of death, I shall fear no evil . . ."

John was trying to frighten her, to make her cower and cry. It was a tactic that had always worked. Until today. Rhonda was willing to do whatever it took to get her baby from the man who was holding her. He wasn't John any longer. He wasn't the man who had beaten Rhonda when she was pregnant with the very baby he now clutched to his chest. No longer was he six feet two inches tall. He was no longer a monster. He was a frightened little six-year-old boy who was insisting on having his way. Rhonda could see it in his eyes. She heard it in his words, and she was not going to terrorize a frightened child. She sat down and looked at the young woman, who was still standing in the doorway.

Rhonda didn't remember who spoke first, but she remembered the conversation. Rhonda had done so many things to make John beat her, he said. John had lied about getting the apartment, she said. Rhonda had called the police on him, and they went to his job and embarrassed him. Her mother was always nasty to him. His mother was nasty to her. When it seemed they were getting nowhere, Mildred jumped up from the sofa, ripped her wig off her head, and threw it on the floor.

"I am sick of this s——! Give her that damn baby so she can get the hell out of my house!"

When Mildred's dog saw the wig slide across the middle of the floor, he attacked it. He grabbed it between his teeth and wrestled it across the room.

"Johnnie, get my wig from that dog. I've got to wear it to work tomorrow."

John tried to take the wig away from the dog. The dog could not be persuaded. Still holding the baby, John grabbed one side of the wig. The dog still had the other side in his teeth. John pulled on his side, the dog pulled against John's grip. John started wrestling with the dog, which was wrestling with the wig. Somehow, in the middle of it all, the baby was transferred from John's arms to Rhonda's arms. By the time the wig was free, Rhonda was sitting in the chair, kissing Nisa's face. She smelled clean. When John realized what he had done, he plopped down in his chair and threw the wig at his mother.

Rhonda turned her attention to the young woman, who had now taken a seat. She had been twisting and turning in her chair like a spectator at a tennis match, trying to follow the words that Rhonda and John were volleying between them. Rhonda spoke to her in a soothing voice.

"What could a man say to you that would make you think it was all right to take him in with a six-week-old baby?"

The woman squirmed in her seat. She looked at Rhonda, then at John. She wasn't sure if she should respond. When Rhonda repeated the question, one word at a time, the woman blurted out an answer.

"He told me you left him. We have been together for almost six months. I have a son, too! I know how to take care of a baby. I love John." Rhonda ignored what the woman had said.

"How old are you?" Rhonda asked her.

"Twenty-one," she answered proudly.

"Thank you," Rhonda said. "The baby looks clean and very well cared for."

John told Rhonda he was leaving her and taking the baby with him. Rhonda kept kissing Nisa's face. *Lots of kisses. Lots of kisses. Babies need lots of kisses.*

When Rhonda stood up with the baby in her arms, everyone else in the room stood up, too. They seemed to be positioning themselves for attack in the event she started toward the door. She didn't. Instead, she walked over to John and placed the baby in his arms.

"I'm going now. I'm going home to clean up a little bit. I should be finished by seven. By eight o'clock tonight, I expect to have my baby home in her bed." She kissed the baby one last time, turned, and walked out the door. Before she knew it, she was back at home. It was 2:30 in the afternoon.

Lady greeted her at the door, obviously feeling a lot better now that she'd eaten. There were piles of dog crap in every room. Rhonda dug around in the boxes and found her rubber gloves and cleaning supplies. On her hands and knees, she cleaned up crap and prayed. She cleaned and sang, "Ain't gonna let nobody turn me around." As she put fresh sheets on her bed, which was the mattress on the floor, she heard the voice again. *Be still and know!* She did know, she really did.

Mothers are very important to children. They provide the lifeblood, the mind energy, and the "soul food" that every child needs in order to flourish. Fathers *show* us how to survive. Mothers *teach* us how to blossom and flourish. The mother must teach, nurture, guide, and provide the spiritual support system that the soul requires to unfold. When a child does not have a mother, some portion of the mind, the soul, and the life of the child remains in a constant state of yearning and want. What the child wants is to be fed and loved in a way that only a mother can love. Only a mother can bring forth the grace, mercy, beauty, and gentleness of the spirit. The spirit of God. The spirit of mothering energy is present in every woman. Whether she knows it or not, a woman is a mother, simply by virtue of the fact that she is a woman. Some fathers are able to mother. Others, like Rhonda's, are not.

When a woman does not know she is a mother, or how to mother, the children around her become lost. She is not sensitive to them or their needs. Her words are spoken harshly. Her actions are abrupt and abrasive. She is authoritarian. She knows the rules of mothering but not the grace. The grace of the mother's love will break the rules, when it is necessary, in order to nourish a child. In the face of an authoritarian mother, a child's growth is stunted. When a child has an unfolded heart, it is too difficult, too painful for her to express how she feels, or what she needs. Unexpressed feelings and needs lead to anger and fear.

When a woman has not touched the part of her spirit that is God, she cannot offer God to her children. She cannot give love, perhaps because she has not received love. She follows the rules that say that love, loving, and the mercy of love are weaknesses. When a woman with a closed heart is placed in the role of a mother, she can't be anything but weak.

The women in Rhonda's life had nourished her with closed hearts. They didn't know it, but Rhonda felt it. All of her life, she felt like a motherless child. She had not been watered by grace, pruned by mercy, or tilled by love. Rhonda had been taught the rules of mothering. She had not been taught how to temper them gracefully. She had been taught how to be strong. She had not been taught the gentle, graceful strength of meekness. Rhonda had heard that the meek shall inherit the earth, but she could not figure out how they would do it. How *she* would do it. She was a stunted child who had not yet touched the woman, the mother, or the essence of God in her spirit. She had not been taught how to do it, but she was willing.

At 4:30, she walked to the pay telephone at the corner to call Daddy's house. It felt so good to talk to Damon. Gemmia wouldn't talk; she just cried. Rhonda asked her father if he would bring the children over in the morning. He said he would, and he told her about an empty apartment on the top floor of his apartment building. It was small, he said, but affordable. Daddy agreed to talk to the landlord.

By the time Rhonda walked back into her apartment, it was exactly five o'clock. She lay down across the mattress. At five minutes to eight, the doorbell rang. Walking toward the door, she could see John's shadow through the lace curtains. She took a deep breath and reached for the doorknob. Rhonda could feel the calm energy that had pierced her body earlier in the day leave her. Her heart began to pound. Her knees grew weak.

By eight o'clock, John was gone, and Nisa was asleep in her mother's arms.

CHAPTER ELEVEN

What's the Lesson
When You Learn the Lesson,
Then Forget It?

For the rest of my life there are two days
that will never again trouble me.
The first day is yesterday with all its
blunders and tears, its follies and defeats.
Yesterday has passed away, beyond my control forever.
The other day is tomorrow with its pitfalls
and threats, its dangers and mystery.
Until the sun rises again, I have no stake in tomorrow,
for it is still unborn.

Og Mandino, in *The Return of the Ragpicker*

RHONDA DID HER BEST to like her newfound stepmother, brothers, and sisters. She was surprised to find that they already knew Grandma and Ray. The boys and girls were excited to finally meet their "big sister" and even more excited that she was their neighbor. Whenever they heard Rhonda and her children leaving their fourth-floor apartment, they would open the door of their first-floor apartment just to say hi. Rhonda did her best to be nice to them, but the fact that they even existed made her furious.

Her new apartment wasn't just tiny, she was sure it was the place that had given birth to claustrophobia. The front door opened into the bathroom and blocked the doorway that led to the children's room. You could turn around in the kitchen, if you did it slowly. The living room was a perfect little box. It had two windows that overlooked the alley behind the building. The first thing Rhonda did was check to make sure there were no dogs in the alley. There was one. When you stepped out of the living room, you were in the bedroom. The only place you could go in the bedroom was onto the bed, which was pushed up against the dresser. The best thing about the apartment was that there were never any BVDs hanging in the bathroom. Rhonda and the children shared the apartment without benefit of male companionship.

It took about a year for Rhonda to get settled in and to realize that she could not raise three children on a $229 check. What didn't go for rent went to feed her three growing youngsters. The little that was left went toward clothing, utility bills, and to cover dire necessities. Nett helped out when she could, but she was a bit miffed that her grandchildren were living in the same building as Daddy and "that woman." John had made it very clear that he wasn't giving Rhonda any assistance unless she had sex with him. Rhonda's brother, Ray, was good for a few dollars on Fridays, when he got paid, but Rhonda would have to get to him before he got high. Occasionally, through a temporary agency, Rhonda got work that she did not report to her welfare caseworker. As the children grew, the apartment got smaller and smaller. She thought about moving, but the money just wasn't there.

When you are in trouble, it is hard to believe that you are being prepared for something better. It is hard to see that the desperation you feel in the pit of your stomach is making you stronger. There is no way to tell that the fear you experience, when the bills are late or the refrigerator is empty, makes you a wiser, more prudent decision maker. When you are in trouble, you feel weak and numb. It is hard to think. It is like waiting for the axe to fall. But because there are so many axes hanging over you, you are not sure which way to duck. Rhonda was beginning to doubt herself. She felt weak, on her way to numbness. She was tired of dodging axes. She could not see her way out of the trouble she was in. Money trouble. Mothering trouble. Rotten-man trouble. John was calling her every day, gnawing away at her resolve to build a better life. It was a bit much for a twenty-three-year-old.

Rhonda eventually married the trouble. She and John exchanged rings and vows in a private ceremony between themselves. Although she was still technically married to Curtis, it was important to her that John wanted to marry her. It worked for almost two years. Then the trouble got stirred up all over again.

John and Rhonda didn't fight. He beat her up. Period. He had stopped slapping her. Now, he would punch her. While she was down from a punch, he would straddle her, choke her, and, if she tried to get away, he would kick her. Most of the time he beat her for spending money. Rhonda liked to spend money. It made her feel good. She spent money on clothing and shoes for herself and the children. While Rhonda was out shopping, John was spending his time with other women. When he came home and discovered the things Rhonda had bought, he would beat her.

Shopping wasn't John's only excuse for beating Rhonda. He beat her because it was Tuesday. He beat her because the moon was full. He beat her if there wasn't enough to eat. He beat her if he didn't like what she had prepared to eat. Slapping, punching, choking, and kicking Rhonda was the way in which John communicated what he wanted her to do and not do. The only thing worse than the actual beatings was the knowledge that if she did not figure out what he was trying to communicate to her, she would get beaten again.

While the children were in school and John was at work, Rhonda would plot and plan how to leave him. Some days, she made wildly elaborate schemes, involving extensive driving and long airplane rides. When Rhonda thought about paying for airplane tickets, or buying a car, she'd have to scale back somewhat. She would envision herself moving from place to place, staying with one person one night and someone else the next. She would see herself carting the kids from here to there, with John in hot pursuit. She always imagined that she would elude him and get away. Then one night John dumped her off the bed, mattress and all. He pulled the mattress off of her and hit her on the head with a bed slat. Rhonda knew she had to do something quickly.

She petitioned the court for an Order of Protection. John could not come within fifty yards of her or the apartment. If he violated the order, she had recourse; she could call the police and have him arrested. Rhonda was in control, and John was furious. She allowed him to visit one day a week to see the children, have sex, and to give her grocery money. Rhonda was sexually addicted to John, but she knew if he stayed in her life, eventually he would kill her. Or worse, he would hurt one of the children. John had never raised his hand against the children, but in the process of him chasing and throwing things at her, one of them was bound to get hurt.

The money John gave her helped meet expenses, but it wasn't enough. The Miss Restoration Plaza Beauty Pageant offered a prize of one thousand dollars, a seven-day, six-night trip to Aruba, and, among other things, a set of luggage. Grandma's dressmaker made the gowns, Nett sprang for a trip to the beauty parlor, and Daddy and his wife watched the children while she went to rehearsals. Entering the pageant not only gave Rhonda something to do besides warding off John; she began to dance again. She prepared her talent presentation as if it were the reason she was born, and the night of the pageant, she executed it with precision. When the mistress of ceremonies announced her as the winner, Rhonda could see the light at the end of the tunnel. It was a small, dim light, but it was bright enough for her to see the handwriting on the wall: You are beautiful! You can make it!

Tony was a bonus prize. He was a radio disc jockey who lived with his girlfriend. He worked for the radio station that had promoted the pageant. After Rhonda won, Tony interviewed her on his program. They hit it off, and eventually Rhonda was spending her days at his house while John and Tony's girlfriend were at work. Every day, Tony would write a new poem for Rhonda; and every night, he would read it over the air. After three months, Rhonda had a glow about her that everyone, including John, could detect.

John was way off base. He accused Rhonda of being a lesbian. He was convinced that she was sleeping with the woman who had served as talent coordinator of the beauty pageant. Sherry was just a friend, Rhonda assured him. She had recognized Rhonda's dancing ability and wanted her to teach the children in the community. John said she "looked like a dyke," and insisted that Rhonda tell her never to call the house or be in the presence of the children. He was so consumed with the mistaken belief that Rhonda and Sherry were sexually involved that it took him a while to realize that Rhonda was seeing another man.

John was coming home more often now, which made it a little more difficult to hide the glow. Rhonda continued to spend as much time with Tony as she could get away with. Little by little, she had shared her pageant winnings with him until they were totally depleted. One gray, overcast day, Rhonda went to Tony's house, had sex with him, then fell asleep. She woke up to find that fourteen inches of snow had fallen, and transportation in the city had come to a standstill. Buses had stopped. Trains were stuck. Cars were being abandoned along the roadside. Rhonda was stranded. Before she could decide what to do, Tony's girlfriend put her key in the door.

Tony shoved Rhonda into the bedroom closet, throwing her clothes on top of her. Eventually, Tony's unsuspecting girlfriend went into the bathroom and closed the door. Tony snatched Rhonda out of the closet, led her through the apartment, and pushed her into the hallway. Rhonda had her clothes in hand and was wearing nothing but one of Tony's shirts. She went down the stairs and into the basement, behind some trashcans, and put her clothes back on. She stomped through the calf-high snow to the closest telephone and called home. John had picked the children up from school and wondered why she wasn't at home when they arrived. Rhonda explained to John that she had been downtown in a store during the unexpected snowfall. When she came out, she said, the buses had stopped running. The lie sounded good to her, but when she finally got home two hours later, she found out that good wasn't good enough.

Very early in her life, Rhonda had learned that if she made people mad at her, they would hurt her. She had learned that when you do not do what people want you to do, they will blame you for upsetting them, making them look stupid, or making them feel bad. She had learned that whatever people do to you as a result of what you have done to them, you deserve. You deserved to be beaten, to be hurt, to be violently abused in a manner totally disproportionate to the alleged offense. Somewhere in the back of her mind, Rhonda believed she deserved to be hurt and beaten, because she was bad, because she wasn't worth the time it took to make her, because she was never going to be anything. Rhonda was a victim, and victims always get hurt.

Being a victim was the unconscious motivation for most, if not all, of Rhonda's actions. It was the thing that motivated Rhonda to do and say things she knew would have a violent impact and a violent outcome. Violence, abuse, being hurt had become a pattern in her life. Most people are always loyal to their patterns whether they are conscious of them or not. Most people will behave in ways that will create what they believe will happen. Rhonda was no different. She knew if John had even the slightest clue that she was messing around, he would beat the living daylights out of her. She knew it because he had threatened her enough, accused her enough times, and acted out his beliefs, without cause, for long enough for her to know what was going to happen. John was going to beat her. Why had she done it? Why had she continued a relationship with another man, allowing herself to believe that John would not find out, and knowing what would happen if John did find out? When a person is in the midst of acting out a pattern that they have come to believe is true as a result of their experiences, they do not think. They act out. They reap the expected outcome.

Rhonda knew that John did not believe her, because he never believed her. Rhonda knew that even if John did believe her, the fact that she had been missing in action for a number of hours meant that he was going to hurt her. And, she was absolutely right.

John let Rhonda get into the house and out of her coat. He spared her the ordeal of questioning her for hours, challenging every response she offered in her own defense. John did not make Rhonda retell her story over and over, giving him the opportunity to catch her in a lie by pointing out to her the events that did not make sense. He did not threaten her, nor did he rant and rave for an hour, postponing the inevitable. That would have been his normal course of action. Today was different. Instead, once Rhonda had taken off her coat, John pulled her to him and began to choke her. He never said a word. Silently, with rage in his eyes, he squeezed her throat until she could feel the life slowly draining out of her body. When her knees buckled, causing her to fall, John became so angry that he punched her in the face. When Rhonda regained consciousness, she could not see. John had beaten both of Rhonda's eyes shut. He was now straddling her on the floor, choking her again. She could hardly breathe.

As suddenly as the episode had started, it stopped. John looked as if he were frozen in time. Rhonda thought she was dying. Instead, John started gasping for air. When he clutched his chest, Rhonda knew he was having a violent asthma attack. John fell against the wall, slowly sliding down until the full weight of his body was on top of Rhonda. Rhonda remained absolutely still, listening to John wheeze while she got her bearings. Slowly, Rhonda slid from beneath him and crawled away, trying to catch her own breath. She stood up, leaning against the wall for support, and stared at John. He was holding his chest, and his eyes were rolling around in his head. He looked pitiful, just like her brother always looked when it was time to go to the hospital. John kept trying to talk, to tell her something. She had never worked out the hand signals with John the way she had done with Ray. But Rhonda knew what he was trying to say. She did not move. A frightened, angry voice in the back of her mind said, "Let him die! Let him lie there and die!" It had taken her a moment to realize that this was not her brother. This was a man who had just tried to kill her. The voice became louder: "LET THE S.O.B. LIE THERE AND DIE! HE'S A PIG!" There was a battle going on in Rhonda's mind. The battle was between the past and the future, between Ray and John, between running and standing against that wall. It was then that Rhonda had another brief and fleeting revelation.

The equation had flipped! Rhonda was now in charge! Rhonda was now in the position of power. She was the strong one. Now she was the one who could *hurt somebody*. Rhonda had never been in that position, and she simply did not know what to do. At that moment, she didn't realize that this was an opportunity to reclaim the power over her own life. She had no idea that she was in a position to change the pattern, to do something different. Instead, the frightening sight of John gasping for air and the implications of him dying threatened her independence. The battle continued in her mind. As brutal as John could be, she loved him. He was no different from anyone she believed had loved her in the past. Besides that, John did love her. He had told her so and shown her love in the ways she had become accustomed to—hurtful, painful, restrictive loving was all that Rhonda had ever known. More important, Rhonda believed she needed John to validate her, to save her, to make a statement that she had not failed again.

When you are trying to get yourself together, you must be vigilant. You must watch yourself carefully. You must pay close attention to what you are thinking, what you are doing, and what you are saying to yourself and others. Getting yourself together means paying very close attention so that you do not send out mixed messages. If you say one thing and do another, you are going to get mixed up, forget what you are doing, and fall right back into the same trap you said you wanted to get out of. When you are getting yourself together, you must eliminate from your modus operandi everything you have done up to the point where you realized you were a mess. You must think a new way, act a new way, and keep your mouth shut. If you start talking about what you are going to do, chances are you will get confused.

When you are getting yourself together, talking takes on another form. It becomes mental language, emotional language, and body language. When you cannot speak all three of these languages in a way that clearly communicates to people what you are trying to do, they too become confused.

Rhonda's mouth had spoken one language: *I can do this.* Her heart spoke another: *This is too hard to do without love.* Her body was saying something completely different: *He must love me. If he didn't, he wouldn't sleep with me.* She had confused herself. She had not been paying attention. If you act like you are married to a man, take his money, and have sex with him, you cannot seriously talk about leaving him. Rhonda knew that, but when she thought about raising her children alone, she forgot. If you stay with a man who brutally beats you, you cannot talk about getting yourself together. She knew that too, but had forgotten because being beaten was familiar. She knew how to survive a beating. It was a pattern she had learned to live with. She had not talked to herself or anyone else about how to survive on her own with three children. She had forgotten that her ability and desire to do that was the only thing that mattered. It was that part of getting herself together that Rhonda had never figured out. It was the part of the language of living she had never learned.

On the way to getting yourself together, you are bound to slip and fall. Sometimes when you fall, you bump your head. The bump may stun you, and your thinking may become cloudy, your speech slurred. You will undoubtedly say and do the wrong thing, over and over again. When Tony told Rhonda he could not see her anymore, she was stunned. His girlfriend had found out about them and threatened to put him out. Rhonda was still sitting in stunned disbelief when John called to tell her that he forgave her, and that he loved her. The fog of confusion had still not lifted several days later, when John came by to visit the kids, beat her within an inch of her life, and left with all three children.

The police said there was nothing they could do. She would have to go to family court on Monday. This was Friday.

"He'll bring them back," Nett said. "They always do. He's just trying to upset you. Besides, this could be a good thing. Give you some time to rest your nerves before you have another breakdown." Nett knew every sordid detail. She had given up on trying to get Rhonda to leave John.

"Upset me? What do you mean 'upset me?' He's been trying to kill me for years!" Nett refused to argue the finer points.

"If he doesn't bring them back, good! Maybe you'll have a chance to get yourself together."

Daddy's approach was more pragmatic. "Is he at work?" It was 9:30 at night. "Try his mother's house. If he's not there, get back to me."

Rhonda got the number for Dial-A-Prayer from one of the free community papers. A woman answered the telephone.

"How can I pray for you today?"

"My husband took my children, and I don't know where they are." Rhonda was exhausted, beaten, and trying to talk and not cry at the same time.

"God will take care of his children. They are not your children. They belong to God. They are safe. The power of God Almighty is protecting the children right now. God hears your crying, Mother. He will not fail to deliver the children."

The woman listened to Rhonda cry a few minutes more, then promised Rhonda that she would hear from the children within twenty-four hours. Twenty-two hours later, John called and asked if he could come home. The children went on and on about Grandma Millie's dog and their Daddy's new car and all the fun they'd had. John and Rhonda didn't speak to one another for the rest of the day. Rhonda waited several hours after John went to bed to make sure he was asleep before she lay down.

She had just fallen asleep when she felt someone shaking her body. Her heart skipped a beat. She opened her eyes and heard a voice: *Get up and leave this house. Leave now!* The voice was familiar and made Rhonda feel completely safe. *He is going to kill you. You must leave this place now! You will be told what to do.* Rhonda could hear her heart pounding at her temples. She eased out of bed and went into the children's room. *Wake the boy first.* She held Damon up until his own legs could support him. She dressed him, then asked him to wake Gemmia, who was still sleeping like a log. She dressed Nisa, then helped Damon with Gemmia, who had collapsed on the floor, refusing to wake up. *Take only what you need.* Rhonda filled four plastic bags with clothing for the children.

They left the house and walked the two and a half blocks to the subway station. Damon kept tripping over the two bags he was carrying. Rhonda carried Nisa on her hip, carried two bags with one hand, and dragged Gemmia along with the other. As she approached the station, it occurred to her that she had no money and no place to go. She and the children stood at the bottom of the fifty or so steps that led up to the platform while Rhonda tried to figure out how she was going to make it to the top.

"Do you need some help?" the man asked.

"What I need is a token for the subway—and a cigarette for me," Rhonda said.

The man gave her both without saying another word and walked up the block. He was out of sight before Rhonda thought to ask him to help her up the stairs. Don't give up five minutes before the miracle. It was a lesson Rhonda would not soon forget.

Rhonda and the children were gone for two weeks before they returned home. One day, after John went to work, Rhonda went to the store and bought the hardware and tools she needed to change the locks on her door. She followed the instructions the salesman had given her, and by the time John came home, his key no longer worked. Rhonda wouldn't let him in, no matter what he said, and she finally heard him retreat back down the stairs.

A few weeks later, she allowed John to take the kids out with him, and while they were gone, she realized that he had gone in her purse and stolen the key to the door. When he returned with the children, he rang the doorbell, and she let them in. Neither of them mentioned the key. Something told her that he'd be back that night. Rhonda knew that if she panicked and became nervous, she would not be able to do what she knew she must do. After the children were in bed, she calmly went to the kitchen and took a large butcher knife out of the drawer. She put the chain latch on, then lay down on the floor in front of the door and waited.

At two o'clock in the morning, Rhonda heard John's footsteps outside the apartment door. She heard him insert the key into the lock and saw the knob slowly begin to turn. Quickly she was on her feet and re-locked the door. John inserted the key again and unlocked the door. Rhonda locked it again. John unlocked it and, this time, gave the door a push, but the chain held, and he couldn't get inside. He stood in the hallway, yelling obscenities at Rhonda, who kept insisting that he leave her alone. The only thing that separated an outraged John from a frightened but determined Rhonda was the little silver chain, and Rhonda didn't know how long it would hold against John's weight. She picked up the knife from the floor and jabbed it through the door opening as hard as she could. She felt the knife make contact. She heard John scream and stumble against the hallway wall, then fall to the floor. After a few minutes, she heard him stumbling down the stairs, cursing and moaning in pain. Rhonda went to the window and looked outside. A patrol car had pulled up in front of the building, and the officers were questioning John, who had slumped to the ground. His blood was brilliant against the snow.

John spent two weeks in the hospital. The doctors said the knife missed his heart by only an inch. When John was released from the hospital, he came looking for Rhonda. He stood outside their window and yelled up at her. He called her every filthy name he could think of, and he yelled it at the top of his lungs.

When you make up your mind to take a stand, forces from out of nowhere will appear to support you. On the second night of John's verbal abuse, an angel appeared in the form of Mr. Johnson, Rhonda's next-door neighbor. In all the time she'd lived there, she and Mr. Johnson had barely spoken two words, but he was always cordial when they passed in the hallway. Mr. Johnson left his apartment, went down the stairs and outside to the street, where John was standing beneath Rhonda's window, screaming obscenities at her. Mr. Johnson pulled a gun from his coat and put the muzzle to John's head.

"I don't know your wife very well, but every time I see her, she's pleasant. The children are always clean and well behaved, and she don't seem to bother nobody." John held perfectly still. "You, on the other hand, Mr. Whatever-your-name-is, are a disgrace to the race. So I'll tell you what—if I ever see you around here again bothering that woman or her children, I'm gonna blow your f———g head off."

With that, Mr. Johnson put his gun back inside his coat and went inside, out of the cold.

CHAPTER TWELVE

What's the Lesson When You Begin to Recognize Yourself as Who You Really Are?

Do not be afraid to look within.

The ego tells you

all is black with guilt within you,

and bids you not to look.

Instead, it bids you to look upon your brothers,

and see the guilt in them.

Yet this you cannot do without remaining blind.

A Course in Miracles

SATURDAY AFTERNOON TEA with my husband is always nice. Today it was especially nurturing and comforting. I thanked him and told him what a blessing he is in my life, then let him get back to his television program. I headed for the showers.

The hot, pulsating water of the shower beating on my back was exquisite. Hot water and black-walnut soap will wash away the shadows that haunt you. I could feel the memories being washed away as I recited the lessons in my mind. If you stay too long in pain, you will get S.O.S. Stuck on Stupid. I chuckled to myself. Rhonda had been stuck on stupid for a long time. It wasn't that *she* was stupid. But the dull ache from the constant pain of her life had rendered her senseless. She had no sense of herself or the power she had to move her life in another direction.

When you stay too long in a place where you do not belong, patterns of pain become etched in your mind. Rhonda had stayed much too long with John. And it had taken her much too long to find the strength, discipline, and courage she needed to get herself together. Discipline comes from doing the very thing you keep praying for the discipline to do. I stood still in the shower and let the soothing, cleansing water wash away the nine years Rhonda had spent in and out of stupidity with John. She had done it. Left him. Refused to speak to him. Refused to be abused or self-abusive. Her friend Ruth had taken her in. Her friend Roseanne helped her with the kids. Her friends Linda and Lorraine supported her and each other, held on to each other, and cried together as things got increasingly better. In the end, it was working two jobs that proved to Rhonda that she could take care of herself and her children.

Taking the soap in my hands, I gently massaged away the years of abuse and neglect Rhonda had experienced at the hands of so many people, including herself. I made a nice lather over the fear, avoidance, and denial. I turned the water up full blast and washed away the suds. Ugliness and unworthiness went down the drain. When I felt clean all over, I started dancing and singing in the shower. "Sometimes I feel like a motherless child . . ." "Momma said there'd be days like this . . ." "I don't believe He brought me this far to leave me . . ." "You've got to give a little, take a little . . ." "Ain't gonna let nobody turn me around . . ." "I am woman, hear me roar!"

"It sounds like you're having a good time." My husband peeked over the top of the shower door. "Are you taking calls?"

"Who's that calling on my phone?" It was a jingle I had made up to the tune of "Who's that knocking at my door."

"It's Karen." Fear shot through my body like a torpedo.

"No. Tell her I'm in the shower," I whispered.

"I told her that."

"So tell her again. Tell her I'll call her back."

There are some things that black-walnut soap and hot water cannot wash away. With Karen, I had stayed too long in a relationship where I did not feel nurtured, comforted, or supported. It had reinforced the patterns of feeling worthless and helpless. Somehow, I had allowed myself to believe that I was a victim. I had told myself that I was powerless to stop people who overstepped their boundaries in my life. I thought about Rhonda's next three years. Years of loneliness. Years of isolation. Years when she wasn't sure, but she kept on moving. Years when she wore a hard shell to cover her bruised and battered soul. Years of working, not working, looking for work, not finding work. Three long years of insecurity and instability. I lathered myself up again and let the water wash those years away.

Then it hit me. Some people don't know how, and others never think about going back and cleaning up their crap. Most people want to start today and feel better tomorrow. They want to take a yoga class, listen to a meditation tape, rub a crystal on their head, and believe they have fixed their lives and healed their souls. You cannot create a new way of being in one day. You must take your time remembering, cleaning up, and gaining strength. If you push yourself too fast, before gaining the strength you need to go in a new direction, you are going to fall and bump your head. I was not ready to talk to Karen. I had not yet figured out why I had stayed so long in a relationship that did not nurture me. And I still had to figure out why I was afraid to fire her. In order to do that, I needed to remember what happened to Rhonda when she got strong and moved forward into new challenges. How we deal with new challenges is always a reflection of how well we have healed.

I had the urge to take a nap. *Don't go to sleep on the job. Rest, do not sleep.* I would rest in my prayer room. It was the only room in the house that the dog knew she was not allowed to enter. I dried off and wrapped a large bath towel around myself and went into the prayer room. I sat down in my favorite chair, pulling a blanket up to my chin. I began to pray so that I could remember just a little more. *Delight thyself in the ways of the Lord and He shall give you the desires of your heart . . . Dear God, it is my desire to know You and serve You. It is my desire to acknowledge You in all that I do. It is my desire that Your will be done in my life and through my life. It is my desire to be a light, Your light unto the world. Please show me those things about myself that are no longer pleasing in Your sight. And when they are known to me, I ask You to please take them away so that I may be all that You have created me to be.*

Rhonda had prayed for guidance. She had stopped working nights, because the children were getting into too much trouble when she was away. They would do their homework, but they also had friends over in their mother's absence. Baby-sitters were often hard to come by. The good ones were always busy, and the not-so-good ones ate too much. She held onto her welfare benefits just for times like this when she needed to be home more. But that meant going to the welfare office.

It was a dismal, nasty place, where people got paid to find ways to treat other people like animals. Rhonda always showed up on time. She wore the same outfit she always wore when she went to be recertified for benefits: cheap jeans, a white sweatshirt, and sneakers. She always had the required papers with her, and that helped to make the trip a little more bearable. Not pleasant, but bearable.

There was a big commotion going on in the welfare office when Rhonda arrived. A client was cursing, a caseworker was screaming. Everyone was watching and waiting for someone to throw the first punch. Rhonda sat down next to the two women who were arguing. Several more people got involved in the controversy, including the woman Rhonda was scheduled to see. As she watched, she vowed to herself that she would find a job, or perhaps go back to school. But she would not spend the rest of her life coming in and out of places like this.

A caseworker in the middle of the room began shouting at a client, "All of you welfare mothers are just alike. Someone should take you all, put you on your knees, blindfold you, and shoot you! What you do to your children is criminal. You should all be shot!"

"I wonder if she thinks she's talking about me?" Rhonda thought aloud. "I am not a 'welfare mother'! I'm outta here!" Rhonda didn't wait to see her caseworker. She gathered her papers and left. She talked to herself all the way to the bus stop. "I'm outta here! That's it. I'm done.

When they start talking about shooting people, shooting poor people, I'm gone!" She boarded the bus. She was furious. "How dare she! She must be related to Grandma, talking to people like that!" Rhonda thought how tenuous the temporary-job market was, and fear crept into her voice. "How am I going to feed my children, pay my rent, buy shoes!" Realizing that she was talking out loud, Rhonda looked around the bus at the people who were now staring at her. That's when she saw the advertisement: *If you are ready to change your life, come to Medgar Evers College.* Rhonda got off the bus at the next stop and transferred to the bus that would take her to the campus. Twenty minutes later she was standing in the admissions office of Medgar Evers College, filling out an application.

Rhonda discovered that she was not at all stupid. After taking the placement test, she was told that she did not need to take remedial classes. There was an angel in the financial aid office who told her how to fill out the applications in order to get the maximum benefits. There was another angel in the registration office who told her how many credits to take and how to fit all of her classes into four nights. Armed with piles of papers about returning to college, study habits, how to write term papers, and child-care services, Rhonda went home to wait for her acceptance letter. It came three weeks later, as did the financial aid approvals. Two months later, at the age of twenty-nine, Rhonda started college.

Daddy and his wife said she was crazy to give up her welfare benefits. Grandma agreed. Nett said she would help type her papers. The children wanted to know if they could come with her. Ruth invited her to come over and have a drink to celebrate. Linda and Lorraine volunteered to help with the children. John hung up on her. Rhonda was so excited she thought she would burst open. The week before classes started, she was offered a three-month temporary assignment. It all seemed so easy. Rhonda wondered why she had not done it before.

By the time she was a sophomore, Rhonda had learned how to use a thesaurus, how to footnote a term paper, how to make stew in a Crock-Pot, and she had a 4.0 grade point average. She discovered that she was a decent writer. So decent, in fact, that one of her professors had accused her of plagiarizing a paper. The professor told Rhonda that she couldn't believe a freshman could produce that caliber of work. Rhonda was mothering by telephone, becoming involved in political activities, and having a good time in her life. She had made new friends, and for the first time, she was having wholesome, nonsexual relationships with men. She and her male schoolmates talked about things that did not involve money or sex. It was a new experience for her. Besides that, Rhonda had a new boyfriend. His name was Eddie.

Rhonda met Eddie on a boat. She and some friends had taken a cruise up the Hudson River. As they were leaving the boat, Rhonda tripped over his foot. When she turned to apologize, Eddie smiled and asked her where she was going. He followed her off the boat to a club in Brooklyn, where they danced for hours. The next morning, when Rhonda rolled over in his bed, she realized she had just had her first one-night stand. It was a one-night stand that lasted for five years.

Eddie was kind and gentle, unlike any man Rhonda had ever known. He was three years younger than she was, but he was far more responsible and attentive than John could ever hope to be. Eddie helped out with the children when Rhonda was in school; he came over on weekends to take them out while she studied. He made Rhonda happy. Not just sexually satisfied, but happy to the bone. Theirs was a quiet, loving, and fulfilling relationship. This, too, was a new experience. There were just two little problems: Rhonda wanted to marry Eddie; and Eddie did not want to marry Rhonda. He stated quite clearly that he did not want a ready-made family.

"Don't get me wrong," he'd say, "I love you and I love the children. But this is not what I want for myself."

Rhonda heard him, but she was sure she could change his mind. Every now and then, the subject would come up again, and Eddie would say the same thing. She would listen, get mad, cry, and then try to figure out what she needed to do to help him change his mind. Eddie never did change his position, and Rhonda began to suspect that Eddie was seeing other women. He was.

By the time she was a junior in college, Rhonda had learned some very important lessons at Medgar Evers and from Eddie. She had learned that when you are smart, attractive, and hardworking, some people will like you, others will despise you. She had learned that you cannot make people do something they are not willing or inclined to do. She had learned that if you make yourself available for people to use you, they will use you. She learned that if you work hard, stay focused, and put your mind to it, most of the time, things will work out for the best. She also learned that sometimes, no matter how hard you work, things just don't work out the way you think they should.

There were also some things that Rhonda had not learned. You cannot *make* people like you no matter how hard you try. She didn't know why she was so into people-pleasing. She had not learned that what you think about yourself is more important than what others think about you. Rhonda did not know why she still felt bad about herself. She still had not learned that people will lie to get what they want from you, and when they get it, they will lie on you. Why did she allow people to lie to her? And when she knew they were lying, why couldn't she tell them so? She had not learned how her relationship with her father was impacting her relationships with men, and she had not learned that she could live without a man in her life. Rhonda still yearned for her father's approval. She thought if she had a college degree, her father would be proud of her. Rhonda needed to belong, and she was completely unaware of how that need motivated her behavior. She had not learned that, in her life, *she* mattered the most. Rhonda had not learned that when you do the right things for the wrong reasons, it never works out.

Father, forgive them for they know not what they do. Father, forgive me, because I didn't know what I was doing. It had gotten hot in the prayer room. I got up to open the window and stared at the lovely trees in my front yard, reflecting on how hard Rhonda had worked to get through college. She was so caught up in working, raising her children, and going to college, that she had never stopped to celebrate herself or her accomplishments. But Rhonda had not done all that work because she wanted it for herself. She had done it to prove something to other people.

She had done the work to protest the caseworker's comments about welfare mothers. She had done it to prove Grandma wrong. She had done it so her father would tell her she was smart and that she'd done a good job. Rhonda had worked herself into a frenzy trying to prove to the world that all teenage mothers are not destined to fail. And she had done it all so that she could provide a better life for her children. At no time did she sit down and say: This is what I want to do for myself; this is what I want to do because I matter.

Looking back, I realized how unfulfilling Rhonda's college experience had been. Most of the time, it was fun. But it did not fill the void Rhonda felt in her life. Neither did Eddie. Perhaps that is why she never felt successful. She had not learned that success means having the desire to accomplish something, then doing it to your own satisfaction. Rhonda was not even focused on material success. She was struggling to achieve what she thought would be some measure of personal success. For Rhonda that meant having someone say to her, "You did good." The truth is, she didn't want just anybody to say it, she wanted her family to say it. Unfortunately, she was so busy trying to elicit those three little words from them, she never said them to herself. When her family didn't offer their approval, it reinforced Rhonda's belief that she was neither worthy nor valuable. It reinforced her belief that she just wasn't good enough. She handled it by working even harder to get the desired effect.

Oh my God! I thought, that's what I want. I want Karen's approval. I want her to tell me that I am doing a good job. I believe that if I do what Karen wants me to do, she will approve of me. Is that what this is all about? It can't be! Surely I've grown more than this. Do I still care that much what other people think about me? Layer upon layer. Each time you peel back one layer, you discover a new level of healing that needs to be done. Sadly, I had to admit to myself that I still needed and wanted external approval and acceptance. I, like Rhonda, was willing to put up with anything to get it. It was something that Rhonda had lived with all of her life. If you don't do what people want you to do, they will disapprove of you. They will get mad at you. They will hurt you and leave you. Karen had rescued me. I was behaving like a victim. *People are out to get me. I need somebody to rescue me.* To protect me the way my father and brother never did.

I felt like I'd been kicked in the stomach. I doubled over and fell back onto my chair. I realized that it was about more than just seeking approval. I was doing what I thought I needed to do to make someone like me. Because Karen had rescued me, I wanted her to like me. It felt like being six years old again, feeling ugly and unwanted, and trying to get someone to like me. I also realized that I felt indebted to her for all she had done for me. I wanted to prove to her that I was grateful. When you are grateful to someone, you must show it. One way to show it is to let them do whatever they want to you. You let them beat you and don't fight back; you lie there and let them rape you.

I squeezed my eyes shut and could see the little piles of crap in my own mind. Rhonda's crap had shown up in my life in a hundred ways. Not asking for what I wanted. Being afraid to tell people what I was really feeling. Not speaking up for myself if I thought it would make someone mad at me. People-pleasing and self-denial. Never feeling like I had done enough, or that I was good enough. Always needing someone else to determine my worth. Each of the little piles had a different shape and form, but at the core they were all the same. I was still looking for love. As far as Karen was concerned, I was afraid of losing what I thought was her love. It was a huge, gaping wound that I still had not healed.

When the telephone rang at seven o'clock in the morning, Rhonda thought it was Eddie. It was Nett. She was not feeling well and wanted Rhonda to go with her to the doctor.

"What's the matter?" Rhonda asked.

"I don't know. I've been up all night long. I get so cold. I've been vomiting, and I have diarrhea. I'm so weak, I can hardly stand up."

"Let me take the kids to school and I'll come get you."

"Thank you, Ronnie," Nett said. "I appreciate it."

Nett was one of the few people Rhonda knew who always said thank you. She always said how grateful she was for the little gifts that Rhonda would bring her. It made Rhonda feel good to do things for Nett, like driving over in her beat-up old Chevy and taking Nett to the supermarket. The car was a family joke. It cost Rhonda exactly one hundred dollars. It was painted a color that Nett called "puke green." And it had one brown door and an AM radio that worked. Rhonda would get dressed in her finest outfit, her ragged old mink coat that Grandma had handed down, and drive away in the worst-looking car on the block. The children thought it was hilarious, but on chilly winter days, the car always started.

Nett looked awful. When Rhonda saw her face, she told her, "You are the same color as the car." Nett was always fragile, but now she was sweating, stooped, and very pale. Nett was admitted to the hospital that afternoon. Rhonda felt almost as bad as Nett looked. She stayed until Nett was situated in her room and hooked up to an IV. The possibility of losing Nett had not yet hit Rhonda.

The next six weeks were horrific. The doctors tested Nett for everything, but they could not find the cause of her debilitating illness. One week they thought she had a kidney ailment, the next week it was a rare form of anemia. Each week they tried a different medication, and frequently Nett would have a bad reaction. She had become so thin and weak she could barely lift her arms. Every morning, Rhonda would drop the kids off at school, visit Nett in the hospital, and then leave at lunchtime to attend classes. After school, she would go home, feed the children, and head back to the hospital.

She never knew in what condition she'd find Nett. Some days she was bloody from a blood test gone bad. Other days she would be in tears because no one had fed her or put her on the bedpan. Rhonda would bathe her, change the bed, comb her hair, and wait for her to fall asleep. She was spending an average of six to eight hours a day at the hospital.

Nett had been in the hospital four months on the day Rhonda visited and found a large group of nurses and interns standing outside of Nett's room. She wanted to run down the corridor, but she was too shocked and afraid. The closer she got to the room, the weaker she felt. The crowd at the door parted to let her through. When she saw what was going on in the room, she almost fainted.

There was blood everywhere. Nett had a tube down her throat and one in her nose. There were new machines at the side of the bed that whistled and beeped. But the worst sight was modest, fragile Nett lying naked and uncovered on the bed with male doctors standing casually about talking.

"What happened? What the hell is going on?" Rhonda screamed at the doctors. She tried to cover Nett with the sheet that she had picked up from the floor, but the sheets were bloody, and there were too many tubes in the way.

"Your mother went into respiratory arrest. We had to intubate her. We think she's okay now, but we'll need to run some more tests."

"No more tests!" Rhonda screamed at them. "Get out! Get out! You're killing her! Get out of here. Now!"

"You're just upset." The doctor's tone was patronizing. "Come outside and we'll talk about it."

"No, you go outside! Get out now!"

The doctors obliged, taking their conversation out into the corridor. Nett was unconscious, and her eyes were swollen. The large tube extending out of her mouth had been taped to her face. Her hair was a mess. Rhonda walked up the hallway and grabbed a stack of sheets and towels off a linen cart. As she removed the dirty linen from the bed, she found two of Nett's front teeth, broken and chipped, under a pillow. She looked at the teeth, then at Nett's face, and fell to her knees. She put her face in her hands and cried. Rhonda realized that she was going to lose her best friend.

Scandal, disgrace, and disappointment marred Rhonda's graduation. Nett was home from the hospital and living with Rhonda and the children. Rhonda had bought her a new outfit and had sent a hairdresser to the house to do her hair. But when Eddie went to the house to pick up Nett and the children, Nett was too weak and too sick to attend.

Daddy said he didn't come because he didn't have carfare.

Rhonda had maintained a 3.99 GPA and was valedictorian of her class. She was also president of the Student Government Association. She had been one of the principal players in a student protest that resulted in the president of the college being removed from office. Two weeks prior to graduation, a group of students accused Rhonda of sleeping with her professors in order to receive good grades. They put signs all over the campus. Some members of the committee that had brought the president up on charges accused her of betraying them in the media and with local politicians. As a member of the committee to search for and appoint a new president of the college, Rhonda was being wooed and solicited by candidates for the job. When she informed them that she intended to vote her conscience, they called her a sellout. People she had once considered friends were now questioning her character. People who were supporting her privately were ignoring her publicly. Rhonda was confused and hurt, but she stood up for herself.

Rhonda made herself a beautiful white dress of English eyelet for graduation. At fourteen dollars per yard for the fabric, it was the most expensive dress she had ever worn. The children wore matching white outfits. When Rhonda walked across the stage to receive her degree, the children walked with her. Damon did a little jig in the middle of the stage to the delight of the audience. Eddie and his entire family came. Even Grandma came and took pictures. Though she never praised or congratulated Rhonda, it was clear that Grandma was proud and excited.

Without Nett or Daddy there, the graduation meant little to Rhonda. She had worked so hard to prove to them that she could do it, and they were not there to see it. She understood Nett's not being there. Daddy's excuse was totally unacceptable.

Rhonda spent the summer taking care of Nett in and out of the hospital. Nett would get better, then worse; and the doctors still did not know what was wrong. Finally, Nett began to steadily improve. She grew stronger, and the color came back to her face. She was released from the hospital three weeks before Rhonda was to enter law school. A week later, Eddie decided it was time for him to say good-bye.

They were sitting at the kitchen table, discussing the Stevie Wonder concert they had just attended. Eddie was smoking and drinking rum.

Rhonda got up and stretched. She was tired and ready to go to bed. Eddie announced that he was leaving and that he was not coming back.

"Where are you going?" Rhonda asked him.

"Home," Eddie answered.

"What do you mean you won't be back?"

"I'm not going to see you anymore. This is it for me."

"What?"

"I'm ready to move on, to settle down. I've always told you that this is not what I want for myself. I think I'm ready to get married."

"To whom?"

"I don't know yet, but I'm ready."

"Well, okay. If that's what you want."

Rhonda heard it, but she didn't believe it. When Eddie didn't call her for three days, she began to think he was serious. She started frantically calling his house, his mother's house, and Dial-A-Prayer. She elicited the help of friends to watch his house so she'd know of all his comings and goings. But she still did not believe that he was serious. It took about two more weeks for her to get it. When she did, she sent the children to Daddy's house, pulled the shades down, got in her bed, and stayed there for a week.

On the day she finally got out of bed, Rhonda got dressed and went directly to Eddie's house. When he opened the door, she didn't know what to say. They made small talk for a few minutes, and then Rhonda asked if she could come in.

"This isn't a good time," Eddie said. "I've got company."

"What does that mean?" Rhonda asked.

"I have someone upstairs."

"I don't care! I need to talk to you."

She stepped quickly to the side, darted past Eddie, and headed up the stairs to his apartment. When she got inside, Rhonda couldn't believe her eyes. The woman standing in the middle of his living room had her same haircut, size, and height. The woman ran into the bathroom and shut the door. Rhonda sat down, and Eddie offered her something to drink.

"Is that your wife?" Rhonda asked.

"No," Eddie said, "she's just a friend."

"What are you doing? Please help me to understand just what it is you think you are doing."

"What do you want me to say? I've been telling you the same thing for the past four years. I don't want a ready-made family. It's not you. It's not the kids. It's me. It's just not what I want."

Rhonda sat there, letting the words sink in. The other woman crept out of the bathroom and asked permission to use the telephone. When she finished her call, she said to Rhonda, "Look, I don't know what's going on, but I'm sorry."

"You don't have anything to be sorry about. This is not about you," Rhonda told her. "This is about learning how much of myself I'm willing to give up for somebody to love me. I thank you for being here."

The next time Rhonda saw Eddie was when he visited her in Philadelphia, where she'd moved to practice law.

CHAPTER THIRTEEN

What's the Lesson When You Lose Someone You Really Love?

There is a place in you
where there is perfect peace.
There is a place in you
where nothing is impossible.

A Course in Miracles

THE FACE OF THE WOMAN sitting across the table had become grossly distorted. Even in the semidarkness, Rhonda could see that. Her voice had changed, too. She was speaking, she said, in the voice of Nett's mother, Ivy Brown.

"I do not want her to suffer," the voice said. "I want her to rest."

"Can you make her better?" Rhonda asked, unsure of what she was seeing and hearing.

"If you will place a slice of bread, a glass of water, and a piece of purple cloth on a table for me, I will make sure that she does not suffer." Rhonda agreed to do it.

The woman speaking was a spiritualist. Rhonda had learned a great deal about spirits and the people who talked to them. She had gone to one to find out the real reason for Eddie's departure. She had gone to one for a lucky number to make the money she needed to start law school on time. She had read books about them, and she had called them on the telephone. Now she sat across from a spiritualist who was telling her what to do to help Nett get well. Rhonda had lived through a great deal, but she did not believe she could live without Nett.

She was searching. Searching for answers, searching for guidance, and searching for herself. Her life was changing radically, and she felt unprepared. Rhonda was aware of the changes, but she didn't know what to make of them. Who and what she was becoming was radically different from anything she had ever known. In many ways, she was strong and clear. But in other ways, she felt weak and off balance. She had so many questions about so many things that she felt insecure.

Her support system had dwindled. Her dear friend Ruth had been murdered. Her college buddies were off working. Nett was semicoherent most of the time. There was no man in Rhonda's life, and her circle of friends was intimidated by her drive to move ahead. As far as they were concerned, Rhonda thought she was too good to be their friend anymore. She was meeting an entirely new set of people in law school, most of whom came from backgrounds and places that Rhonda had only read about.

Being in law school was not like being in college. The people in law school were more intelligent and quite arrogant. It made Rhonda feel inferior and stupid like Ray had said she was. Her classmates had read books she had never heard of. They knew things about the world that Rhonda never imagined existed. Her law books weighed almost as much as she did. They were big, intimidating texts full of words Rhonda had never seen before. Her biggest problem was that there was no one to talk to about how she was feeling except the spiritualist who told her she was courageous to undertake the awesome task of becoming a lawyer. Rhonda felt alone and tired. She kept searching.

During the day, Rhonda attended classes. At night, she worked at whatever job she could find to help make ends meet. Damon was fourteen and working as a messenger and often gave Rhonda the money she needed to buy lunch at school or dinner at home. Two weeks prior to her first semester finals, Nett went into the hospital for the third time in fourteen months. Rhonda was forced to leave law school so she could care for Nett and work full-time to pay for private-duty nurses. When she wasn't working or visiting Nett, Rhonda was searching for and visiting spiritualists.

When Rhonda set up an altar at home and told the children about the spiritual things she had been doing, they thought she'd lost her mind. They knew she was serious about her spiritual search, so they went along just to make her happy. But when she explained how they could do spiritual things to help Nett, they began to take it seriously, as well. Watching Nett deteriorate before their eyes was a painful and frightening experience for the children.

Nett had been diagnosed with lupus. By the time the doctors had finally made this diagnosis, they had knocked out most of her teeth, and she had a permanent trachea tube protruding from the center of her neck. The massive doses of steroids they had given her had made her partially blind. The doctors' prognosis for Nett was not good. But Rhonda wouldn't accept that. She prayed, lit candles, went to church, and did whatever she could in an effort to save her friend, her mother.

When Nett was ready to be released from the hospital, not only was she in bad shape physically, she hallucinated frequently. The doctors recommended that Rhonda place her in a nursing care facility. Nett's older sister, Sharon, agreed. Sharon had recently retired and did not want the responsibility of caring for Nett, though she said she was willing to help out as much as she could. Rhonda did not agree. She knew that taking Nett into her home would put a strain on her household, but she felt she had no other choice. Rhonda moved her family into a three-bedroom apartment to make room for Nett and the medical equipment and supplies she would need.

Rhonda moved Nett into one bedroom, she took another, and her budding teenagers shared the third room. Damon, Nisa, and Gemmia were so happy that their Nana was out of the hospital, they didn't mind sleeping on top of each other. Seeing Nett with tubes coming from every orifice was especially hard on Gemmia. Nett was her best friend, and every time Gemmia looked at Nett, she would cry.

It took several weeks, but eventually Nett could use the bathroom and feed herself—with a little help. Nett loved to look at television, though she couldn't remember what it was called. Nett's only physical feature to survive her eighteen-month ordeal intact was her hair. The long, jet-black hair that Rhonda had so admired as a child was now a beautiful salt-and-pepper mane that framed Nett's thin, pale face.

Nett was sitting in her wheelchair one night, watching television while Rhonda combed and brushed her hair, when she started hallucinating. Nett, who could never deal with the sound of someone screaming, began screaming loudly and waving her hands frantically in the air as if to ward off some imaginary attacker. The children ran into the room. Damon crouched down in a mock karate pose, ready to defend his Nana.

"What's the matter?" Rhonda said, trying to calm Nett down. "What's the matter?"

"Help me! Please, help me!" Nett cried out. "Don't let it get me!" She was terrified.

"What, Nana? What's trying to get you?"

"Help! Help! Please, help me!" Nett was crying. Rhonda tried to maneuver the wheelchair in another direction so that whatever Nett was seeing would be out of sight.

"I'm not going to let it get you. What is it?" Rhonda asked.

"It's a goat! I'm afraid. Please help me."

"We won't let it bother you. Damon, take it away!"

Damon caught on fast. "See, Nana. He's nice. He's not going to hurt you. I'll put him over here." Nett stopped swinging her arms around long enough to watch Damon move the goat.

"Who brought that thing in here?" Nett asked.

"It came by itself. I'll put it out. Okay, Nana?" Damon was in complete control. He walked over to the door, opened it, put the goat out, and closed the door. "See? It's gone."

"Who let that nasty thing in here? I'm afraid of them, you know. Why did you let it in here?" Rhonda tried to think of an answer.

"Oh, Nana, you know how they are. They're all over the place."

The scene was more than Gemmia could handle. She was standing in the middle of the room, wailing. She was inconsolable; she couldn't believe what was happening to her grandmother. She was sure that her Nana was dying. Her Nana, who made perfect pancakes and played war and never forgot your birthday.

"She not dying, Gemmia," Rhonda assured her. "She's sick and she's getting better."

"Well, I don't even know who she is anymore! And she doesn't know who I am most of the time. It's just like she's dead."

Rhonda felt the same way, but she wouldn't admit it to the children or to herself. It was true that, as the voice of Nett's mother, Ivy, had promised, Nett wasn't suffering anymore, but she certainly was not the same person Rhonda had known most of her life.

Visiting nurses were in and out every day. Medical supplies were being delivered every other day. The electricity bill was outrageous. Nett's hallucinations were traumatic for everyone who witnessed them. The children needed some peace at home. Gemmia, in particular, was a nervous wreck. Rhonda needed to get back to law school. She was doing all she could do to care for the only mother she had ever known. But she was quickly approaching the point where she would have to let go.

Three months after Nett moved in, Rhonda decided to move her back to her own home. Rhonda had continued to pay the rent on Nett's apartment in the projects, hoping that one day Nett would be well. She never thought she'd be sending her back there under these circumstances. She talked to the children about it, and they agreed that Nana would be fine at home. They offered to visit and help out when Rhonda returned to law school. She called the Department of Social Services, and they approved the hiring of a full-time home attendant to care for Nett.

Rhonda had to get up the courage to tell Nett. When she did, Nett cried. Rhonda was heartbroken; she felt as though she had failed to do for Nett what Nett had done for her most of her life. The spiritualist had told Rhonda that she was not a failure, that in fact, she was doing a courageous thing. Rhonda chose not to believe her. Then Nett, sounding like her old self, told Rhonda: "I know you have things to do. You go on. I'll be just fine." A few days later, Rhonda called an ambulance to take

Nett home. Before she left, Nett asked, "Will you bring me pizza?" Even with no teeth, Nett loved to eat pizza, and Rhonda promised that she and the kids would bring her pizza as often as she liked.

It was getting dark outside; the trees had become shadows against the evening sky. I sat in my prayer room, remembering and crying. Whenever I think about Nett, I cry. She was Rhonda's best friend, the light of her world. Nett was the only person to ever love Rhonda unconditionally. I had to admit that Nett could sometimes be mean and abrasive, but only when she was frustrated. I understood why she was frustrated with her life, herself, and at times, with Rhonda.

Nett was a phenomenal "sight" artist. She could draw anything she could see. She had had dreams of being an artist and had won a scholarship to the city's art school. Her parents were poor immigrant workers who could not afford the ten cents a day she needed for carfare, but Nett was willing to walk the mile to school, regardless of the weather. Nett was responsible for her younger brother, George. Each morning she would get up and fix George's breakfast and get him ready for school. And each morning, George would freak out when Nett tried to leave for school. He would follow her out of the house and into the street. It would take her three or four attempts to get him calmed down. By the time she did, she was late for school. After three weeks of this routine, she was informed that if she could not get to classes on time, she would lose her scholarship. Eventually, Nett had to drop out of school and go to work.

Much of Nett's adult life revolved around Rhonda's father. She had spent years and years trying to build their relationship and maintain their marriage. When that didn't work out, Nett seemed to lose all hope for herself and for her life.

Thinking about Nett and her failed dreams made me sad. Nett knew what it was like to watch your dreams go up in smoke. She also knew what it felt like to have a special talent and be unable to use it. If it had not been for Nett, Rhonda never would have known that she was smart or that she could move beyond the experiences she had lived through. Sometimes Nett would become frustrated with Rhonda and tell her,

"You're not trying; you've got to keep on trying until you can't try any-more." Boy, did I miss her. I was sure Rhonda missed her, too. I'm sorry that Nett never got to see me make it. I know she would have been ex-cited.

Daddy never got excited about anything. I remembered the day Rhonda told her father that she was going to be initiated into the priest-hood of the Yoruba culture.

"That's nice. What is it?" he asked. Rhonda explained that it was like becoming a minister. In this case, instead of going to seminary, you had to undergo a seven-day initiation process, followed by a year of study and apprenticeship.

"Why in the world would you want to do something like that?" Daddy asked without looking up from the potato he was peeling.

"It feels good to me. For the first time in my life, I think I understand God in a way that makes me feel good. Yoruba helped me do that. All of my life, I wanted to know God in a way that didn't scare me out of my wits."

"That's good," Daddy said. "That's very good. But how come you can do this Yoruba stuff, but you can't come to the temple with me?"

Around the time that Rhonda had separated from John, Daddy had become a disciple of Paramahansa Yogananda. He had changed his name and diet, and went to temple three times a week. Daddy had taken his grandchildren with him on several occasions, but Rhonda always re-fused to go. Maybe it was the strange noises Daddy made when he did his breathing and meditation exercises. Maybe it was because he stood on his head a lot now. Whatever the reason, Rhonda knew that yoga and East-ern philosophy did not ring in her soul. It was the African energy that ex-cited her. She loved the music and the mystery that Yoruba offered, and she told Daddy so.

That was the first time Rhonda and her father ever had an actual conversation. They talked about the differences between Eastern, West-ern, and African philosophy. They talked about God, karma, and rein-carnation. They argued, debated, and yelled. He conceded some points to her. She conceded some to him. He agreed that African culture had been widely misrepresented throughout the world, and that African people had the oldest recorded spiritual history. But he was less than thrilled that his daughter was involved in something he couldn't spell, let alone pronounce.

"Do they cremate?" Daddy asked.

"I sure hope not," she answered. "Who wants to be burned? Not me. I am not that fond of fire."

Daddy became reflective. "I want to be cremated."

Rhonda was stunned. "Are you serious? Why are you talking about that?"

"Make sure that Edna and Ma have me cremated."

Rhonda stood up to leave. She was ready to walk out.

"Ronnie, sit down; shut up and listen." Rhonda had never heard that gentle, yet stern, tone in her father's voice before.

"I know I have never told you this before, but I think it's time. God and only God knows why you are here. God has something for you to do, and God knows, I don't know what that is. What I do know is that you can do anything you want if you put God first in your life. It doesn't matter what you call God, or if you know God the African way. Just put Him first."

"How do you know God is a He?" Rhonda asked. Daddy thought about it a moment.

"I don't know, and neither does anyone else."

Rhonda was in a state of shock and disbelief. Daddy had become a philosopher. Not only that, but thirty years into her life, he was sharing his philosophy with her. This was new. This was different. It made her very uncomfortable. Daddy said he wished he'd known earlier that God had something for him to do. He sounded remorseful, yet deeply reflective. He was making Rhonda very nervous.

"So, are you coming to my ceremony? This is a very big step in my life." Rhonda wanted Daddy to be there and was disappointed, but not surprised, at his response.

"I don't think so. I mean, when is it? I can't. I have to go to temple."

One of the many spiritualists whom Rhonda had sought out told her that it was her destiny to be a minister. She never dreamed it would be in the African tradition. The only ministers she had ever known were the ones she'd seen at Grandma's church. She had stopped going to church as a young woman, because she was still a "sinner." According to the Holiness church, everything was a sin. Rhonda got tired of ministers telling her that she was going to burn in hell for smoking, for wearing nail polish, and most of all for having and enjoying sex. She figured if she left Jesus alone, Jesus would leave her alone.

To be a Yoruba meant that you did not go to church. All of your spiritual work was done in your home or the homes of other priests. It meant that your Bible was the Oracle of Ifa, the sacred scriptures of the Yoruba people, which predated the Christian Bible by two thousand years. It also meant that you had to study about herbs, planets, numbers, and all sorts of things that Grandma's church frowned upon. Rhonda didn't care; she would risk going to hell if it meant getting her soul in order. To be a Yoruba priest, Rhonda was told, meant learning how to be whole, mind, body, and spirit, and how to minister to the whole person. You must know how life and the universe of life function. You must understand that life is more than what we can see; life is tangible and intangible, with visible and invisible spheres of energy. It is the priest's job to help people maintain their balance on all the levels of life.

Of the seven-day initiation process, the actual ceremony took only three. The other four days were spent listening, learning, and resting. During this time, Rhonda was occupied with ritual bathing and praying. If someone wasn't washing her, they were praying over her. If they weren't praying, they were giving her something to eat, drink, or wear on her neck, wrists, or ankles. She was a *yawo,* a baby. It was a time when the elder priests were glad for her and with her and waited on her hand and foot. Rhonda had never seen so many people willing to serve her and happy that she was alive. When the seven days were over, she went home dressed in white from head to toe. She would wear white every day for the next year. It was after she got home that the dreams and the voices resumed.

Rhonda's dreams became clearer and more exciting each night. She remembered most of them, but some of her dreams moved so fast she couldn't remember anything when she woke up exhausted. Three months after the initiation, Rhonda had a series of dreams that were of great significance.

In the first dream, the doorbell rang, and Rhonda went downstairs to answer the door. Standing outside was the image of death. It was a tall figure, dressed in a hooded black cape. It had no face. When Rhonda slammed the door on the image and turned to walk back up the stairs to her apartment, the figure was standing at the top of the stairs. It walked into her apartment and closed the door. Rhonda sat straight up in bed; she was wide-awake. She jumped out of bed and ran through the house, looking for the image. She was standing in the kitchen when she realized she'd been dreaming. Her heart was beating wildly, her mouth was dry, and she was shaking like a leaf.

The next night she had a similar dream. This time, the figure was standing at her apartment door when she opened it. Startled, she stepped back. The figure moved through her body, down the hall, and into the children's room. Again, Rhonda awoke in a panic. She ran to check on the children. The children were fine. She left the light on in their room, and instead of going back to bed, she prayed. Rhonda prayed in every language and faith she knew. She asked Daddy's Yogananda to help her. She asked Grandma's Jesus to help her. She prayed at her altar and asked the ancestors to help her. Someone, she knew, was getting ready to die. It couldn't be Nett, who was now eating on her own and walking and talking. It's Damon, she thought. Something is going to happen to Damon. Rhonda promised God that she would pray and fast for three days in order to receive a message. She needed to know what to do to save her son. She never went back to bed, and she refused to let Damon out of the house all day.

The next night, Rhonda had the most frightening dream of all. This time when the doorbell rang, the image of death was standing over her bed, staring at her. She was paralyzed with fear. "Yea, though I walk through the valley of the shadow of death. Yea, though I walk through the valley of the shadow of death." Rhonda was screaming and crying in her sleep; tears were streaming down her face. The ringing bedside phone woke her up. "Hello!" she screamed into the receiver.

"Ronnie?" It was Edna, Daddy's wife.

"Sorry for yelling," Rhonda said weakly. "I was having a bad dream." She tried to calm herself down, but the image was still vivid.

"I've got some bad news. Your daddy is dead."

Without waking her children, Rhonda dressed herself in her white clothes, jumped in her green car with the one brown door, and made it to Daddy's house in record time.

He looked like he was asleep. Daddy was lying on the bed, his arms folded across his chest. Edna said she had gone to temple, and when she returned, she had found him just as he was. She tried to wake him, and when she couldn't, she went in the kitchen and made herself a cup of tea. When she returned to the bedroom, she found the note:

> Dear Ed,
>   Please tell Ma I'm sorry. I am sorry.
>   Harry

That's when she realized he was dead.

Edna was pretty calm, and so was Rhonda. But Daddy's five children were anything but calm. As soon as Rhonda would get one quieted down, another one would start up. When the children were finally all calm at the same time, Rhonda and Edna sat them down and served them tea and juice. After the medics arrived, pronounced Daddy dead, and covered his face, all the children fell apart again. Rhonda stared into the bedroom, trying to comprehend what was going on within her. *My father is dead. I am sitting here looking at my dead father, and I am as cool as a cucumber. What does this mean?*

Rhonda had been at Daddy's house for twelve hours before the medical examiner's office came to remove the body. Before they arrived, neighbors and friends came and went. Each one voiced their shock as they crept into the bedroom to look at Daddy; and each one expressed some version of "He doesn't even look like he's dead. He looks like he's asleep." The landlord came, the mailman and the garbage man came, and neighbors from every floor in the building came by for a peek.

When Grandma arrived, Rhonda braced herself. She wasn't sure how Grandma would react, and she wasn't sure what she would do if Grandma broke down. Like everyone else, Grandma crept into the room and stood silently at the foot of the bed where her only son lay dead. She shook her head from side to side, then put her hands over her mouth. Her voice was muffled, but Rhonda could clearly hear her say, "He looks like he's asleep." Slowly, Grandma walked out of the room and into the kitchen, where she spent the rest of the day greeting people and ushering them through the apartment.

Ray never went beyond the kitchen. When they took the body bag out of the bedroom and out of the apartment, Ray stayed in the bathroom. Nett, of course, did not come by.

Rhonda sat on the sofa the entire day, refusing Edna's insistent request to go get her children "so they could see Grandpa" before they took him away. Rhonda was trying to find some sense of grief or loss somewhere in her body or in her mind. She sat there, trying to cry for her father. When Edna announced that there would be no autopsy, Rhonda agreed. Still, she did not feel a sense of loss at the thought of strangers dissecting her father's lifeless body. He was, after all, a yogi, a disciple of sorts, and it really didn't matter why he was dead, he was dead. According to his faith, an autopsy was unnecessary. Besides that, they all knew how and why he died. They knew, but no one said a word.

The next day when she got the call that she would have to go to the morgue to identify the body, she was angry, not sad.

"Why do I have to go?"

"Because you are the next of kin," Edna said, her voice displaying her attitude.

"Well, you're his wife." Edna was silent because she knew Rhonda knew the truth.

"What time do we have to go?"

"Sometime before noon."

"I'll pick you up at 10:30. Did you tell them about the autopsy?"

"That's why we have to get there before twelve so that you can sign for the body before they start cutting on him. I found the cup with the stuff in it."

"What stuff?"

"I don't know what it is. Whatever herbs he mixed together. He went out to the park the other day and brought back all this stuff he said he wanted to bathe in." Edna's voice was starting to waver. "I should have known what he was doing. It was too much stuff to bathe in. He knew all along that . . ." Feeling her chest begin to tighten, Rhonda cut Edna off.

"There is no way you could have known what he was doing. He was always mixing herbs and stuff. I'll pick you up at 10:30." Without saying good-bye, Rhonda hung up, and still she didn't cry.

The waiting room at the morgue was freezing. Perhaps, Rhonda thought, that is why the attendant looked like he too should be lying in one of the boxes. She told him her name and the reason for her visit.

"I've come to identify the body of my father, Horace Harris."

"I don't think he's back yet."

"Excuse me?"

"I don't think . . . Wait. Black male, sixty-four or so."

"Horace Harris." Without responding, the attendant stood up and walked from behind his desk. Several minutes later they heard rumbling. It stopped. The black curtain on the floor-to-ceiling glass door in the room was ripped open to reveal a gurney. On the gurney was a body, covered by a white sheet.

"Over here. Come over here," the attendant called out to them. Edna didn't move. Rhonda walked up to the glass.

"Are you ready? Let me know when you are done," the attendant said as he pulled the sheet back and walked away in one move.

Now he looked dead. Rhonda could see the dried blood on the side of his head. She could see the stitches behind his ear and on his chest. Turning to Edna, who still hadn't moved, Rhonda asked, "Did you tell them no autopsy?"

"They're not supposed to do it until you identify the body."

"It's done. It's already done." Rhonda walked back to the attendant.

"Who gave you permission to cut his body up?" Rolling his eyes in her direction, then peering over his shoulder, the attendant shoved a clipboard in Rhonda's direction.

"Sign here. Your name and your relationship." Without saying a word she signed the papers and left.

Running up behind Rhonda, Edna asked, "What do you think they will find?"

"Nothing. If my father mixed a batch of herbs to kill himself, they will never detect it in his system."

Even at the thought that Daddy had taken his own life, Rhonda could not shed a tear. Several weeks later, when she received the death certificate, the cause of death was listed as inconclusive.

The plans for the funeral were, at first, elaborate. Cars, flowers, and a boat to carry his ashes up the Chesapeake Bay. But Daddy hadn't worked steadily in a long time. He had no money and no insurance. Because of his discharge status, he was not entitled to any veteran's benefits. When the family realized that there was little, if any, money to bury him, the plans were scaled down drastically. Rhonda withdrew every penny she had in her bank account to help bury her father. She called friends to furnish the flowers and the food.

Rhonda didn't attend the wake, preferring instead to stay in the apartment and prepare the food. When friends and relatives arrived, Rhonda had everything ready. Many of the relatives had not seen Rhonda since the card parties in Aunt Nadine's basement and the summers in Atlantic City. Some seemed surprised that Rhonda had survived to grow up. They were delighted that she had children. When she told them that she was now an African minister, they said, "That's nice. What does that mean?"

Rhonda did attend Daddy's funeral. She sat in the front row, holding onto Damon, Gemmia, and Nisa, who were very upset. Grandpa had been good to them. Rhonda showed and felt very little emotion through the ceremony, even when Grandma broke down and cried out loud.

When it was all over, she went home and waited to feel something to cry about. It never happened.

Three days after the funeral, Rhonda had what she thought was a dream. The doorbell rang late one night after she had gone to bed. She thought she was dreaming and ignored the bell. When it rang again, she got up, put on her robe, and walked to the window. She looked out, saw no one, and went back to bed. The doorbell rang again. This time she went downstairs to open the door only to again find no one there. Had her feet not been so cold, she would have believed that she was indeed dreaming. She went back upstairs into her apartment and shut the door. As she passed the kitchen, she noticed that the light was on. She saw Daddy sitting at the kitchen table, holding a pencil.

She wasn't afraid or even shocked. "Daddy," she called out to him. He turned to look at her. "What are you doing here? You know that you cannot be here, Daddy. You must leave here right now." Daddy put his pencil down, stood up and disappeared right before her eyes. The next morning, when Rhonda awoke, the light was still on in the kitchen and the pencil was still on the table where Daddy had left it.

A week later, Edna called to find out how Rhonda and the kids were doing. She said that while she was packing Daddy's things, she had found a few items that she thought Rhonda might like to have. It took Rhonda a week to get up the courage to retrieve the pile of papers that had been rubber-banded together. On the top of the pile was a handwritten note. Rhonda decided to wait until she got back home to go through everything. Sitting at her kitchen table, she removed the rubber band and read the note that Edna had placed on top:

> Dear Ronnie,
> Thank you. If you ever need me, this is for you.
> 913 319 510 326 306 105 700 976.

Each number represented an address, a birthday or some significant date in her or her father's life. The *700,* for instance, was from the license plate number of the Cadillac Daddy bought after Rhonda had given him the numbers she got from Sarah in her dream. That was the clue that told her exactly what to do with the numbers. Whenever she needed money, Rhonda would go to the Off-Track Betting Office and place a bet on the Exacta, just like Daddy had taught her. It never failed; she always won.

I was ready now to leave the prayer room and get back into a tub of hot water and rose oil. It was just what I needed. Rhonda's father never gave her roses. He never gave her a compliment. At the time of his death, he had never put his arms around her and told her that he loved her, or that she was his pretty little girl. Rhonda's father abused and neglected her, and still she loved him unconditionally. Rhonda didn't know it, but I knew it.

I knew that Rhonda spent so much time being angry with her father for what he had and had not done, she never took the opportunity to appreciate who he was. Daddy was a wounded little boy doing his best to raise his little girl. He could not do for her what had not been done for himself. He had never been taught how to love and therefore did not know how to express love to his children or to himself. I know that he did the best that he could. I could get into a tub of hot water and cry the tears that Rhonda couldn't shed. She didn't know about judgment and forgiveness. She didn't know about unconditional love. Rhonda had spent her life yearning for something she already had: the best her father could give.

Unconditional love does not mean that you accept or condone mistreatment. It does not mean you excuse people their faults and frailties. It does mean you see them, accept them, and love them, despite the things you may not like about them. If Rhonda had known that, she could have learned to laugh with her daddy, to have fun with him when he was available. When he was not available to her, she would not have blamed herself. She would not have believed that she lacked anything she needed to get love.

Rhonda loved her daddy unconditionally. That is why she never talked badly about her father. That is why she kept trying to get his attention. When you give love, you want to feel that it is being reciprocated.

What Rhonda didn't know was that love does not have to come from the place or in the same manner you give it. Nett was the love Daddy could not give. Ruth, Eddie, and her children were expressions of love. God's love. Rhonda did not realize that no matter how bad it got, something or someone always came along to lift her up and love her. Not because she was special, but because she was lovable. Love always begets love. After all that she had been through in her life, she was not a violent, vicious, or malicious person. She always found someone to help, someone to love. She was so fixated on getting love in a certain way, from a particular person, she missed the love that was all around her. It was never enough. She could have filled the void by celebrating the love she was, and the love she had.

Rhonda had been taught love and loving require doing and getting. If you do this, you will get love. If you don't do this, you will lose love. She learned that love was a bargain, when in fact, love is a principle. It is a state of being that we experience as what we do and how we do it. Because most of the people in Rhonda's life inflicted pain on her, she closely associated love with pain, whether mental, emotional, or physical. Love hurt Rhonda. As a result, when she loved someone, she would hurt herself rather than hurt them.

As the scent of the rose oil filled the steamy bathroom, I was beginning to get clearer. I had been bargaining with Karen. I was doing and getting rather than loving unconditionally. She had shown up at a time in my life when I was in need. She was a tool being used by God to fulfill a need; she was a sign of God's love. I didn't owe Karen anything but love. And I did not have to be hurt to give her love. She was loving me in the only way she knew how, and it was up to me to determine whether or not it worked in my life. If it didn't, I could love her and let her go, without malice or anger. I did not have to feel bad or get hurt in order to get what I wanted. All I had to do was love. Now I understood how that related to Rhonda and Daddy, and even to Karen and myself. What I didn't understand was John. What in the world was Rhonda doing with John? I let my body ease down into the hot water in the tub before starting down that path.

The white clothes Rhonda wore during her first years in the priesthood always attracted people's attention. Drunks on the street asked her to pray for them. Catholics asked if she were fulfilling a "promise." Many of her Christian friends said they would pray that she didn't burn in hell. Her colleagues in law school were too busy writing briefs or studying for the bar to notice what she was wearing. Rhonda was adjusting well to being back in law school. Nett was getting stronger, and the children were doing well. She was studying spirituality and feeling good in the process. And Rhonda had a new beau.

Adeyemi was Rhonda's childhood sweetheart. She had fallen in love with him when she was thirteen years old. He was dating her girlfriend at the time, and Rhonda had learned to let her love for him lie dormant, believing they would never be together. Rhonda had kept up with Adeyemi through the years and knew that he was married and had five children. He had created a life of community work and political activism. He and his wife had been separated for about a year when Rhonda and he began working on a project together. Their working relationship soon developed into something more intimate. Adeyemi knew Rhonda was a priestess and sought her spiritual advice and counseling for his situation at home.

They sat in Adeyemi's car one night after he had driven her home. He asked if he could kiss her. No one had ever asked! "I cannot be in your head and in your bed," Rhonda explained. If he wanted her to counsel him, kissing was out of the question. It took him only a few seconds to choose. A few days later, as they were walking along, he reached out and took her hand in his. No man—not Daddy, Gary, John, or even Ray—had ever held her hand. Rhonda was thirteen again; all the love she had suppressed for eighteen years came rushing to the surface.

Adeyemi's work brought them to Albany, New York. Rhonda was sitting at his desk in the State Capitol, when a secretary told her she had a telephone call. Thinking it was one of the children again, Rhonda answered, "What's the matter now?"

"John is dead," the unknown caller said.

"What?" Rhonda asked.

"I'm sorry. This is Pat, how you doin'? I'm sorry to bother you, but the kids gave me this number." Pat was married to John's cousin Paul.

"You're not bothering me. I just can't believe what you're saying."

"He died yesterday afternoon. He had an asthma attack on the A train."

Rhonda knew that in many ways this was a tragedy. John was only thirty-six years old. He had a new wife and a two-year-old daughter. John was also the father of Rhonda's daughter, Nisa, and he had helped her raise her children. But Rhonda had an irresistible urge to laugh. And as soon as she hung up, she did. When she told Adeyemi why she was laughing, he told her she was a disgrace. So she stopped laughing and started dancing. It was absolutely disgraceful. A priestess dancing all over the hallway of the State Capitol because the man who beat her for seven years was dead. Rhonda's only regret was that she couldn't throw a parade.

By the time she got home, she had regained her composure. She told the children and had difficulty reading their reactions. Nisa started crying, but when she noticed that Damon and Gemmia weren't crying, she stopped. They all knew the truth about their fathers. Rhonda let them decide whether or not they wanted to go to the funeral. They all chose not to go. Rhonda went alone.

She went to the funeral home an hour before the family was scheduled to arrive. The casket was open. John had grown a beard, which Rhonda thought made him look quite distinguished. He was wearing a blue suit, which made him look much older. "This is it," she said to herself. "Let me put an end to this right now." Rhonda knelt down on the cushioned stool at the side of the casket. She looked at the flowers, the walls, and the ceiling; she could not look at his face. She told him exactly how she felt.

"When they told me you had died, I danced. I'm sorry, but I did. I was so glad to be rid of you. But now that I see you lying here, I want you to know how really sorry I am." She lowered her eyes to his face and remembered something she was learning in her priesthood training: Always be grateful.

"Before you go, I wanted to tell you thanks. Thank you for teaching me so much about myself. Thank you for showing me how to defend myself. Thank you for giving me all the time I needed to learn how to take care of myself. I know you didn't know that's what you were doing, and neither did I. Thank you for Nisa. She is my precious baby, and you don't have to worry about her. You know I don't like your mother, but I will make sure Nisa gets to know her. Thank you for all the help you gave me raising my children when their own fathers wouldn't do it. Thank you for the time you got out of bed and came out in the snow to fix the flat tire on the car I would not let you drive. Thank you for teaching Damon how to use his fly. Thank you for trying."

When Rhonda realized tears were rolling down her cheeks, she put her hand on John's hand, took a deep breath, and continued.

"I forgive you. I forgive you. I forgive you. I know that you did the best you could. I forgive you for lying to me and for lying to yourself. I forgive you for abusing me and abusing yourself. I forgive you for all the women you slept with when we were together. I forgive you for leaving me when I was pregnant. I forgive you for all the things you accused me of doing. I forgive you for your inability to see how desperate and wounded I was. I forgive you for everything, and I ask that you forgive me. I forgive you, and I want you to rest."

When Rhonda felt as if she had no more to say, she leaned over and kissed John's cheek. John's mother, Mildred, and her sister Dorothy were coming into the parlor as Rhonda was leaving. Mildred didn't speak at all. Dorothy glared at Rhonda and said snidely, "Well, look what the cat dragged in! What are you supposed to be? We know you ain't no nun."

"I'm sorry for your loss, Millie. How are you, Aunt Dottie?" Before either could respond, Rhonda walked away.

She saw John's wife standing at the entrance to the funeral home.

"I'm Rhonda and I'm sorry for your loss. This is my number. If you ever want the children to get together, please call me." Again, Rhonda walked away without waiting for a response. She stopped just outside the door to see if she had any more tears to shed, tears she did not want to take home. She didn't.

Rhonda almost fainted when she saw a letter taped to the front door of her apartment. She knew the rent was due. But the letter was from the Department of Human Resources and requested that she report to the Federal Office of Investigation to answer charges of welfare fraud.

On her first visit to the office, Rhonda found out that Sharon, Nett's sister, had placed a trace on one of Nett's disability checks. An investigation revealed that the check had been signed and cashed at a time Nett was hospitalized. Rhonda had nothing to hide. She explained that she had cashed the check, just as she had cashed many of her mother's checks, to pay the rent. She told the investigators that she had used the money from the check in question to rent an apartment so that Nett could live with her. Sharon, apparently, had failed to share that information. The investigator informed her that her actions were illegal and that she could possibly go to jail.

Rhonda was explaining that her mother knew she was cashing her checks, when one of the investigators asked, "Where is your mother?"

"She's at home."

"Home where?" Rhonda gave him Nett's address.

"It is our understanding that that is Lynnette Harris's address. We want to know your mother's address."

"I don't understand."

"Mrs. Harris's sister has informed us that Mrs. Harris is not your mother. She is your stepmother."

Rhonda turned Nett's favorite color of "puke green." They offered her some water. When she refused, she was told to return in two weeks with a copy of the lease and proof that Nett had lived with her. Rhonda went directly to Nett's house.

"Did you know that Sharon is trying to have me arrested?" Nett was silent. "Do you know that if I get arrested, I cannot practice law in the State of New York?"

"Sharon wants her money back. She needs her money." Nett was referring to the money her sister had willingly contributed to the private-duty nurses hired to care for Nett.

"She's trying to ruin my life! If I am arrested on a federal forgery charge, I cannot practice law!"

"She needs her money, and blood is thicker than water."

Rhonda was speechless. The only thing she could do was stare at the woman sitting in the wheelchair before her. This was not the Nett she had known and loved. This was a woman who would not, could not see her. This was not the Nett who had kissed her, cared for her, stood by her, and had promised Rhonda she would someday be somebody. To keep herself from feeling too bad, Rhonda told herself that she did not know who this person was.

"I've got to go," Rhonda said, trying to decide if she should kiss this woman good-bye.

"Okay," Nett said. "Would you ask Damon to bring me some pizza?" Rhonda left without responding.

I slid further down into the tub and remembered how hard Rhonda had prayed that night. Once again, her heart had been pierced. She hadn't heard anything about her mother in so long, she actually *believed* that Nett was her mother. The mind is wonderful. It lets us believe whatever we need to believe in order to survive. It can block out pain and information that might send us into overload, or shut us down. Rhonda's mind had blocked out a great deal of information. Now, as she began to pray for clarity and guidance, the information surfaced. But she still had not learned to accurately discern it. Rhonda was still looking on the outside. The truth she needed was on the inside.

Father forgive them, for they know not what they do! She was being punished. Not by other people, but by herself. Rhonda was not punishing herself for anything she had done but for what she believed. She still believed that she deserved to be punished. She still believed that she was not worthy of love. What Sharon had done reinforced what Rhonda believed about herself. I could clearly see another pattern that had emerged in Rhonda's life. It was a covert pattern of which Rhonda was unaware. In order for something good to happen, something bad had to happen first. During the times when Rhonda should have been her happiest, there was always something bad lurking in the shadows. She would not allow herself to enjoy the fruits of her labor.

I sat straight up in the bathtub, splashing water over the rim and onto the floor. That's it! Oh my God! That's it! I am too successful! My books are doing too well; I am doing too well. Rhonda feels she doesn't deserve to do well. She has to be punished. Rather than being able to fully enjoy what I am doing, I place myself in situations in which I feel bad. In which I cannot be happy. Oh my God! This thing with Karen is a covert pattern that sabotages my own happiness. As long as I am unhappy about Karen, what she does, what she does not do, and how I think she treats me, I am not happy, and Rhonda is being punished.

Then I realized that somehow Rhonda must have realized that she was reacting according to the pattern. Perhaps it was the praying, or her deep desire to prove herself to other people. Perhaps it was that her mind was changing, and she realized that she did not have to be punished. I knew I was close to the answer. I had to remember what happened next.

Rhonda returned to the Federal Office of Investigation with the papers they had requested. They told her to have a seat; they couldn't find her file. They looked for hours, and the file was never found. They told her she was free to go. Rhonda was relieved. But she was still hurt by the whole affair, and it affected her law school graduation. Like her graduation from college, the ceremony was anticlimactic. Because Rhonda had gone to law school for the wrong reasons, graduation did not bring her the fulfillment she was seeking. So many people had doubted that she could ever make it, and she had proved them wrong. But Daddy was dead, and Nett was too ill to attend. So neither of them was present to witness her accomplishment.

The three years of law school had been grueling. Rhonda hardly had the strength to celebrate. Constant money problems had taken their toll. Trying to understand briefs and motions and Supreme Court cases was mentally and physically exhausting. Trying to remember all of the things she was supposed to know about being a priest, and constant worry about Nett, even after the betrayal, had added to the heavy burden she carried with her all through school.

The children were ecstatic. Their mother was going to be a lawyer! They were famous people on the block. Rhonda knew she was "famous" in their minds, but that wasn't enough, because she blamed herself for what she had put them through. Watching them get dressed on the morning of graduation, Rhonda wondered if it had all been worth it. Damon and Gemmia had after-school jobs and were handling most of the household bills. Nisa, who was trying her best to get through puberty, was having a great deal of trouble. She had a reading disability and was falling behind in school. She needed her mother in a way that Damon and Gemmia never had. Rhonda had had neither the presence of mind nor the ability to give her the nurturing and support she craved. Rhonda had never learned how to do that. She had only learned the rules.

Adeyemi was wandering. Every now and then, he would have a little fling, and each time he did, Rhonda would find out about it. They had tried living together, but in the end, Rhonda moved out on her own. Their relationship was changing, and it was frightening to her to realize that many things in her life had changed significantly. Graduation from law school meant things were about to change even more. She wasn't sure how much more change she could take.

Rhonda was offered a job in Philadelphia. She wanted to go, but she didn't want to leave Nett. Adeyemi didn't want to leave New York. He didn't want to be that far from his children, and he was in school at Lincoln University. Rhonda had many decisions to make. Graduation meant that she didn't have long to make them.

She spent most of the summer studying for the bar exam. Once it was over, she asked Nett if she wanted to move to Philadelphia. She was sad but relieved when Nett said she didn't want to go. Again, Nett understood that Rhonda had to get on with her life. Rhonda understood that she had to put some distance between herself and Nett, for her own good.

The month before Rhonda was to move to Philadelphia, Adeyemi decided he was going to give his marriage another try. Rhonda had seen it coming this time, but she did everything in her power to avoid it.

"All of the things I have learned in our relationship, I need to share with her," Adeyemi explained. "She stayed with me for fifteen years. She is a habit that is hard for me to break. I know that if you and I are meant to be together, we will be. But for right now, my wife and my children are what I need."

Rhonda sat on the edge of her bed and stared at the man she had loved since she was thirteen. She knew he was leaving and that all she could do was cry.

"Don't do that. Please. You have so much good ahead of you. Don't cry. You have to believe that this is for the best."

She did not believe that at all. She believed that he was a dog, a pig. He was just another in a long line of men who had used her, then dumped her. She didn't say any of that to him; she just cried.

There always comes a time of elimination. The earth sheds each year. The trees and flowers let go of their identity. As the old identity dies, a new identity is born. The body sheds constantly. Some of it happens invisibly, so naturally and silently that we do not realize it is happening. The heart and the spirit also shed. They shed the emotions and experiences that we no longer need. They shed the things that stunt our growth. This, too, is an invisible process. Yet because of the energy involved, the emotional energy, we often feel the emotional and spiritual shedding. It feels as if we are dying. We are. Just like the flowers and the trees, we are dying to an old identity. This shedding, or death, is not the end of us. It is the beginning.

CHAPTER FOURTEEN

What's the Lesson When You Have Mastered All the Wrong Lessons?

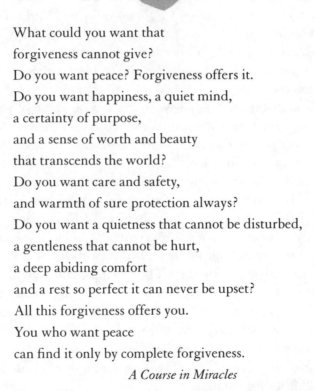

What could you want that
forgiveness cannot give?
Do you want peace? Forgiveness offers it.
Do you want happiness, a quiet mind,
a certainty of purpose,
and a sense of worth and beauty
that transcends the world?
Do you want care and safety,
and warmth of sure protection always?
Do you want a quietness that cannot be disturbed,
a gentleness that cannot be hurt,
a deep abiding comfort
and a rest so perfect it can never be upset?
All this forgiveness offers you.
You who want peace
can find it only by complete forgiveness.

A Course in Miracles

1. Not asking for what I want.
2. Not saying exactly what I mean.

3. Not saying things when I think it will upset other people.
4. Not telling the truth.
5. Telling only half of the truth.
6. Not honoring (paying attention, acting on the basis of) what I know is true.
7. Waiting too long to tell the truth that I know.
8. Not saying anything when I have something to say.
9. Doing what will cause me the least amount of pain or discomfort. Also known as taking the easy way out.
10. Asking other people what they think I should do.
11. Being overly concerned with what other people say about me.
12. Being overly concerned with what other people think about me.
13. Not asking for help when I need it.
14. Waiting until the last minute to ask for help.
15. Waiting until the last minute.
16. Doing things I believe will make people like me.
17. Needing to be liked to my own self-detriment.
18. Being afraid to say no.
19. Staying in a situation when I know it is causing me pain.
20. Ignoring the pain in fear of losing a familiar situation.
21. Taking on more than I can possibly do (so that people will like me).
22. Not keeping my word (because I have taken on more than I can possibly do).
23. Not exercising every day.
24. Trying to control people and situations when I believe I can get hurt.
25. Not having a constructive way to express anger.
26. Being afraid to express anger.
27. Believing that I should not get angry.
28. Making decisions in fear.
29. Making decisions that I believe will bring material rewards only.
30. Not acknowledging the consequences of my decisions.
31. Not taking the time to assess all options available.
32. Doing things the same way I have always done things.

33. Not paying attention to the way I do things.
34. Being afraid to admit that I know what to do.
35. Acting like I don't know what to do.
36. Letting other people believe and treat me like I don't know what to do.
37. Allowing myself to be pressured into making decisions based on what others think I should do.
38. Being afraid to make a mistake.
39. Being afraid that a mistake cannot be rectified.
40. Feeling afraid that I want too much.
41. Trying to be like everyone else.
42. Being afraid to be myself.
43. Not trusting myself.

I acknowledge that there are things that I do which are not in my own best interest. I forgive myself for doing the things I have done that are not in my own best interest.

I acknowledge that, most of the time, I have no conscious awareness of the things I do that are not in my best interest. I forgive myself for being unaware of the things that I do that are not in my own best interest.

I acknowledge that when I have been consciously aware that my actions were not in my best interest, I chose, in response to the fear I experienced, to continue the course of action. I forgive myself for choosing in response to fear.

I acknowledge that I have been an active, although unconscious, participant in the creation of pain and discomfort in my life and the lives of others. I forgive myself for unconscious participation in the creation of pain and discomfort for myself and others.

I acknowledge that there are occasions on which I have been an active and conscious participant in the creation of pain and discomfort in my life and in the lives of others. I forgive myself for conscious participation in the creation of pain and discomfort for myself and for others.

I acknowledge that I have made conscious choices and decisions being aware that the decision or the choice was not in my own best interest, but in pursuit of monetary gain or reward. I forgive myself for placing the value of money before my best interest.

I acknowledge that when I experience fear, I do not tell the truth. I forgive myself for not telling the truth under all circumstances.

I acknowledge that I have allowed myself to believe things about myself that are not true. I forgive myself for believing things about myself that are not true.

I acknowledge that I have been angry with myself for not being able to change my behavior. I forgive myself for being angry with myself.

I acknowledge that I have been angry with others and held them responsible for my inability to change myself. I forgive myself for being angry with others. I forgive myself for holding others responsible for my actions and my life.

I acknowledge that I am a child of God. I acknowledge that I am valuable, worthy, and lovable. I acknowledge that God is the source and the center of my life. I acknowledge that only God can change the false beliefs I have held about myself. I acknowledge that my acknowledgment of God can and will heal the wounds I have experienced as a result of false beliefs, fear-based choices and decisions, anger-based choices and decisions, and ignorance of God's sovereignty in my life. I forgive myself totally and unconditionally. I now ask the Holy Spirit of God to heal my wounds, to eliminate all false beliefs I have held, and to open my heart to true unconditional love.

For all I have received and all that is about to come, I am so grateful!

It was so clear—all of the wrong lessons that Rhonda had learned, and how they had influenced her life. All of the crap she had held onto and believed and acted upon because she did not know any better. I understood how her patterns, the patterns that had been etched into Rhonda's consciousness, had become a part of my life. I also realized that until I acknowledged those patterns, until I could see them and accept them, there would be no way I could heal them. And until I healed them, I would continue to experience their effect on my life, consciously and unconsciously.

I wondered to myself if what I had discovered was true for everyone. I wondered how many people walk around totally unaware that there is another person, another level in their being, that is in total conflict with the ever-emerging newness unfolding through their consciousness. How many people realize that there is an "old you" that has never forgotten? The old you has made choices and judgments of which the "new you" may be totally unaware.

The old you is still afraid of things that the new you has long forgotten or never remembered. The old you has attachments based upon survival needs and fear, while the new you is courageously trying to break free and grow. The old you has found a comfortable place, a way of being, a safe place, and will fight to stay within that comfort zone. The new you recognizes the need to take risks, to move beyond the familiar, and is willing to do so. When the two states of consciousness are in conflict, the experience is frustration. "Why does this keep happening?" we ask. "Why can't I seem to move beyond this place, this experience?" That had been my experience. I wondered if the same were true for everyone else.

I felt a little embarrassed and a little ashamed. How can I run around trying to heal the world when I am still so wounded? Isn't that being dishonest? When I thought about it for a moment, I remembered what my godfather taught me, "You can only teach what you need to learn." Then something Maya Angelou wrote came to mind: "Take a day to heal yourself, and then go and heal somebody else." Realizing how much I have learned, how much healing I have done, I knew that I had nothing to be ashamed of. All that I learn, I teach. All that I teach opens the way for deeper learning. Although it seemed that I was learning the same lesson over and over, I realized it was at a deeper level each time. Each level held a new way of looking at things. Each level offered an opportunity to put a theory into practice as a teaching tool and a standard of learning.

Rhonda had mastered all of the wrong lessons. She was a master of living in pain, struggling for recognition, dishonoring herself, and covering up what she was feeling. She was trying to get my attention. Unfortunately, she had mastered the art of attracting negative attention. Attention that caused her more pain. Attention that further dishonored and devalued her. Unconsciously, I had embraced her patterns. I had failed to recognize and acknowledge them as they played out in my life.

Rhonda had no concept of who Iyanla was. The life Iyanla knew had unfolded moment by moment, as a function of her faith and what she believed about herself. In many of those moments, I, Iyanla, found myself running to catch up with my life. Things were growing and unfolding faster than I could imagine. Rhonda, the old me, was also running, trying to catch up. She did not want to be left again. More important, Rhonda was trying to figure out what was going on. Iyanla's experiences were totally foreign to her. Loving, caring people surrounded Iyanla, because that is what she believed she deserved. Rhonda never knew love that was not attached to pain and suffering. Iyanla has an abundance of good things. Rhonda was taught not to expect good, and that she did not deserve to have anything good. In response to what she had been taught, Rhonda expected the worst, and usually, that is what she experienced.

Finally, I understood why Karen had come into my life. She had come to help me heal Rhonda. She had come to show me what Rhonda believed and to give me an opportunity for a deeper level of healing. I had not done a good job of integrating Rhonda's experiences with Iyanla's experiences. I had not honored the role that Rhonda had played in Iyanla's emerging life. Had it not been for Rhonda, Iyanla never would have been born. I needed to forgive myself for ignoring her and for being mad at Karen. I also needed to go back and see how the breakdown between Rhonda's consciousness and Iyanla's consciousness had occurred. Before I could do that, I needed to give Iyanla a little boost.

There is something magical that occurs when a woman turns forty. She becomes more attractive in a sensual and seductive way. It's not that her body gets better, but I think she becomes more comfortable with her body and learns how to maneuver it better. At forty, a woman's eyes begin to sparkle. Not with lust or excitement, but with wisdom. She has seen some things, done some things, and learned some things that show through her eyes. At forty, although there are things on a woman's body that lie down, at the same time, other things stand out. They become clear. A forty-year-old woman finds her voice, gets her vision and her footing. When I turned forty, I became too old to try to be somebody else, so I stopped trying.

As I thought about it, I realized that I didn't have any sense at all until I turned forty. At twenty-three, I thought I had all of the answers. When I turned forty, I realized that I had no idea what the question was. My life coach once told me that whatever shows up in your life is the answer. You job is to figure out the question. I had lived through many abrupt, harsh answers. At forty, I was committed to remembering the question. For me, the main question I had lived my life trying to find an answer to was, "Why can't people love me the way I want to be loved?" At forty, the answer magically popped into my head, *"Because you don't know how to love yourself!"*

I had read a great deal about learning to love yourself. I had all types of formulas, writing exercises, and physical activities that were offered as surefire ways to bring about my loving essence. Most of them worked for a while, but in the crunch, I was the first one to turn on me. I was the first one to beat up on me. To doubt me. To judge and criticize me. How do you learn to do something you have never experienced? I discovered that you must first find out what love looks like and feels like when it is offered in an unconditional way. The only experience of unconditional love I remembered was what I had experienced when I was praying.

In the midst of deep prayer, I could feel the coolness, calm, and peace of God's presence. Based on everything I had heard and read, that presence was love. I decided to find a way to stay in that presence. To re-create it time and time again, regardless of where I was, or what I was doing. I remembered something that my friend Shaheerah had once told me. She said, "It is not necessary to re-create something you have experienced. If you simply remember it, if you allow yourself to remember what the experience felt like, you can have the same experience wherever you are, whenever you want to have it." I decided that was what I wanted to do, to re-create love within and for myself. It took two years for me to figure out how to re-create that love experience. By my forty-second birthday, I had a plan.

There were many women in my life who had loved me unconditionally. They had seen my life go up and down. They knew most, if not all, of the sordid details of my life. No matter where I was, or what I was going through, I could call on these women, and they would be there for me. These were women I told the truth, because I knew no matter what, they would stand by me. I learned that telling the truth was a big part of loving yourself. You must respect and trust yourself enough to know that no matter what you do, you are worthy of love and support. I had been blessed with friends who had loved me in my most insane moments. I needed the blessing, love, and support of these women as I moved forward in my life.

I had once read that life takes place in seven-year cycles. Every seven years, the focus and energy shifts in your life. From birth to seven years, the beginning of life, you are learning how to live. How to breathe on your own, to walk, talk, eat, and essentially, how to take care of your basic needs. From eight years to fourteen years, you are learning what works and what doesn't work, based on what you have been taught and what you have experienced. Fifteen to twenty-one years is a time of testing. Now that you have some idea of what works, you are testing yourself and your concepts and ideas in order to determine if what you have discovered is true. Twenty-two to twenty-eight years is a time of reevaluation. Now that you know what works and what doesn't, what is true for you and what is not, you must find new or improved ways of being. You must now break the pattern or remain loyal to it, regardless of the outcome.

Twenty-nine to thirty-five are the hard years. This is when your concepts about yourself, about life, and about how to live are put to the test—again. Life is going to test you to see if you really know and believe what you say you know and believe. Most of us still know only what we have been taught and told. We may think we are doing something else, but what really happens is that our subconscious patterns begin to emerge. Thirty-six to forty-two is the healing cycle. Because we have now seen our patterns and subconscious beliefs come to life, we must decide what we will carry forward and what we will not. At forty-two, I had seen enough! I had seen what the lack of love had done in my life, and I did not want to carry that into the next life cycle. I had seen what fear, confusion, and subconscious patterns had created in my life, and I knew I had to do a new thing.

Six weeks before my forty-second birthday, I went on a three-day fast, asking Spirit to tell me what to do to break the cycle. What to do to create more love in myself, for myself. On the third day of the fast, the answer magically came to mind: *Surround yourself with those who love you.* Not until that moment did I realize that I had never celebrated myself. I had never had a birthday celebration.

I have a wonderfully diverse circle of friends and comrades. These women, most of them deeply steeped in spiritual practices and knowledge, have taught me a great deal. They have knowledge of everything from Zen Buddhism to Native American lore. Some of these women are ministers in the most traditional sense. Others are priestesses and sacred-pipe carriers. Some have been my students who have now branched off into other areas of study. Some honor the Goddess, while others pursue more esoteric studies. I made a list of forty-two women, most of them older than me. All had two things in common: they led an intensely spiritual life, and they loved me unconditionally. These were the women I chose to participate in my "rites of passage."

I rented a tent and decorated everything in my backyard in rich purple-and-gold fabric. My daughter Gemmia, another friend who specializes in vegetarian cuisine, and I prepared every morsel of food with our own hands. I had spent the preceding three days in prayer, asking God, the Goddess, the Holy Spirit, my ancestors from all nations and cultures to cleanse me and guide me in a new direction, away from all past errors. When I wasn't in active prayer, I was silent. It can be pretty challenging to remain silent while preparing for your first birthday party, but I knew it was something I needed to do in order to get centered. To let my past thoughts and feelings rise to the surface.

The women came from all across the country. As they began to arrive, I could feel a sacred energy rising through my home and around me. It was the presence of love, and it was all focused on me. I had asked each of the women if they would conduct a ceremony on my behalf, based on their own spiritual philosophy. I asked that their gifts, if they chose to give one, be something that was sacred or meaningful to them.

We began with an ancient African ceremony, washing of the head. Each woman over forty years old was asked to pray for me while washing my head with clear, cool water. By the time the third woman came to wash me, the entire circle was in tears. They prayed for my safety, clarity, and health. They blessed me with love and claimed abundance for me. When my daughters Gemmia and Nisa knelt before me to wash my head and pray for me, the entire circle fell to pieces. By then, most of the women were wailing. We made it through to the next ceremony, the consecration of my body.

Women have always bathed together and bathed one another. When women enter the water together, it is a very sacred act. Since we were in a backyard, we thought it best not to have forty-two naked women splashing around in a metal washtub. Instead, the women surrounded me, holding up white sheets while the two oldest women in the group stripped me and cleansed my body with herbs. Of course, those in the circle watching made all sorts of jokes about my body—the things that were lying down, the things that were standing out, trying to be noticed. Most of all, we laughed about the neighbors who were undoubtedly peering out of their windows, trying to figure out what the heck we were doing. When the bath was completed, the women dressed me in a white outfit that my elder daughter, Gemmia, had picked out for me.

Following the bath, one of the women led us in a Native American ceremony called "baking." I was lying on a sacred blanket on the ground with all of the women around me. Each of the women sat on the ground and placed her feet firmly against my body. After several deep cleansing breaths, the women began to chant the one hundred and nine sacred names for the Mother, the mercy, grace and beauty of God. The energy that poured through the women's feet into my body felt like electricity. I could feel myself vibrating. I could also feel pain, sadness, and grief leaving my body. When they were finished, I needed support in standing as the women formed a circle around me and began to pray.

It is one thing to think you know what people think and feel about you. It is another thing to hear it said out loud. One by one, each of the women told me how she viewed me, what I meant in her life, and what she wanted for me. Of course, we all cried! We were all holding on to each other as the circle grew smaller and smaller. As the women blessed me, thanked me, and issued decrees for goodness in my future, I realized for the first time in my life that I really did matter, that I wasn't all bad, and that I was worthy of love. It was just the boost that Iyanla needed.

As I remembered that day, those women, their prayers, and the love I felt in that circle, I began to cry. I knew that I was not and would never again be alone. I knew that there were forty-two magical women who walked beside me, wherever I went and whatever I did. I realized that after all I had experienced in life, I was blessed, and that I could love myself. Recalling that experience gave me the strength I needed in that very moment to go back and lovingly bring Rhonda into alignment with Iyanla. The strength I needed to forgive Rhonda.

CHAPTER FIFTEEN

What's the Lesson When You Try to Cheat on a Test?

Have the courage to admit your mistakes
so that you can forgive them and release yourself
from pain, struggle and deceit.
There is no mistake that cannot be corrected.
There is no trespass that cannot be forgiven.

Paul Ferrini, in *Love Without Conditions*

BALÉ LOOKED GREAT! This was a man who never seemed to age. I had not seen him in fifteen years, and he looked exactly the same. I was looking forward to getting caught up on what had been happening in his life, and I knew he wanted to know about mine. That had been Balé's job most of my life, making sure I did not go too far off center. If and when I did, he had a special way of bringing me back.

"How are the children?"

"They are fine. Damon is in the navy. He fell in love with a girl in high school. When she enlisted, he did the same. He's stationed in Virginia. Gemmia is wonderful. She has learned how to braid hair and is working with a friend of mine. She is so beautiful and smart as a whip. Nisa is having a difficult time. She has been placed in a special education class because of a reading disability. She feels out of place, but she's a good girl. She's very athletic, and she's working with retarded children for extra credit in school. I guess they're pretty normal teenagers."

Balé was an excellent cook. He had studied cooking most of his life. For him, cooking was therapy. To help him with his therapy, I was eating as fast as I could, but he kept interrupting to ask questions.

"Where's Ray?"

"Ray got married a few years ago. He and his wife are living in Jersey."

"And the drinking?"

"I think he stopped drinking and is doing other things. The last time I heard from him, he was still working and still complaining."

I told Balé that my brother had a habit of getting drunk or high every holiday, then calling me at one or two o'clock in the morning. It wasn't the fact that he called so late that bothered me. It was the fact that he always called to complain about how horrible our lives had been. How badly Daddy had treated him, and how stupid I was for refusing to be mad for all of the things we "suffered" as children. After a few years of Ray's calls, I told him to stop calling me if that was all he had to talk about. He got so mad at me that, unless he needs money, he doesn't call anymore.

"And whatever happened to your grandmother and Nett?"

"Grandma moved back down South after Daddy died. She was living in the family's old home, Uncle Jimmy's house. I don't keep in touch with her. I think I had about as much of her as I deserve in one lifetime."

I was too busy eating to tell him about what Grandma had done to me the day after Daddy's funeral. I had gone by the house to pick up something. Edna let me in. We were standing in the kitchen talking, when all of a sudden Grandma burst through the beaded curtains that hung between the kitchen and the living room and started screaming at me.

"Nobody is going to watch your kids. They're your damn kids! Take them with you!"

Edna and I looked at each other, and then at Grandma.

"Nobody is keeping anybody's kids," Edna said. "Go back and lie down." It must have been the strain of losing her only son. Or perhaps

Grandma knew that I had grown too big for her to intimidate me any longer. Whatever the reason, as I opened the door to leave, Grandma pushed past Edna, lunged at me, and with both hands, shoved me out of the apartment. I went flying out of the door, across the outer hallway, and fell into the door of the apartment across the hall. The children were screaming. Edna was trying to hold onto Grandma so that she would not attack me before I could get to my feet. I stood up and gave Grandma a look that would peel the paint off a wall. In a fierce and hushed whisper, I said to her, "You are a sad and sick old woman. I feel sorry for you." The last I saw of Grandma, she was struggling with Edna and yelling obscenities at me.

"What about Nett?" Balé asked. I took time to swallow the food in my mouth before answering, because I wasn't sure what to say. Nett was still a very painful topic for me to discuss.

"Nett died about six months after I left New York. Apparently she got sick again and went back into the hospital. No one bothered to call me until she was already dead. When I spoke to Ms. Ethel, her home attendant, she told me that Nett would ask for me every day. Ms. Ethel told Sharon, but Sharon said she did not know how to get in touch with me. That wasn't true, but I am sure she had her reasons for wanting to keep me away. Anyway, Ms. Ethel said that after about three weeks of being in the hospital, Nett refused to eat. She refused to open her mouth for food. They tried to force-feed her, and when that didn't work, they fed her intravenously. Her body was weak from being ill for so long. She died in her sleep from starvation. Ms. Ethel told me she knew that Nett would have eaten for me, and she didn't understand why no one called me."

I told Balé about the incident with the check. I also told him about my decision to put some distance between Nett and myself. I was afraid that if she had died with our relationship being as close as it was, I would have lost my mind. Talking to Balé reminded me of something I had not thought of until that moment: Nett's bangles. I had no idea what had happened to the bangles Nett had promised me would be mine once she passed on. The thought made me so sad I had to choke back the tears. Balé must have felt it from across the room.

"You know, her sister probably has most of her things. Have you ever asked her if you could have something special to remember Nett by?"

"No. After I decided not to go clean out Nett's apartment, her sister kinda stopped talking to me. Damon went with her, and he did get the photo album, but everything else is just gone."

"Well, you've got her in your heart. Even with the difficulties you had at the end, she will always be in your heart, and that's all that matters." He was right. Balé was always right.

Over dessert, an apple crumb something, with nuts and raisins, I told Balé that I hated practicing law. I had failed the bar exam twice and didn't want to take it a third time, but I would have to in order to keep my job. Whenever I said that to people, they told me I was crazy: "You come from a welfare check to a paycheck as a lawyer, and you don't like it? You are crazy!" Balé didn't feel that way. He got still and serious. He looked me squarely in the eye and asked a question only a man with his wisdom could ask.

"What were you looking for when you went to law school?"

I wasn't sure if it was the question or the hot raisin, but I spit the contents of my mouth onto the plate. "What do you mean, looking for?"

"Don't play with me. You know I already know. The question is, are you ready to tell the truth about it? What were you looking for?" The force of his words made my heart pound and my head feel light.

"I thought I wanted to be a lawyer, to save the world, to do good things for other people."

He was staring at me. Obviously I had given the wrong answer. The stillness made me nervous. I had to think of something to say. Breathe. Just breathe. I closed my eyes and allowed the words to spill forth truthfully.

"I was looking for a way out. I felt powerless, and I was looking for a way out of pain. A way to feel powerful. I was trying to prove to myself and to other people how smart I was. I thought if I could finish law school and become a lawyer, no one would ever call me stupid again. I was looking for a way to prove to people that I was not stupid."

The tears running down my face were falling all over the apple crispy thing.

"But you didn't believe it, did you? You know that's why you didn't pass the bar, and that's why you are so unhappy. Do you want to practice law?"

"No."

"What do you want to do?"

"I want to make up to my children for all the years I couldn't give them the things they needed and wanted."

"What do you want to do?"

"I want to prove to people that I am not a bad mother."

"What do you want to do? *What do you want to do for you?*"

"I have no idea. I just don't know."

"Good. Now have some more dessert." Balé got up and left the room. I wiped my face and stared at the apple stuff. I felt sick to my stomach.

The rest of the evening went pretty well. I was shaken by Balé's words and by my own. How did he do that? What did he do? I wanted so badly to ask him, but I knew my godfather. He would tell me in his own time and in his own way. We talked about his family, what he had been doing, where he had been. His mother and sister were still in Florida. His father had died. His son was still in New York. I told him what I knew about all the girls from the dance club. I did not tell him that I was sneaking around seeing Adeyemi behind his wife's back. I was too embarrassed.

As I was preparing to leave, Balé gave me a box. It weighed about twenty pounds.

"What's this?"

"These are books. I want you to tell me the major differences between them."

"That will probably take me about a year."

"No. It will take you until Saturday. When you come back next Saturday, I want you to tell me what each book reveals and the major difference between the books."

The box contained the Holy Bible; The I Ching, or Book of Changes, translated by Baynes and Wilhelm; *The I Am Discourses,* by Saint Germain; *The Autobiography of a Yogi,* by Paramahansa Yogananda; *Essays,* by Ralph Waldo Emerson; *Esoteric Astrology,* by Alice Bailey; and the Holy Qur'an. Each book looked to contain between three and six hundred pages.

"I can't read all of this by Saturday! I've got cases. I have to be in court."

"Well, call me when you are finished."

I loved Balé, but he could be a bit weird and a bit demanding at times. On the way home, I tried to peek into the books while I drove. It was very frustrating. After I got home and had a chance to review each book, I was even more frustrated. Three weeks later, I was only sixty pages into the first book, *The Autobiography of a Yogi.* I called Balé.

"You're not finished, are you?"

"I am trying. This stuff is very hard and very confusing. Why do I have to read this?"

"Because you are a priest. A priest has to know what the people need. How do you expect to serve people? You have to be prepared."

"I want to be prepared, Balé, but how do I get prepared and earn a living?"

"God prepared you. Your job is to remember what you have been prepared to do so that you can do it with excellence. Come Saturday at 7 P.M."

It was on that evening that Balé performed my naming ceremony. It was on that day that my life totally changed. At first, I didn't notice the change, but Balé's words, his description of Iyanla, the person I was destined to be, kept ringing in my ears. I wanted so badly to believe that Balé was wrong, but I knew he was right. I knew that I had not been living up to my potential. I knew that I was repeating certain patterns in my life, patterns over which it seemed I had no control. Your name is your nature. I knew that there was something different, something powerful about me. I had experienced it in fleeting moments, moments in Snapper Five, moments when I went deep into prayer and silence. I knew that I had seen things and heard things that could only be explained in spiritual terms, but I was so afraid of what it meant that I had shut down on my own inner exploration.

What if Balé was right and Grandma had been wrong? What would that mean? How much time had I wasted? And how would I ever make it up to myself or to God? What if I was crazy? Or Balé was crazy? What if he was right and people thought I was crazy as a result of what I would become—a teacher, a healer, a woman of great power, prominence, and importance? I thought about all the powerful women I knew. More important, I zeroed in on all the powerful, spiritual women I knew and realized they all had one thing in common—they were alone. They had no man! Oh my God! I had to admit to myself that I wanted a man. No. I needed a man. Was it possible that if I stepped into my power I would be alone? Manless for the rest of my life? It was on that day, sitting at my godfather's kitchen table, that I realized I had to make a choice. I had to choose a way of living and being. I had to choose God's way or my way. It was in the process of making that choice that I began the work of integrating Rhonda and Iyanla in order to become a whole person.

I didn't sleep much that night. I thought about all the mistakes I had made, all the mistakes I made trying to correct the mistakes. I thought about all the things I had done and not done that demonstrated I had not yet developed the kind of character that Balé was talking about. I wondered if I ever would become who and what he said I was destined to become. Just how was I supposed to know? Why didn't somebody tell me that God had a plan? It would have been nice to know that every experience was a part of the plan. Why didn't *God* tell me He had a plan? And if He had one, why did it have to be so harsh, so cruel? What if I had died? Suppose I had succeeded in killing myself. I realized that the attempt at taking my life was also a part of the plan. It was confusing! It was all so confusing! No. I was confused.

I realized all the things I had done and not done to put myself in harm's way. Bible verses kept popping into my head. *"Desires of the flesh . . . The ways of the world . . . Seek ye first the kingdom . . . Suffer little children . . ."* I thought about the children, my children. All of a sudden a chill went through my body. I thought about how my children had suffered as a result of my suffering. I thought about all the days they hadn't eaten, all the days I had left them alone. I thought about how often I had spoken to them, or treated them, the way I had been spoken to and treated. I thought about how painful and confusing that must have been for them. And, while I could not find the compassion to cry for myself, I cried for my children. I cried for the rotten, abusive, neglectful mother I had been. I cried because I could not remember ever telling them that I loved them. I hadn't told them, because I had never told myself.

Then, just before dawn, I stopped crying. I walked to the bathroom mirror, looked myself dead in the eyes, and quietly whispered, "I love you." A chill went through my body as I quickly averted my gaze. When my head stopped spinning, I opened my eyes and said it again: "I love you. I love you." The thought of it made me cry. How could I love myself when I didn't know anything about me? I knew what I had been told. I knew what others had said to me, about me, but I honestly did not know myself. I felt so wounded and battered. I felt tired. No. Exhausted. I wanted to love myself, and I knew in order to do that, I would have to understand myself. I remembered the questions Balé had given me. I ran to my purse and retrieved my notes. Sitting on the edge of my bed, I tried to answer the questions on the list. I was surprised how difficult it was to answer some of the questions, but I worked until long after the sun came up to find a suitable answer to each one of them.

What is your favorite color?
Orange.
What is your favorite food?
Chicken.
What is your favorite song?
"Lean on Me."
What is your most valued possession?
My Bible.
What is your greatest strength?

Sense of humor.

What is your greatest weakness?

I usually jump to conclusions, expecting the worst.

What is your best skill?

Oral communication.

What was your greatest mistake?

Mistaking sexual attraction for love.

What is your greatest fear?

People will not like me and will talk about me.

What is your greatest accomplishment?

Telling Aunt Nadine about Uncle Leroy.

What is the one task that you are least fond of doing?

Paying bills and handling money.

If your life ended today, what is the one thing everyone who knows you would say about you?

She had a great sense of humor.

What would you want them to say?

She was a person of good character.

Why wouldn't or couldn't they say what you would want them to say?

Because they don't know Iyanla. They only know Rhonda.

One day, several weeks later, I returned to my office after a brutal morning in court and visiting clients at three different prisons. The office was dark. I flipped the light switch, but the lights did not come on. I tried again. Nothing. I walked to the office next door and asked a colleague if her lights were working. "I think so," she said. She got up from her desk, where she had been working by the light of her desk lamp, and flipped the light switch. Her lights came right on. I told her I couldn't get my lights to come on. She returned with me to my office and flipped the switch on and off—twice. The office was still dark. She did it one more time.

"You'd better get your eyes checked. These lights are on. They work fine."

I stood watching her as she left my office. When I sat down in my chair, trying to figure out what was happening, I heard a voice. It was so clear, I turned to see who was standing behind me. *Leave this place. Leave now and never come back.*

Gemmia met me at the office late that afternoon so that we could go shopping. When I left, the framed pictures of my children were on the desk, my law degree was hanging on the wall, and I had tea bags and honey in the bottom drawer. I never set foot in that office again.

CHAPTER SIXTEEN

What's the Lesson When You Don't Love Yourself First?

It is through hearing—and obeying—the demand to make
a life adjustment that the ability to face oneself grows.
In fact, many abilities grow along with self-trust . . .
As each correction is made, the bond between self and Self
grows stronger, thus giving more power to the voice of Self,
more clarity and purpose to the individual life.

Marsha Sinetar, in *Ordinary People as Monks and Mystics*

I HAD BEEN UNEMPLOYED four months before someone told me that I could collect money because I wasn't working. My employer paid me for two months while I was trying to make up my mind about what I was going to do. I knew I would have to take the bar exam again, but I also knew that I did not want to practice law. By the time I got to the unemployment office to file for benefits, things were pretty tight, but they were also pretty exciting. I had finished reading all of the books Balé had given me, and probably fifty others. I stopped seeing Adeyemi, and he moved to Atlanta—without his wife. Gemmia had gone off to college. Nisa was making it through high school, and Damon was still chasing his wife around the globe.

I was making the changes I thought were necessary in order for Iyanla to emerge. Although I still didn't know what I wanted to do, I didn't feel lost or idle. I was spending a great deal of time in prayer and meditation, and a great deal of time with Balé. We talked about everything, and he taught me many things about the duties of a priest. I watched how he handled the people who came to him for counseling. Before long, I too had developed a client base, checking everything first with Balé, including what I said and what I advised the clients. I was very careful to do the necessary follow-up. My satisfied clients always recommended me to their friends. My name and reputation spread pretty quickly, which did not make the other priests in the city very happy. I was stealing their business. I was taking people away from them, and they had been in the priesthood much longer than I had.

One of my clients asked if I would be willing to talk about Yoruba culture on the radio. I was delighted. During the show, I talked about the culture of the people and spiritual philosophy. Most of the callers were interested and receptive. Others were downright angry. They called me a heathen, the "anti-Christ," and had no problem telling me that I was going to burn in hell. That helped my support base. The host of the show got so many calls, he asked me to be on his show every week. This grew into me sitting in when other hosts were on vacation. Before long I was cohosting a show. The show helped increase my client base, and the clients in turn supported the show. Looking back, I recognize that, thanks to Cody Anderson and the WHAT family in Philadelphia, this was the beginning of my public image and career. Things were moving along great until I lost track of what I was doing.

Doing spiritual work purely to make money is not a good thing. I am not saying that people who do spiritual work for other people should not get paid, but making money cannot be the only reason you do spiritual work for other people. When the unemployment benefits ended, I was doing spiritual work as a means of supporting myself. This means that I accepted clients not because I loved them or the work, but because I needed to pay the rent. I accepted clients who had all kinds of problems not because I could help them, but because I had a child to feed and a daughter in college. It meant that when I was tired or in a bad mood, when I didn't have time to pray or meditate, I accepted clients. It also meant that when I had no clients, I would panic because I was focused on the money, not on the work. I panicked because the clients had the power and the control. I did not.

Whether you are doing spiritual work for the joy or for the money, you must be very careful that people do not make you responsible for running or ruining their lives. I hadn't learned that lesson yet. Once you do a counseling session with someone, they believe it is no longer necessary to make their own choices and decisions. Some feel they have a right to call you for every little thing. If you are working for money, they can call you. You talk to them because you are afraid that if you don't, they won't call back. One woman I counseled was in a very bad relationship. I tried every way I could to tell her that the man she was seeing had other women, and that she should not bank on marrying him. She wanted me to make him marry her.

"I don't do that kind of work."

"Well, do you know somebody who does?"

"No. I don't. Perhaps you should start seeing other people. Perhaps if he thought he was going to lose you, he would take the relationship more seriously."

"Well, who should I see?"

"Oh, I'm sure if you put your mind to it, you will meet somebody."

"Can you ask your shells who I should see?"

"I can only ask a question that can be answered with a yes or no."

"Well, can you ask if I'll meet him at work?" Without thinking, I asked the question. The answer was no.

"Can you ask if I'll meet him on the bus?"

I knew where she was heading, but she was a good client and I didn't want to upset her. The answer again was no. By the time it was all over, we had asked about the supermarket, the laundromat, the bank, the elevator, and whether or not she should put an ad in the singles paper. When she asked me if she should join a church to meet her intended, the answer was yes. When she asked for the telephone book so that we could figure out what church she should join, I ended the consultation.

Many people who seek out spiritual consultation have the wrong idea. They think that a spiritual consultant is tantamount to a magician. They want you to make specific body parts bigger, or eliminate particular body parts of others. They want you to make people do things or stop doing things. When you explain to them that you are not equipped to do those things, they ask for a referral to someone who can. Others believe that everything that happens to them has a spiritual meaning and significance in their lives. If you are a spiritual consultant, they expect you to know what the significance is. One male client came to see me because crows kept circling his house. He wanted to know the significance. I had to choke back a laugh when he told me he lived near a cornfield. I suggested that perhaps the crows were just passing by and not looking for his house at all. A few days later, I got another call from him at 7:30 in the morning.

"Iyanla, I had a very profound experience this morning and I wanted you to help me make sense of it."

"Tell me what happened."

"When I woke up, there were three pigeons sitting on my windowsill. They were just sitting there, looking in the window at me. I watched them for a few minutes, but they didn't move or anything. Then, when I got up to walk over to the window, all of them flew away. But it's not just that they flew away. They flew away one at a time. First the gray one, then the one with the black spots, then the other gray one. What do you think it means?"

"I think it means you need to clean off your windowsill."

"Is there some special spiritual cleaner you can make for me to use?"

"No, baby, soap, water, and a little bleach is all you need."

The purpose of individual spiritual development and spiritual work is empowerment and to remind you of your divine, spiritual identity. Through the power of your spiritual identity, you become conscious of your ability to create life experiences. Spiritual work must be done in service to and recognition of God. God expects us to serve one another. This requires discipline, focus, and knowledge of spiritual law or principle. It also requires purity of intent and heart. When these elements are absent, you are not building a good character. You are not doing spiritual work for the good of the world. You are doing something else that is bound to blow up in your face. I learned this through experience.

Clients mixed with fans. Fans became students. Students were coming to learn about Yoruba culture. Fans, who thought I was famous because I was on the radio, were asking for my autograph and other favors. I had become a fad. People thought I could and was doing things that I actually knew nothing about. Clients, fans, and students do not mix well. They each want something different from you. People I had no business being around surrounded me. People were beginning to whisper. The other priests heard the whispering and joined in. Clients and students began comparing what I was doing with what they were hearing. The gossip was running rampant. People who were in my home and in my face were talking about me behind my back.

I was so focused on keeping the rent paid, I didn't know what was going on.

Because people are defective does not mean they cannot see your defects. They see your fears, the contradictions, and your weaknesses. When they see them, they judge them. They assume an interpretation that may have nothing to do with what is really going on. When you hold yourself out to be a teacher, a healer, a light, people will criticize. It goes with the territory. When you are, as I was, unclear, unfocused, and sensitive to criticism, it will cripple you. You will become defensive. You will eventually say or do something that appears to support what people have judged to be wrong with you. If you react, or try to defend yourself, that's when they will get you.

I held a public event aimed at exposing the community to Yoruba culture. It was a free event, not because I could afford to host it, but because I wanted to dispel the rumors that I was taking money from people for other than spiritual reasons. When the other priests heard about the event, they went on the attack. A letter was sent to all priests, warning them not to attend. I was called a series of names, casting doubt on my character and integrity. Some clients and students believed the rumors.

Others didn't care. What could have been a beautiful event turned into a community war between those who believed me and those who believed my critics. Articles were written in the newspaper, people talked about it on the radio. I was defensive and angry and hurt. In the end, over two hundred people attended and thanked me for having the event. But the shadow was cast. The client base dwindled. I was estranged from the other priests in the community, and I had a serious case of self-doubt. I needed to regroup.

What do you want to do? I wanted to use my spiritual gifts to help people. *What are your spiritual gifts?* When I am rested and focused, I can hear the voice of Spirit. I can see the presence of Spirit. *What do you want to do?* I want to use the ability to hear and see Spirit in a way that helps other people. *How are you going to do that?* I didn't have a clue.

I stopped accepting new clients. I kept my students and continued teaching about Yoruba culture. My radio job was paying me, but it wasn't enough to sustain my household. There were times when Gemmia needed money, and I didn't have it to send. At times, she would have to walk fifteen blocks to Western Union to pick up twenty-five dollars so that she could buy food. If the electricity was on, the telephone was not. If the telephone was on, the gas was not. If the utilities were all on, we had no food. I was too afraid, too wounded to take on more clients, and my students were watching me. *What do you want to do?* Right now, I want to eat. *What is your greatest strength?* Oral communication. *What is your greatest weakness?* Jumping to conclusions, always expecting the worst. *What are you expecting right now?* To fail. To fail miserably and have people talk about me. *Why?* Because I am bad. I don't matter. I am nothing; I will never be anything good.

Everything I had learned and had not learned, everything I believed about myself or had ever been taught about myself, had come alive in my life. It contradicted everything Balé had told me. How could I build character while believing I was worthless? How could I build a life while believing I was unworthy? How could I take care of myself when I didn't have a man? When things got really rough, it didn't matter that I was a priest. Beneath all of the ceremony, and all of the knowledge I had gained from the books, there was a frightened, wounded little girl named Rhonda. She was in total control of my life, and Iyanla, who had yet to find an identity, didn't have a clue about what to do next.

Yes, I prayed. But I was really begging God to help me. I was not communing with the divine power within me. I was asking a big God out there to save me from myself, like He had saved me from Grandma. God cannot help you unless you are very clear about what it is that you want. God will not help you if you do not believe that you are worthy of the help. Yes, I was meditating. But when you live in fear, meditation becomes an opportunity for your mind to play tricks on you. You get momentary glimpses of what could be. However, since you don't believe in yourself because you do not understand your own power, you dismiss the insights you gain through meditation. Besides that, I was meditating about my problems rather than meditating on the solution. Balé had gone to Africa for an extended visit. I was trying to figure out what he would say to me, but I was so frightened and confused, I couldn't think. One day, as I was staring out of the window, I heard his voice. *What do you want to do?*

I was coming down the stairs, headed toward the kitchen to make coffee. I'd never stopped my morning ritual, although Nett was gone. I had been praying, asking God to give me a sign that I would be okay. Singer Barry White was being interviewed on the radio. His booming voice filled the kitchen. Just as I hit the bottom step, Barry said, "You've got to have faith!" I stood stark still. It was as if he were speaking directly to me. "You've got to take the good times and the bad times. You've got to be willing to do it for free. If you have the desire and the skill, and you never allow yourself to believe in failure, you're gonna make it. You have to make it." I knew that was my message from God. I didn't know what to do about it, but I knew it was for me.

The day before the marshal was scheduled to remove me and my property from the house, I moved into a friend's basement. I was mortified, but grateful. Nisa, the cat, and I lived in that basement for eight months. During that time, I did everything in my power to get as clear as I could. I worked with the list Balé had given me. I studied everything I could get my hands on. I prayed, and most of all, I worked on myself. I examined every motive, every intention, every choice I made, no matter how insignificant it seemed. I was walking down the street one day when I saw a sign that said "Abundance" hanging in the window of a building. Beneath the word was a date and time. I went into the building, not knowing it was a Unity Church, to inquire about the sign.

"What does that sign mean?" There was a young woman behind the counter in a room that served as a bookstore.

"We are offering a workshop that teaches you how to create an abundance of good things in your life."

"God knows I need some good things to happen to me. How much does it cost?"

"We begin tomorrow night at 7:00 P.M. and continue through Sunday night at 7:00 P.M. The commitment to take the workshop is $450."

My heart sank. I had about $18, but I asked if she could tell me anything about the workshop. The woman took me into a small room, and we talked for about twenty minutes. She asked if I was interested.

"I am very interested. I think this is exactly what I need right now, but I don't have the money."

"Do you want to take the workshop?"

"Yes, I do."

"Well, make a decision and a commitment. Everything you need will be provided."

"I'll think about it. Can I call you?" She gave me her card. As I was leaving, she repeated, "Make a commitment. Let me know by 4:00 P.M. tomorrow, because we start exactly at 7:00 P.M."

I thought about nothing else for the rest of the day. When I got back home, I sat quietly thinking about how I could borrow the money. When nothing came to mind, I closed my eyes and just sat. *What do you want to do?* I want to take this workshop. *Write a postdated check for the amount. Call the woman and tell her you will be there.* I wrote the check and made the call.

"I am not authorized to accept a postdated check. Write the check.

Date it for today, and be here at 7:00 tomorrow." I did exactly what she said, without fear and without hesitation.

That workshop was the turning point of my life. It was there that I learned about the philosophy of Unity Village. It was there that I learned about the mind that existed in Christ and how that mind exists in us all. I learned about the power of the mind and its connection to God. I learned about the power of the subconscious mind and how it creates the experiences we live through. It was at this workshop I learned that I mattered. I learned to trust myself, and I learned the importance of telling the truth.

I was the only person of color in the workshop, standing in a circle of strangers, most of whom were older, wealthier, and more experienced at taking workshops. I had spent most of the time in the room feeling intimidated and out of place. The facilitator was in the middle of an exercise when someone in the group offered a very harsh criticism of him. Without warning, he turned to me and asked, "Well, what do you think?" Every eye in the room shifted to my face. When I didn't respond, he yelled, "Honor yourself!" It was not something that I had ever considered.

"Honor yourself!" He was staring at me. He was screaming at me, "Admit what you feel. Learn to trust and to honor yourself as a divine and unique expression of God by telling the truth. Learn to love yourself enough to tell the truth exactly as you know it at any given moment. Do you love yourself?" I took too long to respond.

"Of course you don't! How could you! No one ever told you that you were worthy of love. Well, I'm telling you that you are worthy, and that what you think matters. Do you believe that?"

"I'm not sure. I think so."

"So are you going to tell me what you think about what that gentleman over there just said?"

"Say what I am thinking, out loud, in a room full of people? A room full of white people? You have got to be out of your mind!"

"No. You are out of your mind. You are in your ego. You are in your fears and your judgments. What I am asking you to do is to learn to trust yourself." He wasn't yelling anymore. "What do you think?"

It's really rather hard to think when your brain is frying and your hair is falling off! "Well . . ."

"No wells!" He yelled at me. "The minute you say 'well' or 'I don't know,' you are saying you don't want to talk about it! You are here to talk. So talk! What do you think about what he just said?" I could feel all fifty eyeballs in the room on me. I could hear Grandma's voice in the back of my mind: "If you don't have anything good to say, don't say anything at all."

I could see Nett's eyes darting across the room at me, giving me that look that said if I opened my mouth I would be swiftly put to death. I could smell my brain matter burning. I could hear Grandma, see Nett, and here was this big person, an adult, standing there and demanding an answer. The words escaped from my mouth before I could examine or censor them.

"I feel the same way. I don't think you have to yell and scream at us to get your point across. We are not deaf. We have paid to be here, which means we are willing to learn. It is hard to learn when you are afraid."

"Are you really afraid of me?" he asked gently.

"No, not really. I think I am more afraid of what you will say or do if I don't give you the right answer."

"What is the right answer?" He was pushing it a bit, but it felt good.

"I feel like the right answer is the one that pops into your mind at the moment. The big question is how do you give that answer without hurting or offending the other person?"

He got down on his knees and looked me directly in the eye. "Honor what you feel by saying it the way you would want to hear it. When you say it honestly, with love, your job is over."

The rest of the workshop went smoothly. On the last day of the workshop, we were informed that if we were not satisfied with what we had learned, the tuition would be refunded. They hadn't cashed the checks! They were still in possession of the check I had given them on Thursday. I considered saying I wasn't satisfied just to get the check

back. Build your character, Iyanla! I decided against it. Instead, I left
with an armful of books by Charles Filmore, the founder of the Unity
movement. Two days after I completed the workshop, I received a telephone call from the radio station. Someone was going on vacation. If I
could sit in, I would make $500. I asked for the money in advance. The
check for the workshop and the books was covered in time.

After I completed the two weeks at the radio station, a client asked
me if I would come to her job and talk to her students about self-esteem.
She was an instructor in a job readiness program for women on welfare.
She knew that I was once on welfare, and she knew that I had worked
my way off welfare. It wouldn't pay much, but she would see if she could
arrange for me to come in once or twice a month. The weekly consulting
job turned into a full-time position that got me out of the basement and
into a house.

I started my first weekly ministry, the Transformation Station, which
met every Sunday morning in the new house. I started with ten clients
and students. Two years later, there was a line to get in. I had learned to
combine the universal principles I was learning through Unity with the
cultural principles I had learned in Yoruba. Going back to my Bible, and
reading the other books Balé had given me, I had somehow found and
could articulate the common thread: God is. God exists everywhere, all
the time, in everything. Eric Butterworth, a Unity teacher, wrote, "We
are an eachness in the Allness of God." I had learned, understood, and
believed that God existed in me. The essence and energy of God are expressed as me. By that time, I had also been introduced to and studied *A
Course in Miracles.* The Course teaches about the power of love, also
about the presence of the ego, which keeps us separate from and unable
to recognize God's love in each other. It was the teachings of Unity, The
Course, and a metaphysical understanding of the teachings of the Bible
that helped me to build Iyanla's character. What I had not yet done was
learn how to love myself. I knew what the books said, but I was still having trouble putting it into practice. I needed a man to help me do that.

He wasn't married. He was living with someone. He was gorgeous.
He was aloof. He would say one thing and do another. Before long, I

found myself doing with him what I had done in the past. I was trying to make him change his mind. I was sleeping with a man who was not giving me all that I wanted and needed. And I was using a relationship as the barometer by which I measured my success. When we were on, I was on. When he didn't call or come over, I felt like everything was falling apart. He brought up all of my worth issues, my abandonment issues, and he helped me to see that I was still looking for love "out there." Once I realized what I was doing, I didn't have the strength or courage to stop. I kept seeing him for more than a year before I remembered the list. *What do you want?* I want a man who is willing to be seen with me in public. *What is your greatest fear?* That I will never find a man to love me. *What is your greatest weakness?* Needing someone to love me. *Why?* Because I don't love myself. *Why?* Because I'm not good enough. *Why?* Because that is what I have been told.

Each time I worked with the list, new questions and deeper insights emerged. I never said a word to my male friend. I just stopped calling. So did he. When he did call, months later, I was well on my way to learning "I am the love I seek."

While working with the women in the program, I had developed a small pamphlet for them. It was a workbook, something they could hold onto when they left the program. Most of it came from the journals I had kept over the years. It revealed the lessons I had learned through many painful experiences. It was an analysis of the things I had done to create the chaos and drama I had experienced in my life. With each new class that entered, I added more to the book. I soon had a forty-page book that I wanted to get published. A friend introduced me to someone in the publishing field who would help me self-publish the book. Self-publishing takes money. I had none. The only thing I had was a commitment to get the book published.

A small business owner who had heard about my ministry and my work said that he would be willing to finance the book. A member of the ministry designed the cover. It took about six weeks. The day the books were delivered to my house, I cried. *Tapping the Power Within: A Path to Self-Empowerment for Black Women* was my first baby. It was a beautiful baby that I sold out of shopping bags to bookstores throughout the city. Gemmia and I made a list of bookstores around the country. When the telephone was working, we solicited orders. Soon I was selling between one hundred and two hundred books a week to stores as far away as Dallas. As the news about the book spread, people began calling me.

I started writing letters to literary agents and publishers, asking if they would like to publish the book. I remembered a woman I had worked with at Doubleday some fifteen years earlier. When someone told me that she was a literary agent, I wrote to her. She responded by saying she would not be taking on any new clients for at least a year. Since everyone else had already said no, and realizing that patience is a part of character building, I decided to wait.

I kept the ministry going and started doing speaking engagements at other job training programs. Working with my list, I realized that if there is something you want that does not exist, you could create it. I started writing to clubs, organizations, and corporations asking if I could come to speak to their students, members, and employees. I had a computer a friend had given me that had no printer. I would type the letter at home, take the disk to Kinko's, and print the letter out. There were many times when I would find a typographical error after I had printed the letter. I would have to return to the copy center and pay for another printout. The carfare was wreaking havoc on my budget. I put my request for a car into the universe.

Without my having said a word to anyone, a member of the ministry called to tell me she knew a man who could help me get a car. She gave me his name and telephone number. I didn't call because I knew my credit rating was poor. I had not paid for my Fingerhut towels, I had a defaulted student loan, and my utility bills were seldom paid on time. I decided I would have to save up enough money to buy a used car. The universe had other plans.

Several weeks later, the woman called to ask me if I had gone to see about the car. I told her no, but I didn't tell her why.

"If you have bad credit, he can still help you. You really should call him." I did. Gemmia and I went over to the lot and I found a beautiful gray Honda with my name written all over it.

"How much can you put down?" the salesman asked. Before I could answer, he said, "I'll be right back."

I was sitting in the salesman's office with Gemmia. She is not just my daughter and best friend, she is the voice of reason. "I don't have any money. What should I do?"

"I don't know," she said. "Ask him if you can pay it off later." The salesman was back.

"I'm having them clean the car up. How much can you give me today? Do you have insurance? I have a guy who can help you out. I'll be right back."

"Oh my God! What am I gonna do? I have to pee. When he comes back, tell him I went to pee."

"I'm not going to tell him that," Gemmia said, shaking her head and laughing. I was freezing. That always happens to me when I get nervous. I sat my cold butt on the cold toilet seat, never thinking it would be a spiritual experience. A voice filled the bathroom. *Write him a check for nine hundred dollars.* I was so nervous I answered out loud.

"I don't have nine hundred dollars!" I was screaming at myself.

God has nine hundred dollars.

"But if the check bounces, God is not going to jail. I am."

Offer him nine hundred dollars and trust God to do the rest.

I walked back to where Gemmia was sitting. The salesman rushed back in, sat down, stood up, leaned over the desk and said, "Write me a check for nine hundred dollars, and I'll guarantee it."

"What does that mean?"

"It means that we will put a guarantee on the check so that if it doesn't clear, we will have access to your account to get the money anytime it shows up." I wrote the check.

When the insurance broker arrived, he asked for two checks, one for $75, another for $250. He explained that it would be at least two weeks before either check was cashed, because they had to be processed through the home office in Kansas.

I drove my car home and went to bed. The next morning I crept over to the window and peered through the curtains.

"Gemmia! Gemmia!" I was screaming and jumping up and down. "It's still there! I have a car!" Gemmia and I did a little jig around the room. We jumped in the car and drove around the city delivering books. When we returned home, I found a check in the mail for $1,225. It was a deposit for a speaking engagement that wasn't scheduled for two more months! I shared the story with the ministry the following Sunday. Together, we all celebrated.

It was a hunch. I read an article in *Essence* magazine, written by its editor, Susan L. Taylor. I was so moved by the article, I wanted to write her. I discussed the idea with my dear friend Marjorie Battle, who lived in New York. Marge and I were always making plans about my career. She thought it was an excellent idea. We composed the letter over the telephone. Marge typed it on "good" paper and sent it to me to by mail. I signed the letter and mailed it to Ms. Taylor. The few people I told about it said I would never get a response. Two weeks later, I got a call from Ms. Taylor's office. She wanted to meet with me to discuss the possibility of the magazine doing my story. *Essence* sent me a ticket, and had a car pick me up at the train station. I had never been in a limousine that was not going to a funeral.

Standing in the doorway of her office, Susan Taylor did not know that I had on a homemade suit. She did not know that the jewelry I was wearing was borrowed. She did not know that my daughter had bought my pantyhose and underwear with the paycheck she earned working at McDonald's. She did not know that my rent wasn't paid and that my telephone was about to be disconnected. The glamorous Susan Taylor, editor-in-chief of the largest magazine ever published for black women, took one look at me and said, "Come here and give me a hug. We have been looking for you for a long time." Susan had heard me speak at a retreat several months earlier. She said she was interested in my story.

Essence paid me and sent me to Los Angeles. Bebe Moore Campbell interviewed me and wrote the story. It appeared in an issue of the magazine with Diana Ross on the cover. I bought twenty-five copies, laid them out on the floor in front of me, and cried over them. *Essence* said that the story elicited more response than any other story in the history of the magazine. People began to call me for speaking engagements. The literary agent called back and introduced me to a small independent publisher who redesigned and published *Tapping the Power.*

Within four months, my life was moving in a direction that I had never imagined possible. Iyanla was emerging through a slow, often painful process. My lessons were grounded in an inability to love myself, to trust myself, and to believe that I was worthy. This inability manifested itself in issues with money. I had success etched into my soul. God put it there. It was my nature. But I had been programmed for failure. I believed what Grandma told me. I believed that I would never amount to anything. Although I was doing the work and enjoying it, I kept waiting for something bad to happen.

The Iyanla I had become was still very sensitive to and overly concerned about criticism. Every decision I made had to be confirmed and affirmed by at least five other people. I needed external validation. I learned a great deal by attending workshops and reading books, but I had not learned how to integrate what I was learning into my own spirit. Although I had chosen to be celibate, I was yearning and looking for the love of a man to make me feel whole. While it appeared to the world that she was a bright and rising star, Iyanla wrestled with feelings of inferiority and worthlessness. At least once a day, I felt like six-year-old Rhonda, cowering in the corner. There were things in my past that I had not healed. There were things in my heart that I believed about myself and could not face. It was a recipe for failure. The only thing that helped and saved me was my ability to see and hear Spirit.

CHAPTER SEVENTEEN

What's the Lesson When You Get the Lesson but Don't Know What to Do With It?

Truth must be realized individually.

It must be realized by you, otherwise it is not your Truth.

Only your Truth, not the truth, is expressed in your life,
    not anyone else's.

How do you find your truth?

By seeking and finding the teacher within.

You see, the Teacher and the Truth within are one.

John Randolph Price, in *With Wings as Eagles*

ALTHOUGH I WAS ASLEEP, I could feel the chill in the room. As the
scenes of the dream unfolded, I began to shiver.

I could see Damon sitting alone on the floor of a huge, dark room. I
was standing in the corner of the room. Even though Damon was not
tied up, I knew, for some reason, he could not move. I called out to him
several times, but he did not answer me. I heard voices that sounded
angry and dangerous. In a panic, I ran out of the room, calling out to
Damon. Again, he did not respond and he did not move.

I saw myself running up a long hallway, screaming Damon's name. I
looked back to see if he was following me, then I saw the men enter the

room. I stopped and watched as the angry men walked over to where my son was sitting on the floor. One of the men hit him. "Please stop!" I screamed. "Stop it!" I ran back toward the room. As I reached the door, I saw that one of the men had a gun pointed at Damon's head. For some reason, I could not step into the room. I stood at the doorway, begging them not to shoot my son. I heard the gun click. One of the men turned and looked at me. I begged him, "Please. Don't do it." The gun clicked again. My heart sank. The telephone rang.

I was sitting up in the bed, shivering and crying, trying to remember where I was, when the telephone rang again. I grabbed for the receiver and knocked it and the clock to the floor. It was 6:30 Saturday morning. I put the receiver to my ear, but I couldn't speak.

"Ma?" It was Gemmia, calling from Morgan State University.

"What's the matter? Why are you calling so early?" I yelled into the telephone.

"Ma, you've got to find Damon. He's in some kind of trouble."

Gemmia recounted the dream that had just awakened her. She had seen a mob of people chasing Damon. She was trying to help him get away, but they were separated. When she looked back to see where Damon was, a huge truck appeared from nowhere and ran over him. She was crying on the other end of the telephone.

I told her to pack. I would pick her up in two hours. My car was in bad shape, so I rented one, borrowed forty dollars, and picked Gemmia up in Maryland. Six hours later, we were driving through the streets of Norfolk, Virginia. I had no idea where I was going or where Damon was.

I knew Damon lived somewhere in Norfolk. His father and I had been there once when Damon first enlisted. I was sight driving, trying to remember what I had seen the last time. I pulled into the parking lot of a motel to ask the desk clerk where the housing complexes in the neighborhood were located. I turned the car off, unbuckled my seat belt, and reached over to open the door. As I looked up, I saw Damon running across the parking lot, headed for the pay telephone.

I never would have imagined that my son would be involved in the sale and transport of drugs, but he had a booming business that he ran from one of the rooms in the motel. A rival dealer had put a "hit" out on him. That morning, two gunmen appeared in his room. They didn't realize who Damon was, and he convinced them that he was not the person they were looking for. He was in the process of making plans to move his operation when I showed up. It took me two days to shut the operation down and take my son back home.

There were few things in my life that I felt guilty about. How I had raised my children was one. When I hear "Iyanla, Great Mother," I cringe. I may have been many things, but a great mother was not one of them and I knew it. Great mothers love and nurture their children. They teach them games and they play with their children. I had not done that, partly because I didn't know how and partly because I was too busy chasing men and creating drama in my life. I did not know how to be a mother because my heart was closed.

In a very secret place in my soul, I felt I did not deserve the children I had been given. When I think of all the days I left them alone to go to work, or go to school, or to shack up with some man, shame grips my heart. When I think of all the nights that I left them to look for John or spy on Eddie, the guilt is almost unbearable. I was a good provider. I was not a good mother. Rarely, if ever, did I tell my children I loved them. I almost never told them when they did a good job. I was a verbally abusive taskmaster, afraid that my children would fail. But I never gave them what they needed to succeed. It was this aspect of understanding my name that gave me more trouble that anything else. How could I call myself "Great Mother" when I knew in my heart that I had not mothered my own children? It felt like such a contradiction. It felt dishonest.

When Gemmia was thirteen years old, she stopped speaking. She went to school, came home, did her homework, and went to bed. If you did not speak to her, she did not speak to you. As busy as I was with my own issues, I noticed it. No amount of prodding or questioning got a response. If she wasn't doing homework or housework, she would sleep. At first I thought she was pregnant. But two years into the situation, I knew that was not the problem.

I think she was clinically depressed. I think I was so crazy, and she had witnessed me go through so much drama, she became depressed. When I thought about it, I had never taught her the alphabet, how to count, or how to tell time. She figured it out on her own. Maybe Damon had helped her. I know I didn't. Still, she was a brilliant, straight A student. One day I was talking to a friend who said she wanted to train young girls in the art of hair braiding. I asked her to train my daughter. Gemmia worked in Tulani's salon for three years. She emerged as a master braider and a great conversationalist. When she was awarded a full four-year scholarship in biology, I knew I had been blessed. I felt like a bad mother, but a blessed one.

I taught Damon the importance of money. I taught him that to get money, you had to work hard, or lie, or be treated badly. I never sat down and said these things to him, but he was watching me. I lived with a man who beat me, because I thought I needed his money. I left my children alone at night to go to work for money. I worked two jobs and went to school, trying to amass enough money to move my children out of the projects. Damon and his sisters watched me work and not be able to make ends meet. They never saw me make a budget, because I did not know how. They never saw me use a credit card, because I didn't have one. They knew when the rent wasn't paid and when that was the reason we had to move. They knew when the light, gas, or telephone was off, and that I had to get beat up to get the money to put them back on. In Damon's mind, why should he end up like me? Why should he work only to end up with nothing? I could have addressed all of his misunderstandings, but I had no idea how to begin.

Once they became teenagers, it was rare to see all my children home at the same time. I remember one particular Sunday morning, they were all sitting on Damon's bed, laughing and talking to one another.

"I need somebody to help me in the prayer room," I said as I passed through the room. "But they have to be a virgin." No one moved. I kept walking. A few minutes later, I came back and repeated the request.

"Who's going to help me? I need all the virgins."

Damon spoke first. "Go ahead, Gemmia. Help Mommy."

"No," Gemmia said, "let Nisa go." Damon could not hide his distress.

"Oh no!" he said. "What do you mean 'let Nisa go'? You go. Why can't you go?" Gemmia stared at her brother. I was staring at Gemmia, who leaned across the bed and pushed her younger sister.

"Go on, Nisa. Mommy needs you to help her."

Nisa shook her head. "Uh-uh, I ain't going. Why don't you go?" Damon was stomping around, saying, "Oh no! Neither of my sisters is a virgin. I can't believe this! Gemmia, Nisa, what happened?" I had all the information I needed. They were arguing among themselves. As I left the room, I heard Nisa say, "I don't even know what a virgin is!"

My children always got along. I had taught them to take care of one another. Damon looked out for his sisters, and the girls looked out for each other. I could detect some distance between fifteen-year-old Gemmia and thirteen-year-old Nisa, but they still enjoyed being together for short spans of time. I could at least give myself credit that I had taught my children to stick together. That was more than anyone ever did for Ray and me.

As my career started moving forward, my children were my greatest support. They were excited about the book, they helped me write and mail the ministry newsletter, and they took a front-row seat every Sunday morning. I wasn't able to keep Damon home very long after the Norfolk incident. He said he wanted to be with his wife, who was still stationed in Virginia. He promised that he was finished with the drug life. He lied.

Over the course of several months, Damon was arrested in every state along the eastern seaboard. Each time he was arrested, he would call me, profess his innocence, and beg me to pay his bail and get him an attorney. On the first two occasions, I did exactly as he asked. I didn't help him because I believed he was innocent. I knew he was guilty. I did it because I felt so guilty. Every time he called with some new trouble, a dagger would stab my heart. Not only had I failed as a mother and caused my son to ruin his life, people were going to talk about me: "How can she be out there saving the world and her son is in jail?" When you hold yourself out in the public eye, people sometimes forget that you are still a human being. They forget that you have feelings, and they forget that you have a history. They act as if you popped out of a pumpkin patch one day, fully equipped to do whatever it is that you are doing. I knew better.

When Damon was arrested in Philadelphia, I called some of my law school buddies. They were willing to help, but I didn't have the money to pay them. When he was arrested in New York, I got the brilliant idea to call his father, an ex–corrections officer, to see if he could pull some strings.

"Gary, have you heard from Damon yet?"

"His friend called here and said that he needed eight hundred dollars to pay his bail."

"I know. Would you be willing to put up half if I put up the other half?" I asked him.

"I have fifty dollars. You can have that if you want it." This from a man who lives in a mansion, receives a state pension, works as a locksmith, and sells used cars.

"You know, Gary, this is the first time in his life that your son has ever asked you to help him do anything. I think this may be a good time for you and him to really build a relationship. He needs manhood training. He needs something that I cannot give him."

"The only thing wrong with Damon is the environment he grew up in. What did you think was going to happen to him? Look where he grew up! Look at the things he grew up around. He is only doing what he saw done in his environment."

I was livid. This is a man who passed through twice a year to give his son twenty dollars and occasionally took him to eat lobster.

"I did the best I could, Gary, but you know what? I don't have to defend myself to you, because you are his father. Right now he needs a father."

"You say he needs manhood training. What is that? I never got that. How am I supposed to give it to him if I don't even know what it is? What he needs is a good butt whipping, but it's kinda late for that now."

"What he needs is a man to talk to. He needs a man to tell him the things it takes to be a man. I sure don't know what that is, because I'm not a man. He is reaching out for you, so I guess whatever you know can help him."

"I don't see why I should be forced to have a relationship with my son. Do you want the fifty dollars or not?"

"Please forgive me. You are absolutely right, Gary. Forgive me for calling you. I have no right to call you about anything pertaining to Damon, because you have demonstrated your commitment to him all of his life. And you know what, Gary? You don't ever have to worry about me picking up a telephone to call you again. As long as I am black, I will never call you about your son. Please forgive me and have a good evening." I hung up and paced the floor for hours, finally resigning myself to the fact that my only son would be in jail.

While he was in prison in New York, Damon was extradited to Virginia to face charges on a three-year-old case. He pleaded guilty and was sentenced to five to seven years. He would be eligible for parole after serving two years. I cried and vomited for two weeks. I don't think I have ever experienced such emotional pain in my entire adult life. I prayed and wrote about my feelings every day, sometimes three times a day. It is not your fault, I told myself. It is his lesson. It is the result of choices he has made. Now he will learn to choose again. It took about two years for me to understand what Damon and I had been going through. When it was clear in my mind, I wrote him a letter sharing my deepest thoughts and feelings:

> Dear Damon,
>
> I have received your most recent letter, and I was very glad to hear from you. I have not blocked your collect calls. I have not been paid for quite some time, and I do not have a telephone. I am thankful for this time to be still and listen to my own thoughts. I recognize that you have grown a great deal and believe you have made great strides in your personal development, but it still feels to me that there are many things that you do not understand. I am sure that you have

an idea that my financial situation is not the best it could be right now, yet you write asking me to do something for you. You and I both know the amount of money you have had and wasted, and that you saved nothing for a rainy day. This is why I am so amazed that when you need something you have no qualms about asking me for help, no matter what my situation may be. I guess that is what sons believe mothers are for. It does not, however, make me feel good.

Every day I pray for you. I pray for your enlightenment and your growth. I ask God to touch you right where you are and bring your heart and mind into alignment with His will for you. I pray that you will become one with God and the spirit of God within you. I know that prayer can get into places that I cannot reach. I know that prayer can straighten out situations I do not understand. I guess I need to pray a little harder and a little longer for you.

I spent twenty-two dollars to purchase the book you asked me to buy. I spent another two dollars and ninety cents to send it to you. I am not responsible if the Department of Corrections loses the book. Now, with my telephone off and no money to pay the rent, you want me to pay to Xerox the book and send it to you. That will not happen. I have sent you more than a hundred dollars' worth of books in the last month. This is more than enough for you to read for the next year. Read them over and over again. Each time you read them, you will discover something new. You may even discover how to get the twenty-five dollars you need to submit your college application. The time has come for you to do for yourself. You must learn how to figure things out and make them work for you. You must pray and ask for guidance.

I am happy that you are studying with the brothers. However, being a Muslim, a Christian, or anything else means absolutely nothing if it does not help you find a better way to live. If your chosen faith does not open your mind to the great possibilities of life, it means absolutely nothing. I know that while you are in prison, reading helps you to pass the time. The issue is how is it going to help you when you get out, if you are still thinking the same way, feeling the same way, acting the same way? You do not need God or Allah to keep you where you are. You want the Creative Force of the Higher Consciousness to move you to a new place in your mind and heart.

I was quite shocked to read in your letter, "a divorce would crush me," and "I want for my daughter what I did not have—two parents." The fact of the matter is, you are already divorced. You do not live with your wife. You do not support your wife. You have broken your marriage vows by being unfaithful and not fulfilling your responsibilities as a husband "to love, honor, and obey." The fact that your wife uses your name, if she does, and the fact that you exchanged vows do not mean a thing. Where is the honor? You have not honored her. She does not honor you "in sickness and in health." Right now, you are in a state of sickness. Where is your wife? "For richer, for poorer." Aren't you poor in spirit and finances right now? Where is your wife? And where were you when she needed you? You cannot correct a wrong, Damon. You can learn a lesson, ask for forgiveness, and move on. You cannot build for your daughter what you did not have, because that may not be what she needs. You can give her what you do have, with the best intentions and unconditional love. It will be up to her to accept or reject what you give her.

The truth of the matter is that you have always had two parents. I have always been your mother. Gary has always been your father. You have always known where I was. You have always known who and where Gary was. We may not have lived together, but you have always had a father. You also had Grandpa. You had John. You had Eddie. You had

Adeyemi. None of them was your biological father, but they were there for you when your biological father was not. You must accept your blessings, however they come. You have always had a man in your life. John, however badly he treated me, never let you children be without everything you needed. You had a home. You had food. God knows you had clothes. While you were growing up, there was nothing you needed that you did not have. It was not until you were sixteen that things got bad for us. Think about it. What did you ever do without? You were eating shrimp for lunch when you were five years old. There was always a man to play with you, nurture you, and support you. There was a male presence there for you at the worst of times. Each of these men treated you the same way they treated their own children; in some cases, you were treated better. It is unfortunate that when they left me, they also left you. I always asked them to speak to you. They chose not to.

If you are saying that you wanted your father in the house, that is a different issue. Knowing the kind of person your father is, tell me what difference would it have made for him to be in the house? He has proven himself to be irresponsible, emotionally unavailable, selfish, and undependable. These are things you have discovered about him. You said, "He is and always has been out for himself." Is that the kind of father you wanted present? Is that the kind of man you would want me to live with? Knowing what you know about him, would you have wanted me to go through life with your father? Think about it. When you love someone, you want them to be happy, even when their happiness means you must make a sacrifice.

Your father separated himself from me when I was three months pregnant with you. He demonstrated that he did not respect me as a woman, nor as the mother of his son. He is not to blame or at fault. The truth is, Damon, I did not respect myself. I did not know who I was or what I had come into this life to do. I was a sick, frightened young girl, with no guidance. I was looking for love in the bed. I was using my vagina instead of my head. There is no reason I should have had sex with anyone when I was sixteen years old. Your father and I did not have a relationship. We were not even boyfriend and girlfriend. I was looking for a daddy. He had a hard-on. It is really that simple. Why you chose, in your spirit, to come through our bodies is part of God's plan for you. If you want to know why, ask God. I realize it is not easy to accept certain things about your mother, but you must remember I have not always been your mother. I came into this life with my own issues, challenges, and obstacles to overcome. When you came into my life, I was knee deep in a pile of crap. Unfortunately, you had to walk through it with me. God knew that it would someday pay off for both of us.

Things happen in our lives so that we can learn from them. The reason I have had so many relationships that have not worked is because I have always tried to build for you what I did not have: a family. It did not work because you have to do what you do because you want to do it, not because you are trying to make up for something else. My lesson in life was to live with what was given to me, see the good in it, and strive to do better. I spent most of my life trying to find the father I did not have growing up. I did not realize it at the time, and I have only recently learned my lesson. Now you must learn yours.

Old eyes can see much better than young eyes. As parents, we often see what our children are doing and want something better for them. Unfortunately, we do not always know how to say what we see, so we say the wrong thing. I have told you from the very beginning, your relationship with your wife was not built on a stable foundation. It always appeared that she was using you to escape the unstable relationship she had with her mother. Perhaps what I should have said was, "Damon, I know our family life has not been what you wanted or needed: however, you can make your own life what you want it to be. If you want the best, you do not have to settle for less than the best." In your eyes, your wife was/is the best for you, but what are you comparing her to? The environments to which you have been exposed have not been the best. The people you have known have not been the best. How can you evaluate what is good and what is bad if you have only experienced mediocre?

I see what you are doing and have done, because my eyes are sixteen years older than yours are. I am not saying that things will not work out for you and your wife. That, I do not know. What I am saying is that, at twenty-three years old, your eyes are still closed. When you have spent more than seventeen of those years in my house, looking at life through my eyes, and another almost three years in and out of prison, how many years have you really used your own eyes? And when you did use your eyes, what did you see? Quick ways to make money and break the law. Ways to make yourself feel important in violation of man's law and God's law. You are still blind as to what life is really all about. The Bible says, "Eyes have not seen and ears have not heard what God has in store for those who love Him." You are still blind as to who you are and what God has in store for you.

If you think God made you to be "crushed" by a mere human woman who comes from the same God you do, you cannot know God. How do you know why God brought you into this woman's life? Maybe you came to save her, to help her, to teach her a lesson. Now you want things to go the way you think they should go, not the way God planned. In the past, you were very good to your wife and her mother. Perhaps you were the tool God was using to help them out.

When God's plan is fulfilled, you must move on to the next phase of the plan.

If you believe God brought your daughter onto this earth for you to take care of, you are not only blind, you are dumb. Kahlil Gibran wrote a book entitled *The Prophet*. In that book he wrote, "Your children are not your children. They are the sons and daughters of life searching for their own. They come through you but they are not from you. Although they are with you, they belong not to you." God has a divine plan for us all. Our job is to tap into the energy of God and bring ourselves into alignment with that plan. Sometimes things do not go the way we plan or the way we think they should go. That does not mean we are wrong or that God is wrong. It simply means we have to dig a little deeper, search a little harder to find the meaning, the lesson.

There are many things I wish I could have done for you and your sisters that I did not do. That is because I had my own blindness and sickness to heal. That does not mean I was wrong or bad. It simply means I had to work to get my eyes open. That did not happen for me until I stopped the drama of looking for a daddy, trying to please Daddy and make him proud of me. In all the time I spent doing that, I was trying to be who and what I was not. Not so long ago, I stopped the drama and said, Okay, God, what am I supposed to be doing? At that point, my life totally fell apart.

You see, Damon, whatever is going on in your life comes from inside you. Even my telephone being disconnected is an internal issue. All the negative thoughts and emotional crap must be cleaned out before God can build a foundation inside us. When the crap starts surfacing, it looks like trouble, it looks like things are going bad, and it looks like we are doing the wrong thing. Nothing could be further from the truth. The truth is, when we go to God, He must tear us down in order to build us up. God cannot build upon our distorted ideas, foolish beliefs, miseducation, and misinformation. All of that must come out as conditions we live through so that we can see what we have been thinking. When things go bad in our lives, we try to fix them because we don't realize God is fixing us. Until we see the bad stuff, we cannot make up our minds not to do the things that brought us to that point in the first place.

I am almost forty years old, and I am just beginning to understand who I am and what God wants me to do. There are times when I doubt. That is when I pray. There are times when I am afraid. That is when I remember, "Fear not, for I am with you." There are times when I want to throw my hands up, go get a real job, working for somebody else from nine to five, and say, "Forget this crap!" Then I remember, "For everything, there is a season. A time to laugh and a time to cry." I have been crying for almost forty years. It is time for me to laugh. In order to laugh, I know I must work through the crap, live through the bad, and have my eyes opened wide to the miracle of life called ME.

Right now, I want nothing more than a family, a home, and a man to love me and work with me, to build with me, and share life with me. I do not want to raise any more children. I do not want to suffer. I do not want to be broke. I want to live my life to the fullest every day, enjoying every moment. I know that is about to happen. I also know, in the divine time and the divine way, it will happen. I am no longer willing to accept less than the best. I still make mistakes, but now, when I do, my eyes are open enough for me to say, Okay, that is a mistake, I cannot do that again. I catch myself in the process and change what I am doing.

You have always wanted to have your way. You have always wanted things to go the way you want them to go. When you get an idea in your head, you will not let it go. I

remember how you would always say, "If it kills me, I will..."
If you do not open your eyes soon, this thing with your wife
and mother-in-law will kill you. It will kill your spirit. It will
kill your mind. I know you have prayed and asked God to
show you. Well, I think He is showing you, but your eyes are
closed. Your wife does not write, she does not send you
money, her hair is more important than your coat. She makes
absolutely no attempt to mend or heal your relationship. You
continue to hold on and insist. Could it be that God is showing you who your wife really is? Could it be that you need to
use your mother-in-law to excuse your wife for what she is
doing? She married you without her mother's permission
and against my advice. She knew you were selling drugs and
stealing cars before her mother knew it. She knew that the
two of you were not prepared and could not afford to have a
baby. When she wanted you, she did exactly what her
mother told her not to do. Now she is showing you she does
not want you, and you want to blame her mother. Why? Because your eyes and ears are still closed. You are still blind,
and you are making yourself dumb.

After all that has happened between you and me, I am
still here for you, doing what I can for you. That is my
choice. I could have said to hell with you a long time ago. I
did not, because I am your mother, in good times and in bad,
for richer or poorer. Parenting, like marriage, is "until death
do us part." That is what it takes in a relationship. You must
take the good and the bad, do what you can, and pray for better. God is trying to tell you something, Damon. I think it
would be wise for you to listen. I know it is not easy. I know
you think you are right and your current situation is not fair.
I know you wish it were another way. Maybe one day it will
be different. If God has it in the plan for you, it will be different. If you want so badly to be with the wrong person,
imagine how wonderful it will be when the right person

comes along. For right now, take your blinders off! Get off your knees! Praying is not a nine-to-five job. Prayer must begin in your heart. Pray for yourself and then for your wife. Remember that what you let go will come back to you if it is yours. Also remember that God never closes one door without opening another.

When I was pregnant with you, a very dear friend of mine offered to help me get an abortion. This was in 1970, when abortions were still illegal. I thought about it for a very long time before I decided that was not what I wanted to do. Something inside of me knew I would make it, no matter what, and you would make it. When I looked in your little face, I knew I had made the right decision. You were a beautiful baby. You were never any trouble. You grew into a beautiful child who was not difficult to love or take care of. You are now a beautiful man. You are strong. You are healthy. You are a master! I was once ashamed to say, "My son is in jail." I would lie about it and tell people you were away with your wife, who is in the navy. Now I want the world to know, because I know you are healing. As you heal, a part of me heals. When I think about it, I was in the prison of needing to be loved for most of my life. Now I know I am loved and that God loves me. I also know God loves you, Damon, even when your wife isn't sure she does.

There are many types of jails. Some people are in the jails of their limited minds. Many people are in the jail of drinking alcohol, taking drugs, working on a job they hate, or living in bad relationships. We are all doing some kind of time. The only difference is that some of us have keys to our cells and others do not. Nobody but you can imprison your mind. Nobody can imprison your spirit. My son was born of the Master, and nobody who makes a deal with the Master can lose!

I love you.

I support you.

I pray for your highest and your best.

I am Iyanla, your Great Mother.

Speaking engagements were coming in, I was still seeing a few clients, I had financial support from the ministry, but I still had money woes. Gemmia decided that she didn't like college and wanted to come home and work. That was a big help. I talked to Balé about the conflict I was having about doing spiritual work and getting paid for it. He told me to start thinking about what I was doing as a business and to charge accordingly. He wasn't speaking about the consultations; he was referring to speaking and writing. I would speak for fifty or a hundred dollars. I would speak for free if I were asked. Balé reminded me that I was a lawyer and a priest and had a right to charge people for my training and my skills. He asked me one of those questions that cause my brain to fry: *"How much do you think you are worth? How much is an hour of your time worth?"*

"I don't know. What do you mean?"

"I mean that people are going to treat you according to the value you place on yourself. If you come cheap, they will treat you cheap."

"But Balé, how can I say I am doing spiritual work and charge people lots of money for it?"

"Gravediggers do spiritual work. They create the space that houses the body that the spirit lives in, and they make a lot of money for an hour's worth of work. If you do not see the business aspect of this, you are never going to reach the place you are trying to get to." It was time to go back to the list.

What do you want to do? I want to earn a living speaking and writing. *What is your greatest strength?* Oral communication. *What is your greatest weakness?* Not having the money I need to take care of my family. *What is your greatest fear?* If I ask people for what I want, they will say no and they will not like me.

I knew I was onto something, and I wanted to do the right thing. I especially wanted to do the right thing for my children. I was bringing a spiritual message to a community that desperately needed to hear it, and I wanted to do it the right way. I thought if I could save the world, then my children would forget what a rotten mother I had been. I was obsessed with the work, I was obsessed with trying to correct my mistakes, and I was obsessed with doing it all the right way. The truth is, I was obsessed by the need to please everybody in the process of doing the right thing. I was losing myself, losing my dreams, and I kept losing my home.

In my mind, the right thing to do was to make sure that I saved the people, all of the people, and I didn't feel like I had a right to be paid for it. I was trying my best to live up to my name, believing that God would provide for me. At that point, I still had a very intellectual understanding of my name, what I was doing, parenting, and God.

Most of my serious messages came to me in dreams. Had I known this particular dream was coming, I would have given up sleeping forever. I saw myself standing in a room, and there were babies all around me. All of the babies were crying. I was trying to pick them up. I was trying to feed them. I was trying everything I knew to stop them from crying. I started calling for help. When I looked up, Nisa was standing in front of me. She was pregnant.

The next morning I told Nisa about the dream. She turned "puke green."

"Are you sexually active, Nisa?"

"What do you mean?" she asked.

"I mean, are you having sex? Do you have sex with boys? You know, doing the nasty?"

"Mommy, please. I don't do that."

"Well, I'll tell you what. When you come home this afternoon, we are going to Planned Parenthood. You are going to get some birth control."

"Why?" I gave her a look that shut her mouth and sent her to school an hour early.

I couldn't be still all day. It seemed like three o'clock would never arrive. Then I had a thought: She's going to run away. I started shaking and could not stop. I told Gemmia to come with me; we were going to pick Nisa up from school. We did and went directly from there to the

Planned Parenthood office. When I signed Nisa in, the clerk asked what services we were interested in.

"She needs to take a pregnancy test." I almost jumped out of my skin when I heard the words come out of my mouth.

"How old are you?" the clerk asked Nisa.

"Sixteen," Nisa answered. The woman turned her gaze back to me.

"In the State of Pennsylvania, she doesn't need your permission to have the test done, and she must authorize us to share the results with you."

"Do you want me to slap the taste out of your mouth?" I admit I was having a very unspiritual moment. "Just do the test!" I stormed away from the desk and flopped down in a chair. Nisa sat across the room until they called her name. It was an hour later when we saw her again. She headed straight for the exit.

"What were the results?" I asked, already knowing the answer.

"They said they will call me in a day or two." I knew she was not telling the truth. I walked back to the desk, to the woman I had threatened earlier. In my sweetest voice, I asked if I could speak to the nurse. She called her immediately.

Nisa and I went back into the office. The nurse asked how she could help us.

"I want to know what is going on with my daughter. She says that her test results will take a few days. I thought the results were immediate." The nurse looked at me and then at Nisa. Then she sat down and offered me a seat.

"We didn't do a pelvic exam on Nisa because we think she's about eight and a half months pregnant. It really isn't in the baby's best interest to do a pelvic exam now. But I gave her some brochures on adoption and foster care. I told her if she needed counseling, I would arrange it for her."

"Eight and a half months?"

"Yes. You mean you didn't know? Nisa said you were not in favor of her keeping the baby."

"Eight and a half months?"

I thanked the woman and left the building. I left Gemmia sitting on the sofa, and Nisa sitting in the office. I was walking up the street like a mad woman. Gemmia was running behind me, asking what happened.

"Ask your sister. Ask her what happened."

"Nisa, what's going on? Are you pregnant?" Gemmia asked her sister.

"No. I don't know what that woman was talking about." I stopped dead in my tracks.

"Are you crazy?" I was screaming now. "Are you out of your mind? You are eight and a half months pregnant! You are so pregnant they can't even examine you! What do you mean, no? Are you crazy?"

"I mean, I don't know how it happened. I've never had sex."

"She's crazy! She is out of her mind! Maybe you never had sex with anybody, but somebody sure had sex with you. You are pregnant, fool. Do you know what that means? What the hell do you mean, you have never had sex? Are you crazy?"

We were standing in the middle of Walnut Street in downtown Philadelphia at rush hour. Hundreds of people were staring at us. I was screaming at the top of my lungs, flailing my arms like a lunatic. The only thing Gemmia could think to say was "Oh my God!" It got worse.

By the time we got home, I was exhausted. I had screamed, cursed, and made a fool of myself. I kept asking Nisa questions, but before she could answer, I was off having another bout of hysteria.

"How?" "When?" "Where?" "Who?" "I have left you home for days. Now that I'm home almost every day, you get knocked up." "How?" "Where?" "Were you in my bed?" I carried on for hours before I got to the real question. "Why didn't you tell me?"

"I didn't know."

"Nisa, you are eight and a half months pregnant. Doesn't the baby move?"

"No. I've never felt anything moving in me."

"The baby has to move, Nisa. It's ready to be born."

Then it hit me. She plays soccer at school. The baby is dead! That set me off again. I didn't know whether to be happy or afraid. If the baby was dead, we didn't have to worry. But that meant that my child, my baby girl, would have to deliver a dead baby. Oh my God!

The next morning I called every clinic, every hospital, and every birth center in the city. I explained the situation, hoping to get an appointment for a sonogram. The earliest appointment I could get was June third. It was May twenty-first.

The next week was torture. I tried to stay away from Nisa because, though part of me wanted to comfort her, the other part wanted to end her life. My worst nightmare had come to pass. My teenage daughter was pregnant. I spoke to the guidance counselor at school. She said she had questioned Nisa, but Nisa had denied being sexually active to her also. I told her the name of the boy Nisa said was responsible. The counselor said she would track him down. When she called to say that she had no record of a student by that name having ever attended the school, I went crazy again. It never dawned on me that I knew exactly what it felt like to be pregnant, sixteen, alone, and afraid. By the time it did, my grandson was born.

The first face he saw when he entered the world was mine. He took one look at me, his crazy grandmother, and he cried. Oluwalomoju Adeyemi Vanzant (we call him Oluwa) was born May 28, 1991, at 7:11 P.M. He weighed in at six pounds thirteen ounces, just like his mother. He was the most beautiful thing I had seen in a long time. The minute I saw him, I forgot how he got here and I fell in love.

The cycles continue. The patterns repeat themselves. Our children bring our subconscious issues into life. They show us the parts of us that we need to heal. Nisa was my silent cry and search for love. Damon was my irresponsibility and rebellion. Gemmia was my creative genius. It was all staring me in the face. This was not about my children. This was about me. This was about me getting myself together at a deeper level. What my children and my grandson did was push me a little further along the path, a little faster than I would have gotten there on my own. This was my lesson in forgiveness and acceptance. This was my unconditional love. This was my lesson in self-value and self-worth. These were lessons that I had missed and now needed to repeat because I had to teach

them to my daughter. She in turn would have to teach them to my
grandson.

I knew exactly what was going on in my life, but I did not know
what to do about it. I knew that I had been chosen by the universe of fate
to create a new and better way of living for my family and myself. I knew
that I was not going to die like my mother or my father, broke, desperate,
having accomplished nothing, leaving nothing behind for their children.
I knew I was not going to end up like Ray, lost in pain. I knew all that I
had lived through and survived, and I knew it was for a reason. Unfortunately, I didn't know how to break the cycle. I didn't know how to re-
create the pattern. One of my favorite passages in the Bible is Matthew
11:28, "Come unto me, all ye that labour and are heavy laden, and I will
give you rest." I was trying my hardest to get to God, but I was afraid
that once I got there, He would be mad at me for all of the things that I
had not forgiven myself for. When I tried to forgive myself, I found myself struggling through the millions of fibers of the pattern that had been
etched into my soul. Just when I thought I had made it through, I would
find myself tangled in another string. I would stumble, and I would forget to lie there and rest before jumping up and running out to do something else.

One major mistake I made in growing into my new identity was not
giving myself enough time to master what I was learning. As soon as I
heard something, I would give it away. I would write, speak, or teach
about it. I guess I was so excited, I wanted everyone to know. I did a
grave disservice to my delicate psyche, which was so hungry for information. I did not let what I learned settle in so that I could see and understand it at a deeper level. That's what happens when we use the intellect
instead of the heart. The intellect is like a computer. It will process the
information in a matter of seconds. The spirit is like a womb. It needs
time to develop new information.

Grandma had taught me how to pray, but Nisa taught me what to
pray about. I was on my knees so much, I shrank two inches. Dear God,
please help me. Please don't let this baby go through what I went
through. Please don't let my child go through what I went through.

What am I going to do? Tell me what to do, God. How is she going to raise a baby? How am I going to raise a baby? What are we going to do with this baby?

I'm sure God felt like Nisa. I was asking questions, but not waiting for answers. I was in a state of panic. It was that panic that sent me running to healers and teachers and books. It was that panic that sent me to meditation classes and more workshops. It was the panic that reminded me of the prayer on the back of the card I had received at my father's funeral:

> In our deepest hour of need, the Creator does not ask us for credentials. He accepts us exactly as we are, knowing that we are His erring children. He loves us and forgives us. Why can't we forgive ourselves?

I had to learn to forgive. First myself, and then everyone else I believed had ever done anything to me. Lesson 121 in *A Course in Miracles* begins, "What could you want that forgiveness cannot give?" I read the text of that lesson all day, every day, for at least two weeks.

Every woman I knew brought something that Oluwa needed. By the time he was two weeks old, we had no place to keep all his things. Nisa was walking down the street one day, and a woman called to her from her doorway.

"Do you need a car seat for the baby?"

When Nisa told her she did, the woman gave her one. We didn't even have a car anymore. I sent Nisa back to school the Monday after the baby was born. Gemmia watched Oluwa during the day. Nisa had him at night. When it was apparent that Nisa couldn't handle the baby all night and school all day, Gemmia took over full-time. I was on the road a lot more now, and the more I forgave myself, the more work I got. Two months after Oluwa was born, I got the call to write *Acts of Faith*.

In his book *Conversations With God, Book One,* Neale Donald Walsch wrote, "When you declare yourself to be a thing, everything unlike you will show up." I wish I had known that back then. I wish I had known that the minute I declared myself to be a teacher, a minister, a "Great Mother," everything possible would show up to test my sincerity. I didn't know it. I didn't recognize the tests. I thought I was being punished and so I doubted myself. Then along came *Acts of Faith*. I had a contract with a major publisher. I was being paid more money than I had ever received since leaving the legal profession. *Tapping the Power Within* was selling extremely well. My ministry had grown out of the front door. My daughter had just had a baby. In the midst of it all, I was being asked to write a book. A whole, entire book. Every fiber of my being was screaming, "You're not good enough! You're stupid! You can't do that. If you do, they will find out. You don't believe a word of what you're saying!" I didn't let that stop me. I wrote it anyway.

When things get bad, people have a tendency to fall apart and stop. I know how to fall apart and keep moving. That has been my salvation. I have been able to move through pain, anger, doubt, worthlessness, value-lessness, and fear without missing a step. If you had seen me on any day during that time, you would have never known that I was on the verge of a complete breakdown. Those close to me knew it. I knew it. I would talk to my best friend and prayer partner, Shaheerah, about what I was feeling. I always told her I felt like I was being dishonest. She would remind me over and over, "You can only teach what you need to learn." Shaheerah and I have been through some pretty rough times together. Had it not been for her prayers, her faith in me, her words, which were at times like buckets of cold water, Iyanla never would have been born. When she was coming, a breech birth, Shaheerah was like a midwife who knew exactly what to do or say to turn me around. Shaheerah and I knew what was at the core of my struggle. We rarely talked about it, but we both knew.

I was disobedient, and God knew it. I kept getting messages, seeing visions, hearing things, but I would not listen. Every time I prayed the same prayer, I got the same answer. It wasn't that I didn't know the answer. It was that I didn't believe the answer. I didn't believe it because I didn't think I deserved to be blessed by God. The answer that popped into my mind, no matter what tragedy, crisis, or challenge I faced, was

"Lean not on your own understanding. Honor me in all thy ways and I will give you the desires of your heart." It was so simple, and yet I chose not to believe it. I chose to do it my way. I would ask for guidance and then make up my own mind. Still, the blessings kept coming. I kept getting the support and assistance I needed when I needed it. Each time something wonderful or tragic would happen, it would force me to a new level of myself where I would ask, "Why me?" When the answer was revealed, I would have to clean up my act a bit more.

Writing *Acts of Faith* helped me to develop an intimate and personal relationship with God. It was in that process that I met God for the first time. I met the God of my understanding. The God I could feel in my heart. It was in the writing process that I learned there are many paths that lead to one road. I realized that God didn't care if I was a Yoruba or a Christian. God wasn't concerned with the fact that each of my children had a different father, and He wasn't keeping track of who I slept with. God wanted me to love myself. God wanted me to honor myself. God had a purpose for me and for my life, and if I would ask and trust, trust and believe, God would make all things possible. It was in the process of writing *Acts of Faith* that I discovered God's love and my love for myself. I gave up the fight. I gave up fighting myself, fighting life, and fighting God.

I had been fighting all of my life. Fighting for attention, fighting for love, fighting for survival. I had been fighting for my children, and fighting for acknowledgment as a human being who mattered. I had been fighting so long that if there was nothing to fight, I would find something or someone to fight. I expected to fight, so when I was confronted with situations, I would pick a fight. I had become defensive, aggressive, and combative. I didn't want to fight anymore. I didn't want to fight fear, or doubt, or even loneliness. What I wanted to do was heal. And I wanted to do it peacefully.

Everything I put in that book was what I needed to get through a difficult period of my life. I was coming to the understanding that God is my defense and my defender. Every morning I would pray, ask God what to write, and God would tell me. If I needed information, I was told who to call. When I needed to talk, someone would call me. The members of the ministry fed my family while I was writing. Some gave us money, others cleaned my house. It was as if the entire universe opened up and sent me everything I needed. Gemmia stayed home and braided hair. Nisa went to school. I wrote all day and sometimes into the night.

When I would get tired or frustrated, I prayed. When I prayed, I felt better. In the process of writing, I reviewed every journal I had ever written. I recalled every conversation I had ever had with Balé. I was hearing the same old things in a brand new way. Things that Grandma, Daddy, and Nett had said to me had a fresh, new flavor. Things I had read became clearer, more focused. I put it all in the book. I put my heart and soul in that book. I put the love I was finding within myself in that book.

One day at Kinko's, while I was printing out my pages, one of the clerks asked me if I was a writer. I told her I was.

"I do typing work at home when I'm not here."

"How much do you charge?"

"A dollar a page, but that includes all corrections, too."

I gave her the pile of papers in my hand, took her telephone number, and left. Now all I had to do was write.

I finished *Acts of Faith* in about two months. I missed my deadline, but I finished the book. I had no idea how good the book was, because I never read it. I figured out early on that the reason I had been assigned by the universe to write that book was to open my heart to God. When I finished the book, I did my list again.

> *What is your favorite color?*
> Orange.
> *What is your favorite food?*
> Chicken.
> *What is your favorite song?*
> "Order My Steps."
> *What is your most valued possession?*

Love.
What is your greatest strength?
God.
What is your greatness weakness?
Not trusting God.
What is your best skill?
Prayer.
What was your greatest mistake?
Thinking I could do anything without God.
What is your greatest fear?
I have no fear. I know God is always with me.
What is your greatest accomplishment?
Learning to forgive and love myself.
What is the one task that you are least fond of doing?
Cleaning up China's crap.
If your life ended today, what is the one thing everyone who knows you would say about you?
That she loved and served God.
What would you want them to say?
She loved God.
Why wouldn't or couldn't they say what you would want them to say?
Because they didn't know Iyanla. They only knew Rhonda.

Shortly after the manuscript was turned in, Gemmia, the cat, and I moved to Maryland. Nisa stayed in Philadelphia to complete a program that was training her to become a home health-care worker. Two years later, on the same date that I had found out Nisa was pregnant with Oluwa, she gave birth to her second son, in my house, on Oluwa's bed. His name is Adesola, which means "the crown has come."

CHAPTER EIGHTEEN

What's the Lesson When You Let the Past Pass?

Soul Surgery changes our consciousness.
And in changing our consciousness it releases us from
  our problems
and prepares us for our good.
But unless our consciousness remains changed
problems will always return.
Unless we can sustain the freedom from false beliefs . . .
We run the risk of having our consciousness attract
back to us the same or similar situations as before.
Richard Jafolla, in Soul Surgery

AS I LAY ON THE FLOOR of my office, it all became clear. There had been a moment, however brief, when I tried to live life on my terms. I had taken my eyes off God and tried to do my own thing. Perhaps that was why I tried to negotiate the contract for myself. Maybe it was when I let myself be talked into staying somewhere I knew I didn't belong. I knew that I had given someone control of my decision-making process. But none of that mattered now. The bottom line was that I had hired Karen because the moment I took my eyes off God and tried to live on my own power, I felt powerless. That state of powerlessness brought up all of Rhonda's stuff, and I had fallen into her pattern of being a victim. My goodness! What a revelation!

It was time for a happy bath. Happy baths are the kind you take when you light candles and put on music you can sing along with. I think I'll do Luther. No. That will give my husband ideas, and I'm not finished yet. Maybe I'll do Patti. "Somebody Loves You, Baby." No, I think I'll do Al Jarreau. "Tenderness." That's exactly what I need—to be tender. I need to be tender with myself, with my thoughts about Rhonda, and especially with my thoughts about Karen. I understood that what I had done had been very unloving. I hadn't meant for it to be, but it was. Whenever we make someone else responsible for our lives, we are not demonstrating love. It was Karen's job to sell my work, but I now understood how I had taken it way beyond that. I had made her responsible for me. I had mixed business and friendship, and I had not honored my boundaries.

As the tub began to fill, I let my thoughts wander. I guess it's hard to have boundaries when you were allowed none as a child. There is never a place for you to just go and be with yourself. You have no privacy. Wherever you are, somebody else is there. When you find a temporary place to be, you never know if or when somebody is going to walk up on you. I didn't have a room or a door as a child. Rhonda had no place to retreat to, no place to go. Besides that, the adults in her life violated all of the boundaries she did have. I had carried that into my adult life. I gave up my boundaries much too easily. I needed to remember that business is business, friendship is friendship, and my life is my life. Whenever I lost sight of that, things got confused. Roles got confused. Now I could see how many times it had happened before. How many times I had lost sight of my boundaries for fear of making someone mad. Or when I thought I needed someone in order to survive. When I thought my survival was at stake, I would allow a person to be in my life in a way they had no right to be. In a way that I did not want them to be.

Slipping into the tub, I remembered something Aunt Mabel told me. It was something that she told me about my mother, Sarah.

❤

I had found Aunt Mabel's telephone number among the handwritten papers that my father had left for me. For some reason, her name stuck out in my mind. I remembered her from Atlantic City and the Saturday night basement parties. I also remembered hearing that Aunt Mabel was Sarah's sister. I needed to know. I needed to know the truth.

Without thinking about how I would explain who I was, or wondering whether or not she would remember me, I called Aunt Mabel. I remember thinking to myself, *Your mother's sister will know exactly who you are.* She answered the telephone on the first ring. I was so startled, she had to repeat her hello.

"Is this Mabel?"

"Yes. Who's speaking, please?"

"Mabel, I don't know if you remember me. My name is Ronnie. I am Sarah's daughter." That was the first time in my life those words had ever come across my lips. There was silence on the other end. I was just about to call her name again, when she spoke.

"Thank you, Jesus! Thank you! Thank you, Jesus! Thank you, Father! You don't know how long I have been waiting. Thank you, Jesus! You don't know how long my baby sister has been waiting. Oh my God, my God. How are you? How are you, my precious baby?"

We were both crying. Aunt Mabel was thanking God at the end of every question without giving me an opportunity to answer.

"Do you know how long I have been waiting and looking for you? Thank you, God. Where have you been? Thank you, Jesus. Nobody could tell me a thing. Thank you. Thank you. They all said they didn't know. My God, my God. God promised me that I would see my sister's children before I closed my eyes for the last time. I prayed and asked God. God answers prayer. Thank you, God. Where is your brother? Where is baby Ray?"

When Aunt Mabel calmed down, I told her that Ray was just fine. I did not tell her that he had a drinking problem. I told her about my children, I told her I had been through law school. When I said that, she started crying all over again. "You must be like your mother. She was smart as a whip." Hearing that made me cry. She asked about Nett and

Daddy. I told her about Daddy and that Nett was fine. We talked for nearly three hours. Aunt Mabel said that she had some pictures and that she wanted to see me and the children. I told her that my boyfriend was coming to D.C. in two weeks, and that I would come with him. She started crying again. When I hung up the telephone, I knew that Aunt Mabel had the information I needed to finally make sense of my life. I knew that if Nett was willing to acknowledge that she was not my mother, I needed to know a little something about my real mother.

Holding flowers in my hand and carrying framed pictures of my children in a shopping bag, I rang Aunt Mabel's doorbell. When I heard feet shuffling up the hallway, my heart started to race. When the first lock turned, I broke out in a cold sweat. I wanted to run. I had to pee. I was freezing. The chain slid off. The doorknob turned. The door slowly opened. Standing before me was a picture of myself. I was short, about four feet ten inches tall. I had a beautiful head of salt-and-pepper hair that was mostly salt. I wore glasses. If it were not for the circles under my eyes and the age lines around my mouth, you would not have known how old I was. I had never seen myself like this before. I was beautiful. No. I was gorgeous.

We stood in the doorway, staring at each other and crying. She was thanking Jesus. I was mumbling, "Oh my God." When she reached forward and touched me, the top of her head came to my chin. I rested my face on her head, and we cried some more. One of her neighbors opened their door and peeked out at us, so we went inside her apartment, still holding on to one another. I didn't let go until I really did have to pee.

When I came out of the bathroom, she was waiting for me in the hallway. She took my hand and led me to the kitchen. She had prepared a lunch of cornbread, collard greens, and iced tea.

"I don't eat no meat no more since I started suffering so bad with pressure. I had to change my diet."

"That's okay, Aunt Mabel. If you fixed this for me, it's just fine."

"Do you still like chicken? You children was some chicken-eatin' somebodies. Your daddy and grandmomma was always travelin' with a bag of chicken for you and your brother, Ray. He still like the wings?"

She knew everything. She knew all about me. I was so full I didn't want to eat, but knowing that she would be upset, I took a few forkfuls before asking her the question. "What can you tell me about my mother. I mean, was she my mother? Was Sarah really my mother?"

"Oh, blessed Lord in heaven! Of course she was your mother. What do you mean? What do you want to know?"

"I never really knew for sure. No one ever talked about her much. I kept hearing little things, but nobody, not even Daddy, ever told me anything about her."

"He wouldn't, that lyin' dog. I know it's wrong to speak ill of the dead, but if I could get my hands on him, I would ring his pretty neck. Was he still pretty when he died? Because he was a real pretty boy when he was alive. And what about his momma? She still livin'?"

"Yes. As far as I know, she is." Aunt Mabel walked out of the kitchen without saying a word. She returned with a large photo album. Using her apron, she dusted the cornbread crumbs off the table, put the album down, and began to give me my history.

Aunt Mabel had pictures of my mother's side of the family dating back to the early 1900s. She was quick to point out all of the "real Africans." Some of the pictures looked like they had been drawn and then photographed. Looking through that album, I met my maternal grandmother, Elizabeth. Her mother, Hortense. I met my grandfather, Samuel, and his mother, Francine. I met cousins and aunts and uncles, and then, I met my mother, Sarah Elizabeth Jefferson. She looked like an older version of Gemmia.

Sarah was five feet eleven inches tall, which made her three inches taller than Daddy. She was slender, with very large breasts. There were pictures of her with shoulder-length hair, but in most of them, her hair was pulled into a bun that sat on top of her head. I saw pictures of her with my father, with her sisters, and with her mother. In some she posed on cars, in others she was standing on steps, or next to trees. When I saw the picture of my mother holding me in her arms, I fell to pieces. I knew then that the lady in the hospital room, at the cemetery, in the kitchen had been with me all of my life. I had a mother who loved me. She was real and she loved me.

Aunt Mabel told me all of the family stories and secrets, who begat who, who begat and lied about it, who begat and gave away. She had told me an hour's worth of hilarious stories before she told me my parents' story.

"Your mother fell in love with a married man when she was sixteen years old. She was headstrong. When she made up her mind, it was made up for good. Anyway, this guy ups and moves from Mississippi to New York, so your mother decides that she will follow him. She got a job working with the Pennsylvania Railroad as a porter. That way, she could travel back and forth to see him without havin' to pay. Half the time, when she got to New York, he wouldn't even see her, and that made her sick. When she and her girlfriends had time off, they would go partyin' and drinkin', tryin' to help your momma get over her broken heart. Them friends was Dora and Nadine.

"Anyway, they was dancin' in a club one night. Your momma sho' could dance. She would swing her little skinny-legged self all over them guys in the club, and they loved it. One night she met your daddy and forgot all about that other no-good-fo-nothin' man. Your daddy was a big-time gambler, and he was pretty. Sarah said she wanted a pretty man to be the daddy of her babies. She decided that your daddy was pretty fine. She called me and told me he was pretty enough to give her some babies.

"Nadine and Dora stopped workin' the trains to get married. Your momma wanted Mr. Pretty Man to marry her, but he wouldn't. We didn't know he couldn't 'cause he already had a wife. He would meet your momma every time she came to the clubs. But just before your brother was on the way, she took sick, had to stop workin', and was stuck in New York.

"When she found out Ray was on the way, your daddy took her in, wouldn't marry her, couldn't marry her, but he took her into his mother's house, right around the corner from where he lived with his wife. When the railroad told Sarah she had to come back to work, she was too sick to go. She had been workin' for fifteen years, but they fired her anyway. Didn't give her no kind of pay or nothin', just fired her. It was when Ray was born that they told her about the cancer in her blood. She didn't pay them doctors no mind. She kept on drinkin' like nothing could ever stop her. By the time she had you, the disease was all in her breasts. Do you drink?"

"No. I never have."

"Well, I guess not. Your mother drank so much carryin' you, you could be drunk for the rest of your life. I think she drank because of the pain. She was always in a lot of pain. Maybe that's why she fought all the time. She was a fighter, you know. We never said nothin' to her about drinkin', because she would fight. She used to fight your daddy. He beat her. Did you know that? Did you know that your daddy beat your mother right there in his mother's house? It was a disgrace. His mother never lifted a hand to help Sarah, not even after she got so sick she couldn't walk.

"We all tried to tell her not to have that last baby. She said she was goin' to no matter what. Well, she had him, and Dora took him. Took him right outta the hospital. See, you and Ray were your mother's children. That little boy was Dora's from day one. Sarah kept you in a dresser drawer right near her bed, but she gave that other baby away. It almost killed her to have that baby. It did kill her. She wouldn't let them take her breasts off. She said she would die first. She said if God let her live long enough to see Ray turn three, she would never take another drink. Ray was gonna be three March thirty-first. She passed on March twentieth. She wanted to give him a party.

"It wasn't until we got to the cemetery that we realized what was goin' on. Your father had her buried in a grave with a whole bunch of other people. When I saw that, I fainted right out there on the cold ground in the cemetery. If only he had asked, we would have put my sister away proper. He never asked. He was Mr. Big Shot. Anyway, I wanted you to come live with me, but your daddy said no. Your mother wanted you and Ray to stay together. Since your grandmother wanted Ray and not you, you both ended up there because your daddy was there."

"Did he really beat her?"

"Listen, your momma loved that man, and when she loved, she loved forever. Your momma could not live without love. We loved her, but she needed the kind of love she got from a man. I want you to be different. Love God. If you love God, he will bring you a man. I love God so much he gave me a husband when I turned seventy-six years old. I just married an old man with a bad heart. But he makes me very happy."

We talked awhile longer, and Aunt Mabel gave me pictures of my parents and other family members. We both knew that I did not want to leave her, but Adeyemi was waiting for me. We were standing in the hallway, holding on to one another, when Aunt Mabel reached up, took my face in both of her hands, and said to me, "When you were born, your mother called me and said, 'Snookie'—she called me Snookie—'she is going to be something great. I can see it in her eyes. Maybe she will write. Or maybe she will be a great and famous dancer. I am going to put my mark on her, because she is going to be somebody one day.' Your momma didn't say that about either of your brothers. She said it about you. Your mother loved you. She and I both knew that you were some kind of miracle. She knew that you were born to do God's good work. I want you to know that. I want you to know I love you too."

I never saw Aunt Mabel again. She died ten days after I walked out of her house.

The similarities between my mother and me were amazing. Aunt Mabel's words kept ringing in my ears, "You have to be different." Until that moment, I thought there was something wrong with being different. I was trying to be like everyone else, but I had to be different. The other thing that kept coming up in my brain was "a proper burial." My mother had not had a proper burial, and neither had Rhonda.

When I asked my husband to dig a small hole in the back yard for me, he told me I was crazy.

"It's midnight. It's freezing, and we don't have a shovel."

"Use a spoon. I don't want to bury somebody, I just need a little hole."

"Aren't you taking this a bit far? What are you putting in the hole?"

"A lot of crap. I need to bury the crap." I knew if I kept talking, he would figure a way out of it. I turned and left him lying across the bed. I went into my office and started looking for pictures of Rhonda.

I was trying to find pictures of myself at every stage of my life before Balé gave me my name. I found teenage pictures, pictures of me when I was pregnant, pictures of me with John. I found a picture of myself smoking and another one where I was naked. *I wonder who took that one?* I laid them all in front of me on the desk, trying to remember the times and experiences of my life. There were some tears and some smiles, but I knew the time had come for me to say good-bye. I needed closure. I realized that all of my efforts would be for naught until there was absolute closure between who I was and who I am. For me, it wasn't enough to forgive, to surrender, or to make peace. I needed a concrete demonstration that it was over. That my life and everything about it up until the day I changed my name and nature was completely closed. I decided to write Rhonda a letter and tell her what I was planning to do. *In all things be grateful.*

Dear Rhonda Eva Harris, also known as Ronnie:
   I write this letter to thank you for all you have been to me. I thank you for all you have been in my life, and for the many ways in which you have served me. We have had many great times together, and while our relationship was healthy and purposeful at one time, I find that our relationship no longer serves me. Our relationship no longer supports what I desire in my life, or the purpose I believe God intends for me. I find that we now have an unholy relationship, which I no longer choose to continue. Therefore, I now release you from any and all unconscious and conscious agreements we have made in the past to continue this relationship. I now forgive you totally and unconditionally for any and all conscious and unconscious thoughts, words, and actions committed by you that have had an unloving, nonsupportive, unhealthy impact on my life. I now ask for and claim your forgiveness for any and all conscious and unconscious thoughts, words, and ac-

tions of mine that have held you in a condition of lack, fear, anger, resentment, guilt, shame, or any other unhealthy emotion. You are now free to pursue your higher and greater good. I am now free to pursue my higher and greater good. I wish for you love, light, peace, and an abundance of every good thing in God's kingdom. I release you. I surrender the energy of you in my being to the presence of the Holy Spirit and ask that any memory of you be transformed to productive and useful energy according to God's perfect plan for my life. I love you. I bless you.

                                                        Iyanla Vanzant

I took the letter and the pictures outside to the hole my husband had dug with a spoon. After saying a brief prayer for Rhonda, I set each picture on fire in the hole, allowing the smoke to rise. I kissed the letter, placed it on top of the remnants of the burned pictures, and covered the hole. After praying again, I knew that I had brought Rhonda's life to closure. The only thing left to do was to bring closure to the things she had put in place in my life, her relationship with Karen.

For three days, I tried to figure out just what to say and how to say it. I wrote it down, thinking I could read it. I practiced it over and over in my mind and out loud. Each time I reached for the telephone, my mouth would go dry and my palms would begin to sweat. I was about to do a new thing, ask for exactly what I wanted. I was prepared to do it in a new way, honestly. I was willing, but I was also scared to death. *What do you want?* I want to tell this woman—a sister and friend who has served me—that our time together is over. *What is your greatest strength?* God. *What is your greatest weakness?* Not trusting God. *What is your greatest fear?* That God is not home today. No. Just kidding. I have no fear because I know God is with me. *Whenever you declare yourself to be a thing, everything unlike you will challenge you!* The remnants of fear were definitely challenging me. What am I afraid of? *Are you afraid, or are you ashamed?* Afraid and ashamed. I think I am ashamed that I did not see this before now. I am ashamed that I stayed in this so long, that I didn't have the courage to leave before now. *What are you afraid of?* I am afraid she will get mad at me. I am afraid she will not like me or love me anymore. *Are you afraid or is Rhonda afraid?*

It was like a bucket of cold water in my face. This was still about Rhonda. Iyanla was trying to move through Rhonda's fear and shame. The same fear and shame that had ruled her life. What should I do? Why is she still so ashamed? My body was beginning to tremble. I was fighting the urge to cry. Ken Kizer, one of my teachers and counselors, had once told me, "When you feel the fear coming up in your body, drop your hands to your sides and let it come up. Don't fight it. Don't deny it the right to exist. It will probably feel like you are about to die. The only thing you will die to is the fear. You will live long enough to see that it will not kill you."

I did exactly what Ken said, I dropped my hands to my sides and let my body shake and tremble. My stomach flipped. Sweat broke out on my brow. What is Rhonda afraid of? What is she so guilty about? The words came from a place in the pit of my stomach. One at a time they entered my brain, *"You are guilty because you killed your mother!"* What? How did I do that? I was crying out loud now. My brain was stuck on the words. *Your guilt comes from the belief that you killed your mother!* I couldn't breathe. I wanted to run, but I couldn't move. *You are guilty of killing your mother!* The only thing I could think to do was pray. *Hold not thy peace, O Lord of my praise, for the mouth of the wicked and the mouth of the deceitful are opened against me. Have mercy, Lord. Forgive me, Lord. Restore me, Lord. Your grace is my sufficiency.* Over and over I said the words out loud until my body stopped trembling. When it did, I put my head down on the desk and cried.

This was too big for me to do alone. I picked up the telephone and called Ken. His wife, René, answered the telephone.

"René. I killed my mother. How did I kill my mother?" I was wailing into the telephone. I don't know how she knew it was me.

"Just breathe, baby. Come on, breathe with me. Take a breath. Now tell me what happened."

I told René about burying Rhonda and trying to release Karen as my agent. I told her about the thought that had popped into my brain and what happened to my body.

"You know that's not what really happened. Take a breath and tell me what really happened. Close your eyes and breathe with me." René and I took several deep breaths together. When I was calm enough to talk, I let the words pour out of my mouth.

"Everyone said that if my mother had not had me, she would not have died. I've heard that most of my life. 'Your mother should have never had you. She should have had the operation.' No one ever explained it to me, they just said it. In my mind, I concluded that somehow, because of me being born, my mother died. Then I blocked it out." René was breathing harder than I was.

"You know that you and your mother had a soul agreement. You both agreed that she would leave you so that you could learn. You know that, don't you?"

"Yes. I do know that. I guess I just forgot."

"Those bastards! You know they did not say those things in love, right? What did they take from you by saying that? Do you know what they took?"

"No."

"Your innocence. You are innocent, Iyanla. Say that with me, I am innocent. I have innocence." I repeated the words with René.

"You are innocent. Please remember that. It is your innocence that allows you to love yourself. You have done nothing wrong. You kept your agreement, and your mother kept hers."

As René and I talked, something else came to my mind. I was too shaken to share it with her, so I thanked her and promised to call later. My thoughts were racing. I grabbed my journal out of my bag, a pen from the basket on my desk, and began to write.

I always thought that Uncle Leroy took my innocence. Now I realize he did not. What he did was misinterpret my cry for love. I was a loveless child, crying out for love and attention. I was willing to do anything to get love and feel love. Uncle Leroy heard my cry, he saw what I needed, but he misinterpreted it. He tried to love me the only way he knew how, sexually. He was not trying to hurt me, he was trying to love me. Just like I misinterpreted what they said about my mother, he misinterpreted my thoughts and my energy. I

felt guilty, and he acted out my guilt. The truth is, I was innocent, and he was
innocent. We were both in the pain of not knowing what to do about what we
were feeling. Uncle Leroy did not steal my innocence. Misinterpretation and
misjudgment did. Today I know that I am innocent of all things, for all times.
I forgive myself for thinking I ever did anything wrong. I forgive myself for
thinking Uncle Leroy ever did anything wrong. We both did the best we could
do based on what we believed to be true at the time.

The minute I put the pen down, my body stopped shaking and the
tears dried up. I took a deep breath, closed the journal, and went for a
walk. I had to be with and integrate this new information.

The day after my revelation, I was still not ready to speak to Karen,
but I knew I had to bring closure to our experience. It was an experience
that kept me in the shadows of guilt. My fear was that I was not yet
strong enough in Iyanla's identity to endure the tongue-lashing I believed she would give me. I called Ken to share with him my dilemma.
"Don't call her, write her. You don't have to be punished. If you really believe she will abuse you verbally, why would you call? The issue here is
not how you do it; the issue is that you get it done. Write her."

What an absolutely brilliant idea! *It doesn't have to be hard, Iyanla. It*
doesn't have to hurt.

I wrote Karen a five-line letter.

> Dear Karen:
> I got it! Thank you. Our time together has come to an
> end. I am so grateful to you for all you have done for me. I
> am grateful for your willingness to participate in my healing.
> I know that sometime in the future our paths will cross
> again. Take care of yourself.
> Be Blessed!
>
> Iyanla

After I mailed the letter to Karen, I notified everyone who needed to
know about the change in our relationship. In the process, I discovered
that Karen was away on vacation and would not be back for two weeks.

On the day she was scheduled to return, I called her to tell her about the letter. She asked me what it said. When I told her, she said, "Oh. Okay. Did I do something? Are you mad at me about something?"

"No, Karen. This is not about you. This is about me learning to take care of myself. You have been nothing but a blessing to me."

"Okay. Just know that if you ever need me I am here."

"I know that, and I thank you."

CHAPTER NINETEEN

What's the Lesson When You Do It All Wrong and It Turns Out All Right?

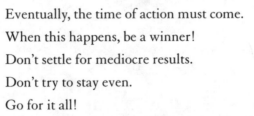

Eventually, the time of action must come.

When this happens, be a winner!

Don't settle for mediocre results.

Don't try to stay even.

Go for it all!

Deng Ming-Dao, in *Everyday Tao:*
Living With Balance and Harmony

I KNEW THE MOMENT I saw him.

We were talking on the telephone for the first time in years. I brought him up to speed on the recent events of my life. And he, in turn, told me what was happening in his life. He was ending a five-year relationship. Four months earlier, I had ended a three-year relationship. Now we were talking to each other about all of the things we had learned.

Adeyemi was still living in Atlanta. He had put three of his sons through high school and was facing an empty nest. He sounded like a mother about to lose her children. Once again, he was turning to me for counseling. I knew this was not going to be a case of me being in his head, but I wasn't quite sure how to say it.

He must have known it too, although I think it took him a little longer to catch on than it took me. I was a different person now. Iyanla had been born. She was still growing, but at least she knew who she was and what she wanted. I also knew that no matter what happened, I was going to love this man for the rest of my life. I would love him no matter what he decided to do. I had learned how to love from a distance, and I was just glad that we were talking.

Over the next few months, we talked a great deal. Every day, in fact. No matter where I was in the country, I would call. He was having a hard time, coming out of one relationship, on the verge of starting another. We talked about patterns. We talked about our unconscious needs. We talked about healing and growth. But rarely did we talk about us. At least not until I laid eyes on him.

Love will take your breath away. When you really experience the "holy instance" of love, it will rattle your brain and take your breath away. I know. It happened to me when I saw Adeyemi waiting for me at the gate when I got off the plane. A chill ran from the bottom of my feet straight to the top of my head. For a second, my sight blurred and my breathing stopped. I wanted to laugh *and* cry. I wanted to bite him and lick him. I wanted to rip my clothes off and dance naked in the airport. But I was cool.

"Hello, Ms. Vanzant."

"Hello, Mr. Bandele."

"How are you? You look great."

"I be fine. Thank you muchly."

We made small talk on the way to pick up my car. I was in Atlanta for a speaking engagement the next day and to see Balé, who had relocated there. Adeyemi and I talked about our children, my books, and his latest project. But we never talked about us.

Several more months went by before I had the courage to approach the subject of us. I had to bring it up because, although we had become intimate, he was considering a relationship with another woman. I wanted him to know that I was not the same person who used to sneak up to Albany to see him. I had too much at stake to be "the other woman."

"I was just wondering," I said, "what it would be like if you and I were to get together again."

"You were? That's interesting, because I've been thinking about that, too." He was trying to hide his excitement.

"You were? What were you thinking?"

"I was thinking that you know me better than any other person does. You know me better than my mother. I was thinking about how well we work together and how much we have been through together. It's funny, but every woman I have ever been involved with knows about you. Some of them have been pretty spooked about it. But they all know that you are the one person in my life who has loved me unconditionally."

It was a lot for me to swallow, so I changed the subject to hide my excitement. Later in the week, I got a call from Balé. He said he needed to speak to me, and he wanted to do it in person. He assured me that nothing was wrong, but that he needed to lay his eyes on me. By the end of the next week, I was back in Atlanta.

Adeyemi picked me up at the airport, I went to his house, and we went to Balé's together. Balé called me into his meeting room. We talked for a few moments before he called Adeyemi. I had said to Adeyemi that the only way we could be together was if we did it the right way, with the blessings of our elders and in public view. I was not going to repeat the same mistakes I had made before. He agreed. But we both knew that Balé was the key. He was very unhappy about the way Adeyemi and I had carried on in the past and spared few words in letting us know his displeasure about the way we ended our relationship the last time. When he called Adeyemi into the room, I expected to be scolded and whipped.

I am not sure who spoke first. I was too busy trying not to wet myself. Balé was saying something. I was trying not to look at him or Adeyemi. Before I knew what was really going on, Adeyemi was on his knees in front of me, asking my godfather for permission to marry me. My heart stopped. I think Balé knew and was trying to give his response before I keeled over and died. As if he were ordering lunch from a menu, he said, "I believe I could give my blessing to a union between the two of you."

I rested my head on Adeyemi's head, which was in my lap. Together, we sighed deeply with relief. The next stop was the home of my surrogate mother and mentor, Dr. Barbara Lewis King.

We didn't announce our coming. I knew she would be home because it was just after church. When she opened the door and saw us standing there, she said, "What did you come to tell me? Are you two getting married?" We all laughed.

Dr. King had been my eyes and ears when I had none. She has nurtured, and guided me in a way that brings my heart peace. She never tells me what to do. She always asks me questions framed in a way that lets me know exactly what I'd better do. When I first began speaking, very few churches opened their doors to me. People were confused about my being a Yoruba priestess. Through ignorance and fear, some people assumed that being a Yoruba priestess was anti-God and anti-Christ. "Dr. Barbara" was the first minister of a large, well-known church to put me in the pulpit. Years later, she also ordained me.

On this day, I sat before her as her daughter, with my beau, asking her to bless our marriage. She spoke just like a mother. It was a side of her that I had never seen. She spoke to Adeyemi first.

"What is your vision?"

"I want to support Iyanla in the work that she does. I believe in her, and I know what she does is very important. I am blessed to be a part of that."

"No. That is not what I asked you. I asked what is *your* vision? Your vision for yourself." I was getting a little nervous. I had never heard Dr. Barbara speak so sternly. Adeyemi's response made me even more nervous.

"I have never thought about it. I'm not sure I have a vision. Right now, I feel so blessed that God has given me another chance to be with this woman whom I love so much. I wasn't thinking about my own vision, I want to help her build her vision. I can't answer your question right now because I'm not sure what my vision is."

"Well, you better get sure. Your vision and Iyanla's vision are not the same thing. That doesn't mean that the two of you cannot work together or be together. I'm not saying that at all. I am saying that it is important for you to have your own vision, because God has your wife on a particular path." I was relieved to hear her say, "your wife," but she wasn't finished.

"You seem to me to be a very nice man. I don't really know you, but I have never heard anything but good things about you. This is what I want you to understand. God has placed Iyanla in the world to do something very special. She is doing God's work. She doesn't have time to cook and clean, and she will not be taken off her path. I know you want to be a part of her vision, but until you have a vision of your own, you must do everything you can to make sure she stays on the path. Can you do that?"

"Yes. I want to do that."

"Okay. Let's pray."

There are few things that I know for sure about me. One of them is that I am married. I am so married that I will probably be married until the earth no longer exists. I am so married that if I ever thought about not being married, I would probably be struck by lightning.

The wedding ceremony was three hours long. Adeyemi's mentor and godfather officiated. Dr. Barbara offered the prayers. Balé and Ray sat in the front row and had to give nods of approval before each part of the ceremony was concluded. The two hundred guests also participated, answering questions and giving their sanction to everything. My marriage was a sacred community affair that reinforced spiritual principles most of us never consider when we get married. I was the bride, and I had not considered most of them.

Baba Ishangi, the minister who married us, is a master teacher and cultural custodian. He wanted to make sure that Adeyemi and I, and all of the witnesses were completely clear about every aspect of the ceremony and what we expected from the marriage. The first ceremony was "tasting the tides of life." Baba presented us with a plate that contained salt, pepper, and honey. He explained to us that life is not always going to be sweet; that as you move through life, you must be prepared to dance your way through whatever comes your way. He placed a spoonful of salt in my mouth. He talked about the bitterness of life and the bitterness that often comes into a relationship as time passes. He talked about the need to know how to move beyond bitterness by dancing over and around the things that really do not matter. With the mouthful of salt, I had to dance around Adeyemi, then he around me. By the time we were both done, my lips were puckered.

Next, Baba placed a pinch of hot, African red pepper in my mouth. While he was talking, I was choking. He talked about anger and fear and things that could make us angry and frightened. I swear he said more when I had that pepper in my mouth than he has ever said to me in my life. He ended his soliloquy by asking me if I understood. I didn't respond. I just started dancing. Adeyemi, who had more pepper in his mouth than I did, repeated the same process.

Then he gave us the honey. What a relief! He told us how to attract goodness and sweetness into our lives. He talked about sexuality and lust. He talked about babies but told us we were too old to have more, that we already had enough children. We danced for each other as before, our mouths full of honey. Next came the egg.

Baba held an egg in his hand as an example of how delicate life is. He explained to us the necessity of being gentle with life and with each other. He explained how fragile the heart and the mind can be, and what happens when they are not handled with care. He placed the egg in my hand, then instructed Adeyemi to take my hand in both of his hands. Together we danced, holding the egg. It was all so beautiful and meaningful, but it was the suitcases that brought the whole room to tears.

Baba presented us each with a separate worn and ragged suitcase. He talked to us about the necessity to come to each other "empty." Our hearts and minds, he said, needed to be empty of every past relationship, every past hurt, everything we had done in the past that could in any way harm our marriage. He made us each visualize taking people, things, and thoughts out of the suitcases. When we thought we were done, he asked us if we now thought the suitcases were empty. Then he made us do it again. I don't know what Adeyemi did, but I pulled Gary, John, Eddie, and Curtis out of my suitcase and threw them into the bushes. I took Grandma, Daddy, Nett, and the old Ray out of the suitcase and offered them each to God. I took my children out, and his children out. I kissed each of them on the forehead and shooed them away. Next, I imagined words floating out of the suitcase into the sky. The words I remember were fear, anger, hate, resentment, jealousy (that was a big one for me when I was with Adeyemi the first time), worthlessness, valuelessness, dishonesty, neediness, and doubt.

Finally, as I began to cry, I pulled Rhonda out of the suitcase. She jumped back in. I pulled her out again. She started to fight me, so I opened my arms and asked her for a hug. When I did that, she ran off by herself.

Baba kept peeking into the suitcases. When he felt the completion, he showed the empty suitcases to Balé who nodded his approval, and the suitcases were taken away.

On a beautiful cold day in May, Iyanla married Adeyemi. We have a "no way out" clause in our commitment to one another. We understand that our marriage has a purpose. Our purpose to is help one another heal. It is not always easy, but we are committed to each other and the process of being healed. Every now and then, Rhonda shows up, as does the child in Adeyemi's mind. When they get busy in our lives, we want to get away from each other as fast as possible. We entertain the possibility of separating. But when we remember that there is "no way out" of the healing process except by learning to love, we get clear. We remember that we have so many things to celebrate, we do not have time to remember the tears.

Epilogue

Life hurts. Life is painful. Life is suffering.
There is nothing in life that does not involve trial.
There is nothing worthwhile that doesn't have a cost.
Yet, we must go on.
There is nothing great that does not require a series of
    small acts.
We must persevere.
If we do, good times are sure to follow.
If we constantly seek, even in darkness,
guidance is sure to come.
If we strive against evil, no matter what the cost,
righteousness is sure to triumph.

Deng Ming-Dao, in *Everyday Tao:*
Living With Balance and Harmony

GIVING BIRTH TO THIS BOOK has been one of the most challenging experiences I have faced in quite a while. It was yet *another* opportunity for me to review my life. It was a blessing in disguise that forced me to search my soul, revisit old wounds, assess where I am, and make some decisions about where I want to go. It was frightening. It has led to many new revelations. It has given me something else to celebrate. It has reminded me of the mistakes I relived because I did not celebrate my learning the last time. Most important of all, this project, unlike any other, has helped me to rededicate my life and my work to God.

When the press interviews me, I am often asked about the tragedy and hardship of my upbringing. On many occasions, the interviewers have been put off or upset by the way I brush over the details and get to the lessons. One interviewer asked me about my unwillingness to discuss my past. I explained that those incidents have nothing to do with me. That history is not mine. It is not Iyanla's. While I am well aware that without every incident, every event in my past, I would not be who I am, I no longer have the need or even the ability to promote that pain. I have told the same story many times. Many people know it by heart, as I do. My goal is to use the story of my life as an example, a reminder that you too can be healed.

I have learned to look at my life as an observer. I stand back, look at what happened, and focus my attention on the place where the wound was inflicted. I do not look at who inflicted the wound or how it was inflicted. That it *was* inflicted is the essence of healing. Find what your wound is, where the wound is being played out in your life, and heal it. Only by doing the work on ourselves that is required to heal mental, emotional, and psychological wounds can we ever hope to be whole in our spirits. I chose to do the healing work because I didn't want to be mad anymore. I didn't want to cry anymore. I wanted to heal so that I would have something to celebrate—myself.

I have also been asked many times who my inspiration was. Who were my role models? Again, people have not been pleased with my response: I wasn't paying that much attention; I had no idea that people were trying to show me anything; I was in too much pain; I was too busy trying to survive to look for role models. The only role model I have had in my life has been the Holy Spirit. It has been the presence of God in my life that has given me understanding. Without that presence, I never would have been able to comprehend what I was looking at, or looking for. I hope that after reading this story, people will have a better understanding of my meaning.

My journey is not over by a long shot. I still have some deep wounds that require intensive care. There are places in my heart that are still closed. Writing this book has helped me to realize that. The difference between Iyanla and Rhonda is that Iyanla is equipped with the skill, knowledge, and ability to do a great deal of healing on her own. I also have sense enough to know when I am not equipped. In those times, I call my teachers, Balé, Dr. Barbara King, Ken and René Kizer, Dr. David Phillips, and Gemmia. I call my friends, Adeyemi, Shaheerah, Marge Battle, Tulani Kinard, Vivianna Brown, and, again, Gemmia. And there are those times when I still call Dial-A-Prayer.

My point is that it never stops. Healing, growing, and learning never stop. Not as long as you are breathing. This does not mean that there is always something you need to fix about yourself. Nor does it mean that there is anything *wrong* with you in the first place. It means that there is always something more for you to learn. Something for you to recognize at a deeper level. Something for you to grow through. It means that each time you learn something, you also learn how to handle the learning better. Learning is a part of living. I am so glad to be alive at a time when it is okay to say, "I need help. I need healing." I believe we are blessed to share the planet with people who have mastered healing techniques and are writing about new ways to heal. It is an absolute blessing to know that whatever you need, God's got it covered.

If there is one point that I hope has come through in this story, it is that children must be celebrated and taught to celebrate themselves. Positive reinforcement is absolutely essential to the development of a healthy sense of Self. When children are allowed to live day to day, making strides, learning, and accomplishing without being recognized or celebrated, their sense of value is diminished. More important, children must be celebrated, honored, and valued, not for what they do, but because they are. We must not only let children know that we love them, we must be glad about loving them. We must begin to have parties for our children "just because."

If, as an adult, you cannot find or do not feel the necessity to celebrate something about yourself, it is probably a reflection of what you experienced as a child. It is a pattern you may choose to want not to continue. I was never celebrated, not my birth, my life, or my accomplishments as a child. As a result, I did not feel welcome. My existence did not matter. I learned what to do but never that it was okay to "just be." In preparing this book, I realized that of all the experiences in my life, the one that had the most devastating effect was not being celebrated or being made to feel welcome. It was worse than any beating or cruelty I experienced. It seems like such a small thing to have someone say, "Thank you for being alive." Or "I am so glad you are here." I will never know for sure, but I feel that to have heard *that* would have made a major difference in my life.

Hoping that this story is your story and that my healing is our healing, I remind you to celebrate yourself and your life each and every day. There is always a good reason to have a party. The reason is you! In closing, I share with you something that I pray will make it easier for you to move through your life experiences. It is something that Grandma taught me when I was six years old.

> *But they that wait upon the Lord shall renew their strength; they shall mount up with wings as eagles; they shall run, and not be weary; and they shall walk and not faint.*
>
> *Isaiah 40:31:*

I am not sure why Grandma, of all people, made me memorize this particular verse, but I do know that in everything *there is a seed of good.*

Be Blessed! I am!

Iyanla